Participation in Human Inquiry

edited by
Peter Reason

SAGE Publications
London • Thousand Oaks • New Delhi

SAGE Publications Ltd
6 Bonhill Street
London EC2A 4PU

SAGE Publications Inc
2455 Teller Road
Thousand Oaks, California 91320

SAGE Publications India Pvt Ltd
32, M-Block Market
Greater Kailash – I
New Delhi 110 048

British Library Cataloguing in Publication data

A catalogue record for this book is
available from the British Library

ISBN 0-8039-8831 1
ISBN 0-8039-8832 X (pbk)

Library of Congress catalog card number 94-068552

Typeset by M Rules
Printed in Great Britain by Redwood Books, Trowbridge, Wiltshire

Contents

Contributors

Lesley Archer is based in the Social Work Research and Development Unit, part of the Department of Social Policy and Social Work at the University of York. Now a Senior Research Fellow, Lesley was a social worker and family therapist with a child guidance centre before she joined the University full-time. For the last 12 years she, with Dorothy Whitaker, has been involved in partnership research with social agencies, on projects such as the quality of life for staff and residents in homes for elderly people, and resettling learning-disabled people coming out of hospital in housing association small group homes. They are currently engaged in 'The prevailing cultures and staff dynamics of children's homes', a three-year study funded by the Department of Health, and in a learning programme, 'Understanding and managing practice in the helping professions', in which middle managers and senior practitioners from social services departments, health, and other welfare agencies are helped to conduct their own research within their own agencies.

John Cosier is an independent management consultant and trainer, specializing in the area of Total Quality Management. He is a skilled group facilitator, with extensive experience in consultancy in organizational change and improvement, and the design and delivery of supportive training at all levels. Although most of his career has been spent in industry, he is increasingly finding application for his skills in the public sector, notably health, education and local, government.

Moira De Venney-Tiernan left school with no exam results, worked in the travel industry and became a mother at the age of 18. As her son grew she became involved with play work, sparking an interest in youth work. In March 1989 she joined Merton Youth Service undertaking the Induction and BBTS course which led her to becoming a qualified part-time youth worker in October 1990. She is still working for Merton as a Youth Worker-in-Charge of two projects and is interested in becoming a full-time Youth Worker – hence the need to research into Accessible Routes to Qualification. She is now involved with Brunel University in setting up such a scheme.

Sara Glennie is an independent social work trainer and consultant whose interests lie in interdisciplinary studies. She is a Visiting Lecturer in The School of Social Studies, University of Nottingham and an active member of its

Professional Development Group. Sara's doctoral thesis explores the impact of multidisciplinary training on individual and organizational change.

Annette Goldband has been involved in youth and community work since 1973, initially as a part-time worker or volunteer and, since 1977, in a variety of full-time posts. She is currently involved in the training and development of part-time and full-time workers in Merton. She was introduced to new paradigm methodology through an opportunity to undertake an MA, and says she has not looked back since! She was employed as an Associate Tutor for Brunel University working with her original collaborators and new ones in other services, to design and provide an Accessible Route to Qualification. She is now Lecturer in Informal and Community Education at the YMCA George Williams College.

Lyn Rackham is married with three children and has been involved in youth work for 14 years, organizing mother and toddler groups and play schemes on a voluntary basis for the local community. She joined Merton Youth Service in 1989 and qualified as a part-time worker in 1990, hoping eventually to do a full-time youth workers' course but found that this was only possible if she gave up both day time employment and youth work in the evenings. As this would have put a severe financial strain on her family she was delighted when Annette invited her to join a group that would design a new route to qualification for part-time youth workers that would not involve giving up other employment.

Peter Reason is Director of the Centre for Action Research in Professional Practice at the University of Bath.

Nancy Reilly has been involved in youth work over the past four years now. She is a qualified part-time youth worker having gained the Brunel Basic Training Scheme in Youth Work and Community Studies in 1990. She works in a voluntary club with 12–18-year-olds. She became involved in the research because of her interest in furthering her career in youth work. She has enjoyed the challenge of being in the group and looks forward to taking up the opportunity of studying for a full-time qualification in Youth and Community Studies through ARQ. She is also in full-time employment as a Recreation Officer at a Leisure Centre.

Hilary Traylen is now Nurse Executive Director on the Canterbury and Thanet Community Health Care Trust Board. She completed her MPhil at the School of Management, University of Bath.

Lesley Treleaven was Staff Development manager at the University of Western Sydney, Hawkesbury, and is completing her PhD at the University of Western Sydney, Nepean, Australia. Her main interest is finding ways to create cultural change within organizations so that they can become diverse, inclusive places where people can both work and learn. Lesley was previously on the academic staff of the Social Ecology Centre at the University. She is now working with the Australian Taxation Office, leading the newly formed Learning Facilitation Team. The team's work is to support managers in developing a learning culture that is integrated into everyday practice in the organization.

Dorothy Whitaker was Professor responsible for the social work course at the University of York before taking early retirement a few years ago. She is now engaged in research on children's homes and with a learning programme designed to assist practitioners and managers in service-providing organizations to design and carry out research on issues arising from their workplace (see notes about Lesley Archer above). This follows a career-long interest in the dynamics of therapeutic and work groups, research processes, and in how people really learn.

Elizabeth Whitmore is known among her friends and colleagues as Bessa. She received her Master's degree in Social Work at Boston University and worked in the inner city during the 1960s and early 1970s. She moved to Nova Scotia in 1973 and taught at Dalhousie University in Halifax for 17 years. Bessa did doctoral work at Cornell University and it was there she developed her interest in participatory action research and evaluation. Since 1991 she has been a faculty member at Carleton University School of Social Work, Ottawa, Ontario.

The most noble kind of knowledge is earned by living

(Meister Eckhart in Fox, 1983: 4)

Introduction

This book is about research as a participative process, about research *with* people rather than research *on* people. It is about inquiry as a means by which people engage together to explore some significant aspect of their lives, to understand it better and to transform their action so as to meet their purposes more fully. The book takes forward the work on the paradigm of co-operative and experiential inquiry, and is a companion to *Human Inquiry: a Sourcebook of New Paradigm Research* (Reason and Rowan, 1981) and *Human Inquiry in Action: Developments in New Paradigm Research* (Reason, 1988).

Since my early involvement with human inquiry I have continued to work with participative forms of inquiry. I have developed the methodology of participatory research – starting from my own work with co-operative inquiry I have compared this with action inquiry and participatory action research and taken some steps to integrate theory and practice. I have reflected on the consequences of a participatory methodology for our understanding of ourselves in our world – concerns for emerging patterns of thought and belief, for ontology and epistemology. And I have worked as a teacher and supervisor of graduate students who have taken the ideals and practices of human inquiry into both their work and their lives.

As I have pursued these questions of method and practice I have realized that a participative methodology needs to rest on a participative world-view. It is not possible simply to tag co-operative inquiry or participatory action research onto a world-view that is primarily forged in a positivist or modernist perspective, with its deep rooted assumptions about the separation of knower from what is known; this would result in an untenable situation, with methodologies which demand a collaborative ethos and practice resting on assumptions that demand separation. This issue became particularly clear to me when I started to ask questions about quality and validity in collaborative research. Of course, I was not alone in these developments: over the past 20 years many people have contributed to the development of a participatory world-view, both in writing and in practical ways. There is a strong argument that we are at a critical turning point in our understanding of ourselves in relation to each other and our planet (see, for example, Tarnas, 1991).

So this book attempts to explore two themes which, while quite distinct, are highly interconnected and in the end inseparable. One question asks, 'How do you practice research in a collaborative fashion?'; and the other asks, 'How can we articulate a world-view which fosters an experience of participation with each other and with our planet?' I cannot tell which question comes first:

considerations of method raise questions of world-view, while the emergent world-view interrogates, informs and supports our practice.

Part I addresses the broader question: the Western world-view is, I believe, changing towards a realization that our existence is based on participation and communion rather than separation and competition. I explore this theme through theory, imagery, myth and archetype, starting in Chapter 1 with a discussion of the alienation and fragmentation which seems so strongly to characterize the Western world at the present time, and by offering an alternative image. Then in Chapter 2 I seek to understand participation as an aspect of human consciousness, exploring first the deep sense of identification and participation that, as far as we can tell, characterized early human consciousness; and moving on to look at the emergence of an autonomous self experienced as separate from environment and the consequent loss of awareness of participation. This development brought much in terms of clarity, control and understanding, and yet brought also in its wake the dislocation and fragmentation of modern times; I draw on feminist and indigenous scholarship to ask whether this alienation was inevitable in the development of human consciousness, and look briefly at alternative visions of human development. In Chapter 3 I argue that a future form of reflective participative consciousness is emerging dialectically out of the contradiction between deep participation and the alienation of modernist consciousness. In Chapter 4 I show how the practice of human inquiry is a discipline which can contribute to this development: my thesis is that participative forms of inquiry are one potentially critical linchpin in the transformation of consciousness through which we in the West are moving and need to move.

In Part II these broad themes are brought down to earth with examples of participatory research which illustrate how we can realize these alternative forms of inquiry in practice. When you or I, espousing this participatory ethos, sit down with a group of people intending to develop collaborative relationships we are confronted with all the practical issues of how to actually do it, how to engage together, to meet each other, to respect each other's differences, and to work together on a common task. As soon as we touch upon the question of participation we have to entertain and *work with* issues of power, of oppression, of gender; we are confronted with the limitations of our skill, with the rigidities of our own and others' behaviour patterns, with the other pressing demands on our limited time, with the hostility or indifference of our organizational contexts. We live out our contradictions, struggling to bridge the gap between our dreams and reality, to realize the values we espouse. So while we need the sweep of a participatory world-view, it is not enough: we need also to learn the practice of participation. One of the questions I have been asked repeatedly as I have talked with groups of people about collaborative forms of inquiry was, 'How do you actually do it?' It is as if many people feel intuitively that a participatory approach is right for their work and are hungry for stories and accounts that will provide models and exemplars.

I believe strongly that a book on participation in human inquiry needs to address both these levels. It needs good stories, good accounts that show a range of approaches to participatory inquiry. It also needs to invoke a participatory world-view. For those of us committed to human inquiry, to research as a participatory endeavour, live in this gap between vision and actuality, always on the edge of what is truly possible. The accounts of participatory inquiry projects contained in Part II of this book are written by people who live on this edge. They started with a vision of what might be possible and spent months and even years of work preparing the ground. They gathered people together, negotiated organizational contexts, facilitated a process of group development, so that in each of the inquiries the participants learned to work together in ways that were more fully collaborative. I believe that through this kind of work special times are created, new possibilities are dreamed and brought into reality, so that for a moment the world is re-aligned towards a new form of participative reality.

The notion of participation carries strong positive connotations for many people; it is often seen as 'a good thing'. It is very easy to espouse participation and yet at times incredibly difficult to practice genuinely. When Bob Hardiman (one of our graduate students) heard about this book he wrote a paper entitled 'On becoming a participant: a view from an iconoclast' – an iconoclast being one who destroys images and attacks established beliefs. He wrote

> I believe there is an *implicit* belief, amongst some of the new paradigm research community, that if only we were all doing participatory research, the world's problems would be solved. There is certainly a part of *me* that believes that. There's a part of me . . . that believes that I ought to participate fully with friends and colleagues in everything I do, and that all such participation should be wonderful and easy, and that all of us participants will smile and be nice to one another. These are the established beliefs that this iconoclast is attacking. (Hardiman, 1993; emphasis in original)

After exploring his own experience of participating through several examples with family friends and colleagues he concludes

> This is all difficult stuff and *that's* what I wanted to say in this piece of writing. If, like me, you find yourself passionately attracted to the idea of a form of research that is participatory, that doesn't do damage to the world, or those upon whom or with whom it seeks to research, then don't imagine it will be easy. It's much easier to be fascist about research, to decide what you want to know, to design the methods, recruit the subjects, run the experiments, draw your own conclusions and write up your own results . . . I have a horrible feeling that it is all too difficult. (emphasis in original)

While it may be difficult, it is certainly not *too* difficult. Part II of this book is made up of stories which tell how the people who initiated the projects found different ways of collaborating with others – how they transformed the people who in orthodox research would be their 'subjects' into co-researchers. You can read how this was accomplished by those with professional training as group facilitators, and how it was done by relative newcomers to working in groups. You can read about projects that were fully funded as part of organizational training and development, and about projects which were taken on the informal initiative of a group of people. I hope that these examples show some of the very different ways in which people actually practise participatory or collaborative research, and that they will inspire those who read them to develop their own approaches. For the stories show that there is no one right way to go about it: each research situation is unique and will respond to different approaches in different ways.

The inquiry accounts in Part II cover a range of activities. You can read about:

- How health visitors in the British National Health Service explored ways in which they could confront hidden agendas in their practice, the unmentionables such as depression and child abuse which haunt their work.
- How participatory research was used to evaluate a pre-natal programme for single mothers – with some of the mothers actually doing the research.
- How a diverse group of professionals worked together to improve the child protection process in their area.
- How a group of youth workers explored the process of learning from experience which contributed to the design of new forms of training and accreditation.
- How collaborative inquiry was used to develop a woman-centred form of staff development which challenged the masculinist culture of an institution.
- How collaborative research can become a partnership between academics and organizations in the interest of improving service delivery.

These examples draw quite widely on different approaches to participative inquiry: they are informed by co-operative inquiry, participatory action research, and action research. They present diverse ways in which groups are formed and developed, and diverse relationships between the initiating researchers and the participants. I have drawn out some of these comparisons in Chapter 10.

How to read this book

It should be clear that this book does not tell you 'how to do it' in the sense of providing a checklist or clear guidelines. Rather, by providing both a theoretical perspective and a set of examples it is intended to open a range of possibilities to a would-be participative researcher, so that their choices may be better informed. It should also be clear that you as reader may be more interested in one part of the book than the other: you may wish to start at the beginning and read through to the end, but there is no reason why you should! You may prefer to start with the examples, and move from them to the more abstract theory of participation. If you want a brief introduction to some participative inquiry methods you will find this in Chapter 4. But I hope that in time you will move between both parts of the book and that the contrast between them will suspend you at that difficult edge between the *vision* of a participative world-view and the *practice* of participation in human inquiry.

Acknowledgements

My first thanks go to those who wrote the chapters which make up Part II of the book – Hilary, Bessa, John, Sara, Moira, Annette, Lyn, Nancy, Lesley T., Lesley A. and Dorothy – who have accepted my comments on their earlier drafts with grace and were so responsive to my requests. And quickly on their heels I offer thanks to all those who were involved in the inquiries reported whose experience contributes so much to our understanding of the human inquiry process.

Several people helped me with my own contributions to the book, notably Judi Marshall and David Sims, who twice took time from their own research to read and comment in detail on my drafts. I am extraordinarily lucky to have such colleagues! My dear friend Philip Raby read the drafts and provided a non-academic perspective and critical comments on my English. And Bill Torbert and Sue Jones provided helpful criticism of an early draft.

In addition to those who contributed directly are all those who provide the context for my work. The postgraduate research students at the University of Bath have been delightful companions and provided immense stimulus for the development of my ideas. Further afield I have held seminars with faculty and graduate students at the Universities of Keele, Boston, Cornell, Boston College, Brandeis, Case Western Reserve, Pennsylvania, Western Sydney at Hawkesbury, and Teachers College, Columbia, at which exciting conversations have provided new questions and insights. I am blessed with many good other friends and colleagues. Thank you all.

Peter Reason
Centre for Action Research in Professional Practice
University of Bath

Part I
Towards a Participatory World-view

Underneath the blanket giants tremble, other cultures begin to sing, the genius of woman emerges, the depths start to rise, and the other side of the moon of ourselves haunts our becoming and demands its tribute. It is the first stirrings of the Rhythm of Awakening. Many have felt it coming. Some have experienced it with joy and hopefulness; others have felt it as a gut-gripping terror, knowing its music, when it comes, demands that they live at their edges.

(Houston, 1982: xv)

1

Inquiry and Alienation

Peter Reason

My field of work for the past 20 years has been human inquiry. I see this as an approach to living based on experience and engagement, on love and respect for the integrity of persons; and on a willingness to rise above presupposition, to look and to look again, to risk security in the search for understanding and action that open possibilities of creative living. I have at times felt that such a genuine human inquiry is one of the greatest virtues of humanity, and might be the greatest gift that Western consciousness has given the world. I love Nietzsche's phrase, 'All truths are bloody truths for me!' (Kaufmann, 1950), suggesting as it does that complete personal engagement, passion and profound risk-taking are central to inquiry, and that science and life are not separate.

Research in the West has traditionally been part of a positivist world-view, a view that sees science and everyday life as separate and the researcher as subject within a world of separate objects. In a positivist world-view the purpose of inquiry is to search for truth, to know more and more about a world of things; it is part of a modern world-view based on the metaphor of linear progress, absolute truth and rational planning (Harvey, 1989). Along with many others I believe that this world-view is coming to the end of its useful life and is no longer a guide to wise action. The ecological, political, social and personal crises we confront at this time need no rehearsing here; fundamental to all these crises is the way we think and how the way we think separates us from our experience, from each other, and from the rhythms and patterns of the natural world. At root the problem is epistemological: I have long believed, with Gregory Bateson, that the most important task before us is to learn to think in new ways (Bateson, 1972), and thinking in new ways implies new forms of practice.

Now, you may say that in attacking the positivist world-view I am setting up a straw man. Surely, you may say, we have moved on beyond the limitations of orthodox positivism, surely our world-view is more holistic than that? In some ways it is true that there *are* stirrings of a new consciousness, of which human inquiry is a part. But in my less optimistic moments I am drawn to Feyerabend's words, who is reported as describing Popper's critical rationalism as 'a tiny puff of hot air on the positivistic teacup' (Horgan, 1993: 17). Despite systems thinking, the 'new' physics, the metaphors of catastrophe and chaos, the reported emergence of a post-positivist paradigm (Schwartz and Ogilvy, 1980) and the postmodern movement (Harvey, 1989), the common epistemology of the Western mind remains crudely positivist.

Human inquiry practitioners assert, in contrast to this positivist world-view, that we can only truly do research *with* persons if we engage with them *as* persons, as co-subjects and thus as co-researchers: hence co-operative inquiry, participatory research, research partnerships, and so on. And while understanding and action are logically separate, they cannot be separated in life: so a science of persons must be an action science. I use the term *human inquiry* to encompass all those forms of search which aim to move beyond the narrow, positivistic and materialist world-view which has come to characterize the latter portion of the twentieth century. While holding on to the scientific ideals of critical self-reflective inquiry and openness to public scrutiny, the practices of human inquiry engage deeply and sensitively with experience, are participative, and aim to integrate action with reflection.

In the context of the epistemological crisis of our times, I have been much persuaded over recent months by the image that the purpose of human inquiry is not so much the search for truth but to *heal*, and above all to heal the alienation, the split that characterizes modern experience. For as R.D. Laing put it

> the ordinary person is a shrivelled, desiccated fragment of what a person can be . . .
> What we call normal is a product of repression, denial, splitting, projection, introjection and other forms of destructive action on experience . . . It is radically estranged from the structure of being. (Laing, 1967: 25–7).

To heal means to make whole: we can only understand our world as a whole if we are part of it; as soon as we attempt to stand outside, we divide and separate. In contrast, making whole necessarily implies participation: one characteristic of a participative world-view is that the individual person is restored to the circle of community and the human community to the context of the wider natural world. To make whole also means to make holy: another characteristic of a participatory world-view is that meaning and mystery are restored to human experience, so that the world is once again experienced as a sacred place (Berman, 1981; Reason, 1993; Skolimowski, 1993).

But what do we really mean by participation, and what are the qualities of a participatory world-view? In particular, does not holism imply a lack of perspective, and so does participation not imply a loss of critical reflective consciousness? Is this not likely to lead to lack of clarity and to superstition? There seems to be a fundamental tension between a holist world-view based on deep participation and an atomist world-view based on dualism. In these first three chapters I explore these questions, tracing different paths in the development of human consciousness, and attempt to show that it is in this tension between a deeply participative experience of our world and the critical consciousness that has developed in the West that a new form of participative consciousness may arise. I will show how the various processes and methodologies of human inquiry can be seen as disciplines of practice which contribute to this development.

But first I want to look in a bit more detail at the fragmentation of consciousness that characterizes modern times; and to contrast this with a story which tells how human experience emerges through the evolution of a creative cosmos.

Fragmentation

Western consciousness is characteristically dualist. As Maurice Ash has recently argued, the very notion of an individual self is at the root of our difficulties because it creates an ontology or world-view in which the knower is detached from the world, rather than implicate within it (Ash, 1992). As Alan Watts puts it with more than a twist of irony, there is in the West a 'taboo about knowing who we really are' – against knowing that we arise out of and are part of the web of being. If we start from the notion of an individual autonomous self, we must separate self from other, knower from what is known, parts from whole, mind from body, masculine from feminine: the whole fragmentation of Western epistemology can be seen as starting from the establishment of the self.

In the story of Western ways of knowing it is objectivity that is most highly prized. Objectivity means standing outside the phenomena being studied, separating the knower from what is known, refusing to 'contaminate' the data, resisting 'going native'. But as Skolimowski points out, objectivity is a 'figment of our minds; it does not exist in nature' (1992: 42); and as we know from many sources, from Heisenberg's uncertainty principle to Zen practice, the observer is inseparable from that which is observed. A participative world-view will move towards forms of knowing that are self-reflexive, that are both deeply engaged and rigorously self-critical. In *Human Inquiry* John Rowan and I coined the term 'critical subjectivity', arguing that the validity of our encounter with experience rests on the high quality, critical, self-aware, discriminating and informed judgements of the co-researchers (Reason and Rowan, 1981).

The separation of knower from known implies a separation of self from other and researcher from subject. Orthodox scientific inquiry is based on the dogma that the researcher is in some way a quite different animal from the subjects studied: as John Heron has pointed out (1971, 1981b), this separation of roles carries with it the implication that only the researcher is able to exercise free will and creative judgement (in being able to discover 'new knowledge'), while those being studied are subject to deterministic laws which it is the researcher's job to discover. A participative methodology in which we conduct research *with* people rather than *on* people attempts to heal this division, proposing that people of all kinds can inquire together into their experience and their practice.

The separation of knower from known leads to the separation of the parts from the whole. Western ways of knowing have, on the whole, encouraged us to divide the phenomena in which we are interested into constituent parts, to measure and count the parts, and then to relate these in relatively simple cause and effect relationships. So we in the West see our world in terms of 'things', constituent parts, and as we do so we reify what is better understood as process (Griffin et al., 1989; Whitehead, 1929). The scientific world-view has been extremely powerful and effective in studying those phenomena that can be seen as 'things', entities that can be identified as separate, real wholes. Thus our times have been described as employing a mechanical metaphor, a view that we live in a 'billiard ball' universe. This perspective co-exists strangely with our knowledge from the further reaches of physics and mathematics that the whole cosmos is an interconnected dance; but it is firmly rooted in the Western collective unconscious. Bateson (1972, 1979) points out that there is a fundamental difference between this world of non-living things and the world of living process, where order arises from the patterns of information flow rather than from physical relationships of cause and effect, and where differences in quality are more profoundly important than differences in quantity.

All these separations on which Western epistemology is founded are closely connected to an emphasis on intellect as the primary means of knowing and to the power of conceptual language. This results in the separation of intellect from experience, so that knowledge that comes in propositional form is valued more highly than intuitive, practical, affective, analogical or spiritual knowledge. It also leads to immediate conscious purpose being valued more highly than systemic wisdom. This reinforces the tendency to think in terms of parts rather than wholes, things rather than processes: naming the parts of the world creates an illusion of real separate objects; concepts drive a wedge, as it were, between experience and understanding. These mental constructions, or paradigms, are immensely robust and self-fulfilling when isolated from experience. We are as a culture beginning to learn that all conceptual knowing is relative, but this learning is not easy: Lawson (1985) has pointed to the sense of vertigo we may experience as concepts crumble and the world as we know it reels off into meaninglessness.

One result of all this abstraction is a loss of the concrete, and specifically a dishonouring of the body and the separation of humanity from the natural world. Berman (1989) writes of the need to 'come to our senses', literally honouring again the wisdom of the body, locating knowing in the experience of sensation instead of in intellectually elaborated paradigms of thought. The body is the lodge of spirit in this life, yet we have an immensely ambivalent relationship to it, often very concerned with the presentation of a 'face', powerful or beautiful, to the outside world, yet being quite out of touch with our physical inner processes. Many approaches to holistic medicine, such as stress reduction and biofeedback, are based on teaching people to pay attention once again to what their body is telling them about its well-being.

Similarly, we may value the natural world from a distance and yet have little idea, and no felt experience, of the damage that patterns of consumption and waste continue to have on the natural world. Much is published about pollution, the destruction of habitats and the extinction of species, but this is not experienced directly as a loss, but at a greater distance. Recently Judi Marshall and I held a discussion with final year undergraduates on the impact of human beings on the natural world. We pointed to many of the ecological horrors reported in the papers over recent weeks – the most startling being the disappearance of fish on the Grand Banks of Newfoundland. What was most striking about the students' response was that they had studied all this at school, and the information no longer had much impact on them. I think on reflection they were as shocked about this as we were. The arguments of the deep ecologists have only just begun to make some of us reconsider the value we place on the natural world (Devall and Sessions, 1985).

The body and the natural world are deeply connected: our body is that piece of wilderness that we carry around with us all the time, a living ecology which provides a home to many creatures and life events, which may be in balance or out of balance. For many city dwellers the body may be the primary contact with the wild, 'a great beauty that seethes with intelligence, that is ever surprising and refreshing' (Swimme and Berry, 1992: 127). Gary Snyder's essays on the 'practice of the wild' (1990) show how we may delight in and savour wilderness. A participatory world-view will appreciate the extent to which civilized life depends directly on the balance of natural living processes, and take us back to experience of the body and of the wild.

As I will explore more closely in the next chapter, all these issues can also be seen in terms of masculine and feminine: language, concepts and analysis are among the archetypal qualities of the masculine; participation is among the archetypal qualities of the feminine. Over 3000 years of Western culture the masculine has been separated from the feminine and overvalued, so that certain masculine attributes have been culturally defined as desirable and certain female attributes as less desirable. As a result our experience and understanding of both male and female qualities is warped and distorted (Marshall, 1984, 1989, 1994).

Western civilization has been sustained by a myth that it is at the peak of civilization and the evolution of consciousness; there is thus a tendency to separate Western epistemology from other ways of knowing. When we look to other times and other cultures we see them through the distorting lens of our own epistemology (Allen, 1992), or project onto them our own violent shadow. Members of mainstream European and North American culture often resent the demands of women and minorities who want their culture and ways of knowing to be honoured, seeing this merely as a demand for 'political correctness' rather than as a deep challenge to narrow-minded ways. I believe that most of us in the West have little idea how separated and defended our civilization and our consciousness actually is. At the very worst, this separation continues to express the European imperialist and genocidal adventure of colonizing the rest of the planet, a colonization which has oppressed other peoples and the planet itself. A participatory world-view would be pluralist, honouring the teachings of different traditions, and finding ways of learning from indigenous perspectives on learning and inquiry.

Finally, in this catalogue of fragmentation, I believe it is essential to acknowledge that as a culture we are separated from the sacred, the numinous, the mysterious. In grasping for control and knowledge we have lost a sense of what is whole and holy (Reason, 1993). One consequence of reductionism is the illusion of understanding; in contrast phenomena as wholes can never be fully known for the very reason that we are a part of them, leading us to acknowledge and respect the greater mystery that envelops our knowing.

The universe story

I find Susan Griffin's term 'split culture' evocative of our time:

> We who are born into this civilization have inherited a habit of mind. We are divided
> against ourselves. We no longer regard ourselves as part of this earth. We regard our
> fellow human beings as enemies. And, very young, we learn to disown parts of our
> own being. (Griffin, 1984: 175)

We need, I believe, a way of knowing which helps us to heal this split, this separation, this alienation. We need a way of knowing which integrates truth
with love, beauty and wholeness, a way of knowing which acknowledges the
essential physical qualities of knowing. We need a new story about our place
in the scheme of things. While I am aware that the current academic vogue has
made 'grand narrative' unfashionable, I agree with Charlene Spretnak (1991)
that the fashion of deconstructive postmodernism is nihilistic, indeed, is an
extension of the alienation of modernism. If voices are just voices and have no
claim to truth, the search for voice becomes the search for any old voice; it no
longer matters what we say about ourselves. I believe it is important that we
consider the quality of the stories we create and consider whether they do justice to human possibilities and our place in the scheme of things. We need to
ask whether we like the story we are creating and in which we play a part
(Kremer, 1992c: 27). New healing stories will, I believe, be based on a vision of
ourselves as deeply rooted in and emerging out of a living and creative universe. Brian Swimme (a physicist) and Thomas Berry (a cultural historian)
offer such a vision in their story of the universe and the place of human beings
within it (Swimme, 1984; Berry, 1988; Swimme and Berry, 1992).

They argue that we are without a comprehensive story of the universe,
without a creation story that is appropriate for our times. People throughout
history in every land have told stories of the universe which gave meaning to
their life in its fullest sense. The modern scientific story tells much about the
development of the physical universe, but sets humanity apart from the natural
world. What is needed, they assert, is a story which interprets the account of
the universe given by modern scientific observation in a way that acknowledges the presence and majesty of the universe and the human place within it:

> the universe carries within itself a psychic-spiritual as well as a physical-material
> dimension . . . the human activates the most profound dimension of the universe
> itself, its capacity to reflect on and celebrate itself in conscious self-awareness.
> (Berry, 1988, p. 131–2)

They start their story from the beginning of time when 'Fifteen billion years
ago, in a great flash, the universe flared forth into being. . . . Originating
power brought forth a universe' (Swimme and Berry, 1992: 7–17). They tell the
story of the development of the physical cosmos, the emergence and development of living beings, and the development of human society, drawing on a
wide range of scholarship and imaginative vision for their understanding.
From this originating power they trace the evolution of matter, of galaxies,
stars, planets; how early life emerged on earth and developed into plants and

animals; how early humans developed the Neolithic village – a stable form of human society to which most members of the human race have belonged – and moved on to develop complex civilizations and industrial societies. As they look at the power and potential destructiveness of modern times, they see people in industrial societies seemingly unaware that they belong to a greater dance, and thus wreaking havoc on the life systems of the planet. We are moving, they say, into an Ecozoic Age in which the well-being of the whole must be our primary concern.

The Swimme and Berry story is of the cosmos as a self-generating, essentially creative process which emerges through *differentiation, autopoiesis,* and *communion.* Differentiation, including the violence of destruction, leads to the creation of more and more complex entities, from simple atoms to advanced life forms; and also to the increasing complexity of relationships between entities. Autopoiesis highlights the self-organizing, systemic dynamics of these differentiated structures, their coherence, their tendency to work according to their own internal organizing principles. Communion honours the essential relatedness of existence, for 'Nothing is itself without everything else' (1992: 77)

> The universe evolves into beings that are different from each other, and that organize themselves. But in addition to this, the universe advances into community – into a differentiated web of relationships among sentient centers of creativity. (Swimme and Berry, 1992: 77)

And here maybe is a special message for humanity and for my consideration of participation in human inquiry:

> The loss of relationship, with its consequent alienation, is a kind of supreme evil in the universe. In the religious world this loss was traditionally understood as an ultimate mystery. To be locked up in a private world, to be cut off from intimacy with other beings, to be incapable of entering into mutual presence – such conditions were taken as the essence of damnation. (Swimme and Berry, 1992: 78)

And so this new story of the universe shows again how participative relationship is of the very essence of all life, and certainly of human life. We are not an alien species set on earth out of nowhere, 'We bear the universe in our beings as the universe bears us in its being. The two have a total presence to each other and to that deeper mystery out of which both the universe and ourselves have emerged' (Berry, 1988: 132).

I believe that the development of a participative world-view requires an imaginative recognition of humanity's fundamental participation in the natural world, a recognition of the way the human mind is engaged in a co-creative dance with the primeval givenness of the cosmos (Skolimowski, 1992). In this vision humanity is 'nature rendered self-conscious' (Bookchin, 1991: 313), one part of the cosmos capable of reflecting on itself, which has evolved so it stands on the threshold of conscious participation in the unfolding of the whole.

2

Participation in the Evolution of Consciousness

Peter Reason

In forging a new story for ourselves and a new vision of human possibilities I think it is important to explore the development of human consciousness. Participation is not simply a matter of interpersonal skill or political constitution – although these are important – it is also about the foundations of human understanding. That it is human consciousness that we must understand is emphasized by Mumford, who argues

> Every transformation of [the human species] . . . has rested on a new metaphysical and ideological base; or rather, upon deeper stirrings and intuitions whose rationalised expression takes the form of a new picture of the cosmos and the nature of [humanity]. (1957: 179)

Of course, any account of the story of human development will be just that, an account, a story; but while we cannot give a 'true' account, we can attempt to be true to our sources and, at the same time 'fashion a myth', as Mumford puts it, which will be of service to our time. The story I tell in these chapters is necessarily my story, grounded in my intuitions, influenced by my reading of the writers in whom I have delighted and on whose ideas I have drawn, and woven in with the texture of my life experience. I have fashioned a myth which I hope provides a vision of a participatory consciousness which helps collaborative researchers map their way through the territory. But as you read it, please remember that the map is not the territory and that to fashion a myth is not to state a positivist truth.

The old (modern) story of progress is one of separate human consciousness battling against the forces of irrationality and of nature, emerging out of the mire of superstition towards one rational scientific truth. This story was amplified by the enormous success of scientific models in explaining the world and technological solutions to immediate material problems. The newer story (which is of course also an ancient story) points out that our rational consciousness rests on an essential foundation of tacit knowledge (Polanyi, 1958; Berman, 1981): underneath our experience of separateness is a profound and mysterious participation. We are in endless open communication with all that is around us, so we can say of the cosmos, 'I am not it, yet it is all of me' (Crook, 1993: 46; see also Ash, 1992).

Modern biologists and systems theorists use the principle of autopoiesis –

a word coined from the Greek words *auto* (self) and *poiesis* (poetry or making) and so literally meaning the self-generating poetry of living systems (Segal, 1986: 127; Maturana and Varela, 1987) to describe the self-organizing property of all living beings. Autopoiesis tells us that all creatures continually participate in the creation of their worlds; the interesting question for the present is the different ways in which we humans do so.

If we look at the evidence, mainly from anthropology and the study of myth and the history of consciousness, a fairly consistent story can be told which suggests that human consciousness has evolved (and is evolving) through three broad phases. In the first phase human consciousness is undifferentiated from the natural world and people live in deep unconscious communion with their surroundings. In the second phase human beings progressively differentiate themselves from their environment, developing a separate sense of self and of community; in an extreme of this phase (which characterizes much of Western consciousness at the present time) participation is denied and people live in an alienated consciousness. In the third phase the sense of participation is regained but in a new way so that human beings participate intentionally and awarely in the creation of their world. This last phase is on the whole more potential than realized.

Owen Barfield's account of this development in his book *Saving the Appearances* (1957) provides a useful frame. He referred to these three phases as original participation, the loss or alienation of participation in the modern age, and final participation. It is particularly important to note that the worlds of original participation, loss of participation, and final participation are literally different: different worlds are created because the forms of interaction between human consciousness and the primal givenness of the cosmos are different. In particular the world of final participation is not the same as the world of original participation – it is more conscious, more choiceful, more self-reflexive (Kremer, 1992a: 173).

In some ways I am uncomfortable with Barfield's terminology. His description of the second phase as loss of participation and as alienated consciousness (he describes it (1957: 43) as a form of thinking that 'seeks to destroy . . . participation') implies a denigration of individualized consciousness and the creative differentiation that it brings. Barfield's terms also offer the danger that both original and final participation will be idealized and seen as bringing about some unreal harmonious world. And as Kremer points out (1992a: 176), it implies that there is one conclusive outcome to the development of consciousness: how do we know that 'final' participation will be final? I shall borrow Kremer's terms and refer to the three phases as *original participation*, *unconscious participation*, and *future participation* since these are fairly neutral. The reader should be warned that these terms are not entirely satisfactory either, in particular since the term unconscious participation is called upon to encompass both the alienation of modern consciousness that I have described, and also the creativity of differentiation.

Original participation

In original participation human beings are embedded in their world, consciousness is undifferentiated, there is no separation between subject and object, and little reflectiveness. Barfield (1957) describes this as a world of representations, collective experiences of the world, which are encountered directly: they have not yet been converted by 'thinking about' into external 'things' with a separate existence in an 'outside world'.

Sukie Colgrave tells the story of original participation through the eyes of Daoist thought. She tells of the Great Nothingness, the undifferentiated Mystery which is the source of everything:

> Before the Heaven and Earth existed
> There was something nebulous:
> Silent, isolated,
> Standing alone, changing not.
> Eternally revolving without fail.
> Worthy to be the Mother of all things.
> I do not know its name
> And address it as Tao. (Colgrave, 1979: 8; quoted from *Tao Te Ching*)

The evolution of all things – the physical world and human consciousness – takes place through a process of increasing differentiation from an amorphous, chaotic and unknowable origin, from the original Great Mystery. Until the beginnings of individual consciousness there is no separation between the world and the human psyche, and thus a deep experience of peace and instinctive harmony – the mythical Golden Age. Whether such a period actually existed is arguable. However, Colgrave points to an ancient period when this radically different human *consciousness* was expressed in early myth and literature, and personified in the image of the Great Mother who appears in a great variety of forms throughout the ancient world.

> She is the universal principle who gives birth to all things, protects them in life and calls them to Her in death. She is the vessel which contains and generates the cosmos, the Dao, or unifying principle, which guards, guides and permeates the infant consciousness of humanity. The distinctions of our 'either-or' consciousness are not relevant to the Great Mother, for in her these polarities are still undifferentiated. (1979: 30–31)

Baring and Cashford's more recent scholarship suggests that early human consciousness was inspired and focused by 'the myth of the goddess', so that the universe was perceived as an organic, alive, sacred whole in which humanity participates: 'Everything is woven together in one cosmic web, where all orders of manifest and unmanifest life are related, because all share in the sanctity of the original source' (Baring and Cashford, 1991: xi). These early mythological images can tell us a great deal about original consciousness and the way it is participative:

> Matriarchal consciousness is a diffuse, undifferentiated and all-embracing vision of the world which knows from within rather than from without, subjectively rather than objectively. It experiences the essential unity of the cosmos, and knows humanity as integral rather than separate from the whole. To this consciousness life and

death are part of one continuous process controlled by Mother Earth. (Colgrave, 1979: 35–36)

Another account of human development is provided by Murray Bookchin. As an eco-anarchist, he is fiercely critical of much current thinking: 'few people know how to build ideas anymore' (1991: xvii). He is particularly impatient with the 'mystical ecologies that are becoming popular today' (1991: xvii) and would probably be alarmed to find his ideas used alongside those of Colgrave. However, from his very different perspective Bookchin takes a remarkably similar line. In his portrayal of 'organic societies' he argues that they were based on a feeling of unity both between the individual and the community and between the community and its environment. As part of the balance of nature, a truly ecological community develops in a way which is peculiar to its ecosystem 'with an active sense of participation in the overall environment and the cycles of nature'.

> The direct involvement of humanity with nature is thus not an abstraction . . . Nature begins *as* life. From the very outset of human consciousness, it enters directly into consociation with humanity – not merely harmonization or even balance. Nature as life eats at every repast, succours every new birth, grows with every child, aids every hand that throws a spear or plucks a plant, warms itself at the hearth in the dancing shadows, and sits amid the councils of the community just as the rustle of leaves and grasses is part of the air itself . . . But nature is not merely a habitat; it is a participant that advises the community with its omens, secures it with its camouflage, leaves its telltale messages in the broken twigs and footprints, whispers warnings in the wind's voice, nourishes it with the largesse of plants and animals, and in its countless functions and counsels is absorbed into the community's nexus of rights and duties. (Bookchin, 1991: 47; emphasis in original)

Bookchin writes of a deep and essentially unconscious sense of community in organic societies, an 'equality of non-equals'. He suggests that our modern words – participation, reciprocity, exchange, mutual aid – are so imbued with our perspective of the separate autonomous ego that they do not begin to capture the deep complementarity that existed between individuals, age groups and sexes.

He sees these societies as matricentric, centred around women's activities of gathering and horticulture. As Colgrave, he sees the world contained by the figure and symbolism of the Great Goddess as an expression of 'the unqualified nature of mother-love itself' (Bookchin, 1991: 60). It is this unconditional love, without expectation of any reward, which 'makes humanness its own end rather than the tool of hierarchy and classes' (Bookchin, 1991: 61).

Bookchin argues that these original organic societies are the fundamental basis for human life, but he does not eulogize them – seeing them as fragile and parochial. In particular, he argues that since their complementarity is unconscious they are completely unguarded against hierarchy and class rule. He contrasts their unconscious complementarity with the ideals of universal justice and freedom, which emerged much later and allow us the ability to extend our sense of humanity beyond immediate kin to encompass all other peoples.

So original participation is primarily to be found in societies based on hunter-gathering and horticulture. In such societies economic activities, myth,

ceremony and story-telling knit together in an integrated whole; individuals
have permeable and fluid personality structures, open to the collective conscious, the world of landscape, plants and animals, and to trance experience.
Such peoples will experience themselves as embedded in and part of their
local ecology. Body, emotions, mind and spirit will all be integrated aspects of
the whole human person, integral aspects of their way of sensing and experiencing (Kremer, 1992b).

It is difficult for those of us in industrial societies at the end of the twentieth
century, wondering what it means, if anything, to be entering a 'postmodern'
age, to imagine such a way of being. It is easy either to idealize or to reject, to
imagine 'how wonderful', or to believe with Hobbes that life in those times
really was nasty, brutish and short. It is worth contemplating that many peoples continued in such a way of being, living in stable societies and balance with
their ecosystems until quite recent encounters with modern culture. It is also
worth contemplating that in such societies economic activities – hunting, gathering and horticulture – took up far less time than do agriculture or industry,
leaving large periods of life free for the elaboration of life through play and ceremony (see for example Reader, 1988: 144; Norberg-Hodge, 1991: 35).

Original participation is also not so far away from us all for it remains at the
ground of our being. John Heron argues that human experience originates in
'a resonance with being'. Human persons 'indwell the world, participate in its
qualities', and experience other presences in our world not primarily by definitions but 'by attunement, resonance and empathy in direct acquaintance and
encounter' (1992: 92). While we may relegate this experience of deep participation to relative unawareness, it remains with us, to touch us, if we will allow
it, at those odd moments of a direct encounter with the presence of otherness.
Such moments are truly wyrd (Bates, 1983) in that they provide an experience
of deep connectedness. It is for this reason that the deep ecologists recommend
wilderness experiences as part of the cure for our alienation from the living
presence of the world.

Unconscious participation

For a variety of reasons, original participation cannot be sustained as the pattern of organization of consciousness. In Colgrave's story, everything – the
physical world and human consciousness – arises through the process of
increasing differentiation from an amorphous, chaotic and unknowable origin,
from the original Great Mystery. In Daoist philosophy it is through the interaction of yin and yang, the primary polarity, that all things evolve. *Yang* can be
described as the masculine, active force which separates and individuates; *yin*
as the feminine principle of relatedness which receives, nourishes and embraces.

The evolution of consciousness can be seen within the myths of the Great
Mother who, encompassing both yin and yang in undifferentiated fashion, was
experienced as all-embracing, all-nourishing, all-protecting. While personified as female, she contained within the seeds of an undeveloped masculine
principle; she was thus androgynous, bisexual, virgin in the sense of being

complete to herself. The emergence of human consciousness is associated with the differentiation of the masculine – the yang attributes of separating, penetrating, cutting, analysis.

> The birth and development of the masculine principle in consciousness revolutionises humanity's experience of itself and of the world. Instead of participating instinctively in the rhythms of nature, being contained and regulated by her laws, a consciousness emerges, which assumes that people, not nature, should be primarily responsible for structuring human life. It seeks to differentiate itself from the old pre-conscious identity with the cosmos and replace the previous acceptance of control by unknown natural forces and law with the ambition to take and order nature through understanding her. Such consciousness searches for independence, autonomy and freedom. It pursues these aims through the development of a number of characteristics and skills which, in different ways, all express the central differentiating impulse of the masculine, or Yang, principle. (Colgrave, 1979: 71)

In the evolution of myth the masculine principle, which carries this task of separation, emerges first as son of the Great Mother who later 'rejects her protection and finally usurps her authority' (Colgrave, 1979: 44). With this emergence of human consciousness more negative images arise of the Great Mother as all-devouring and threatening the emergence of human consciousness: 'the Goddess became almost exclusively associated with "Nature" as the chaotic force to be mastered, and the God took the role of conquering or ordering nature from his counterpole of "spirit"' (Baring and Cashford, 1991: xii). Thus humanity and nature became polarized.

Wilber tells a similar story about the emergence of what he terms the mental-ego. While in early myths the individual usually comes to a tragic end – killed, castrated, sacrificed to the Great Mother, who always triumphs – in the later 'hero' myths the individual breaks free, transforms and transcends the Great Mother: the hero representing the new egoic structure of consciousness. Wilber makes the important point that while the ego, as a necessary course in the differentiation of consciousness, needed to break free from its embeddedness in the Great Mother, 'in its zeal to assert its independence, it not only *transcended* the Great Mother, which was desirable; it *repressed* the Great Mother, which was disastrous' (1981: 187; emphasis in original):

> No longer harmony with the Heavens, but a 'conquering of space'; no longer respect for Nature, but a technological assault on Nature. The ego structure, in order to rise arrogantly above creation, had to suppress and repress the Great Mother, mythologically, psychologically, and sociologically. And it repressed the Great Mother in *all* her forms. It is one thing to gain freedom from the fluctuations of nature, emotions, instincts, and environment – it is quite another to alienate them. In short, the Western ego did not just gain its freedom from the Great Mother, it severed its deep interconnectedness with her. (1981: 187; emphasis in original)

So for Colgrave, Wilber and Baring and Cashford (who base their accounts on the scholarship of others including Campbell, Gebser and Neumann as well as on their own research) the necessary differentiation of consciousness becomes the domination of one form of consciousness over another, and the consciousness of the Western world shifts from original participation to a denial of participation.

Berman (1981) has written an account of the history of this shift since the seventeenth century. He shows how the denial of participation is also the denial of the body, of myth and of the feminine. He points out that even though we repress the connection, the explicit, conscious knowledge of the Western world must always rest on a pre-conscious, tacit knowing; similarly participation is never abolished – we human beings remain an integral part of this planet and of this cosmos however much at times we choose to deny it.

With the denial of participation human consciousness is left uncontained by a greater whole. People living in a culture characterized by original partic-ipation may have lived in fear of the power and unpredictability of their physical and spiritual environment, but they belonged. Once participation is denied, humanity is left drifting, unconnected to the greater whole, open to existential terror at the meaningless and contingency of being. The part can-not contain the whole; conscious purpose can only encompass a limited arc of the ecological circuits of the natural world (Bateson, 1972). The mind develops endless anxiety-driven intellectual systems to fill the void, and the experience of original participation is driven yet further away.

Bookchin's account of the shift from the participative consciousness of organic societies provides a different emphasis, for it is in the emergence of social hierarchy that the old order is destroyed. In those societies that became more complex and differentiated, specialization of tasks was organized on the basis of gender and age: women's work was in the home and men's outside; the young were active producers and the old the source of wisdom and tradition. While it is possible for such specialization to remain fully complementary, it also contains the seeds of domination as separate interest groups develop (particularly the elders and the men) and gain power: differentiation becomes separation as interests are seen as in conflict. The civic sphere outside the home grows and develops a meaning in its own right. More powerful and specialized technologies are developed. Hierarchies emerge and with them 'epistemologies of rule' based on notions of command and obedience and subject–object relationships and a 'transcendental' notion of order over nature and society.

Bookchin makes no bones about his view that this is all bound up with the emergence of patriarchy and the development of a male-orientated society; and that the development of hierarchy in society goes hand in hand with the oppression of nature:

> woman haunts this male 'civilization' with a power that is more than archaic or atavistic. Every male-oriented society must persistently exorcise her ancient powers, which abide in her ability to reproduce the species, to rear it, to provide it with a lov-ing refuge from the 'unfriendly world', indeed, to accomplish those material achievements – food cultivation, pottery, and weaving, to cite the most assured of women's technical inventions – that rendered that world possible, albeit on terms quite different from those formulated by the male . . . The subjugation of her nature . . . forms the archetypal act of domination that ultimately gives rise to man's imagery of a subjugated nature. (Bookchin, 1991: 121)

It would appear that the emergence of patriarchal hierarchy is to some extent dependent on the ecology of the region in which the original community is located. Bookchin argues that hierarchy emerged first among nomadic desert people as opposed to settled horticulturists – and par excellence among the Hebrews. Turner (1980) sees Western civilization's pervasive antagonism towards the natural world as having its roots in the desert cultures of the Near East, which were forced to wrest a living from a reluctant land. Crook (1980; personal communication) has traced the influence of ecology on social organization, and argues that while settled societies based on horticulture may be organized in a complementary and matrifocal fashion, nomadic cultures are more likely to be less settled and more land-hungry, to develop separate arenas for men and for women and thus more likely to develop hierarchical and dominating social organizations. These 'dominator' cultures (Eisler, 1990) subsequently invade the more settled and peaceful horticultural peoples. The development of agriculture on a larger scale, the consequent emergence of a surplus of food production and the growth of cities amplified this process.

To summarize, unconscious participation, and with it an alienated consciousness, appears first in nomadic tribes and seems to have reached a peak in Western industrial societies. Such societies will experience themselves as separate from a hostile and chaotic natural world, and strive for control over it. Mythological process will be unconscious and devalued, and intellectual processes overvalued, science eventually taking over as the new (unconscious) myth. Individuals will have relatively rigid and boundaried personality structures; the experience of trance states will be rare and marginalized (although the whole society in some way remains in unconscious trance). The relationship with wilderness becomes increasingly oppositional. Mind is prized as the most important human faculty; the body either pampered or tolerated; emotions repressed; and spirit devalued or denied (Kremer, 1992b).

Barfield interestingly terms this state of affairs an 'idolatry', because what is in essence a *representation* of the world – the phenomena that arise in the original participation between human consciousness and the primordial stuff of the cosmos – is reified, experienced 'as objects in their own right, existing independently of human consciousness' (1957: 42). This confusion of the image with the real is the essence of idolatry. As he says, 'Idolatry is an ugly and emphatic word and it was deliberately chosen to emphasize certain ugly features, and still more ugly possibilities, inherent in the present situation' (1957: 42). However, he also acknowledges some of the advantages of experiencing objects as separate from human consciousness, to which I shall return later.

Feminist re-visioning of human development

From a feminist perspective, this story of human development in the West is a story of a masculine path. It is clear that the evolution of the Western mind has been a masculine project (Tarnas, 1991) and has been founded on the repression of the feminine – not only the repression of the undifferentiated consciousness of original participation, but also of the feminine wisdom principle, personified in the figure of Sophia who, as Long shows (1992) originally stood alongside and ultimately contained the masculine deity. Feminist writers argue that women in industrial societies carry the muted voice of participative consciousness within patriarchal culture and are aware of the violence done to human and planetary relationships by loss of participation, hierarchy and alienation. Modern feminist scholarship points to potential differences between women and men in styles of thinking and valuing (Marshall, 1993). Thus Gilligan (1982) writes of the importance of relationship and Miller (1976) of affiliation as central to women's identity. Belenky and her colleagues (Belenky et al., 1986; Goldberger et al., 1987) have explored women's ways of knowing and emphasize the importance of dialogue, reciprocity and co-operation. Eco-feminists have asserted the parallels between the oppression of women and the destruction of the planet (Plant, 1989). While this work is important for women in developing their authentic identity in Western society, it is also crucial for humanity as a whole in showing that alienation from participation is not necessarily at the foundation of human consciousness.

So was the route through an extreme form of loss of participation necessary for the development of human consciousness? Did the human ego have to haul itself out of the unconscious thrall of the Great Mother, have to go on to *repress* the Great Mother as Wilber describes, to *exorcise her ancient powers* as Bookchin has it? If we look at the story of Western patriarchal industrial cultures the answer appears to be 'Yes', but with the benefit of this feminist scholarship an alternative perspective emerges: in some societies human consciousness may have evolved without going through this over-masculinized stage of unconscious participation.

Riane Eilser's (1990) thesis, in her study of the development of European culture, is that society can be organized in two contrasting fashions, which she terms the *dominator* model and the *partnership* model. Societies organized on the dominator model tend to be hierarchical, warlike, and in particular to value masculine principles over the feminine; partnership societies tend to be peaceful, agricultural, and, while they may specialize tasks along gender lines, do not raise one above the other. Eisler proposes, on the basis of careful examination and re-visioning of the archaeological evidence, 'the original direction in the mainstream of our cultural evolution was toward partnership, but that, following a period of chaos and almost total cultural disruption, there occurred a fundamental social shift' (1990: xvii). The shift was towards the dominator model, triggered by the invasion of fierce, warlike patriarchal tribes from the Asian and European north and the desert south.

Partnership societies were highly evolved. It would appear from the archaeological evidence that human society emerged from Barfield's original participation much earlier than he proposed. Neolithic civilization was highly sophisticated in Europe, and was the time when 'the first great breakthroughs in our material and social technology were made' (Eisler, 1990: 12); 'early Europeans developed a complex social organization involving craft specialization' (Eisler, 1990: 13; see also Swimme and Berry, 1992: Ch. 9). It is difficult to believe that these complex societies were based on a pure form of original participation: there must have been a high degree of purpose, planning and reflexiveness. Yet the social organization was articulated in terms of equality and partnership.

Thus the picture from archaeology and from myth is different from that presented by Colgrave and Wilber:

> the world of myth was not polarized into female and male as it was among the Indo-Europeans and many other nomadic and pastoral peoples of the steppes. Both principles were manifest side by side. The male divinity in the shape of the young man or male animal appears to affirm and strengthen the forces of the creative and active female. Neither is subordinate to the other: by complementing one another, their power is doubled. (Gimbutas, 1982; as quoted in Eisler, 1990: 27)

The example of Crete is central to Eisler's book, for here was a civilization noted as remarkable by male and female archaeologists and historians, immensely sophisticated, economically successful and highly egalitarian. Eisler characterizes it as a place with 'joyful and mythically meaningful ritual and artistic play . . . [with] equal partnership between women and men. . . . Cretan art appears to reflect a society in which power is not equated with dominance, destruction, and oppression' (1990: 32–6).

Eisler's story is one told for a purpose, to re-vision our view of power, domination and partnership, and to revalue the feminine. Morris Berman has pointed out to me in conversation that her scholarship is seen by many as flawed (Fox-Genovese, 1987; Lefkowitz, 1992). However, the revisioning of society that she offers is timely and has been an inspiration to many. My intention in drawing on her work is not to idealize ancient Crete but to offer an appreciation of a possible society based on very different assumptions from those of the modern West: Eisler offers a new picture of the development of European civilization and offers the partnership model of cultural development. In the Western hemisphere indigenous feminist studies offer a similar picture. Paula Gunn Allen describes Native American tribal cultures as 'posited on the notion of participation . . . all life is a circle and everything has its place within it. Life is really a kind of dynamic sphere in which everything is interconnected, alive, and intelligent' (1986: 26–7).

In her book *The Sacred Hoop* (1992) Allen points out how often Western studies of tribal cultures offer distorted understanding because they force these cultures into a patriarchal frame. She describes tribal cultures as 'more often gynocratic than not, they are never patriarchal' (1992: 2). She points to the complexity and sophistication of these cultures, in which

> a multitude of personality and character types can function positively within the social order because the systems are focused on social responsibility rather than on privilege and on the realities of the human constitution rather than on denial based social fictions to which human beings are compelled to conform by powerful individuals within society. (1992: 3)

One particularly interesting aspect of this for my current argument is that in some traditional tribal cultures there was a much wider latitude in sexual style: passive, nurturing men and assertive women have their place, as do female and male homosexuals and transvestites. It would appear that gender identity was traditionally far less polarized and antagonistic than in the West.

This observation conforms with Watts' (1963) contention that Western epistemology tends to place opposites in an antagonistic dualism while the Eastern
cultures he studied place them in a creative interactional dance.

Allen's essay on the tradition of Native American sacred literature in particular describes a highly developed, self-reflective yet still participative culture:

> The tribes seek – through song, ceremony, legend, sacred stories (myths), and tales –
> to embody, articulate, and share reality, to bring the isolated, private self into har-
> mony and balance with this reality, to verbalize the sense of the majesty and reverent
> mystery of all things, and to actualize, in language, those truths that give to human-
> ity its greatest significance and dignity. (1992: 55)

This is not a description of original participation in the sense of being unconscious and unreflective.

Allen espouses a dialectical form of consciousness in which the boundaries
are fluid and the person can move in and out of deep participation: in the world
of everyday life the person is a distinct being in a world of separate (though interconnected) objects, while non-ordinary reality is far more relative, with the
potential of merging with other beings or with the whole of existence. A full
adult in traditional tribal society is able to experience in both ways (1986: 29).

Thus while the route to future participation for Western civilization may be
through the loss of participation, this may not be so for all humanity. Eisler,
Allen and others (Stone, 1978, 1992; Gimbutas, 1982) point to the past and
present existence of cultures in which a reflective human consciousness has differentiated out of original participation in much more fluid ways.

This cautionary comment is needed if we are not to be misled by Barfield's
framework. The danger of evolutionary or developmental maps of consciousness or personality is that they are usually composed from a mainstream
Western perspective and see Western rationality as the high point of human
consciousness. Some of us in the West are just discovering the limits of the
modern world-view and are seeking a new participative consciousness, which
other cultures may have already developed. In addition, many indigenous
peoples have been forced to live within the tension between their traditional
cultures, which may have strong elements of original participation, and
Western unconscious and alienated participation. As a result, members of
such societies may have evolved further towards a future participation than
any of us in the West (Kremer, 1992b).

Fals-Borda and Rahman (1991), describing the process of participatory
action research with oppressed peoples, specifically celebrate the participative
quality of their cultural relationships. They describe them as 'rooted in cultural
traditions of the common people . . . which are resplendent with feelings and
attitudes of an altruistic, co-operative and communal nature and which are
genuinely democratic' (1991: 5). My first response to this was that it might be
an idealization of oppressed peoples; but if I take seriously the work of Eisler
and her colleagues I see that there may be here an important insight.

As Western cultures move towards a future participation a new relationship
may develop between the industrial and indigenous peoples of the world, with
a revaluing of the gifts of participative consciousness that the latter have to

offer. These cultures may then again begin to develop spontaneously as imperialist and genocidal pressures subside. As the representatives of indigenous peoples assert in the Kari-Oca Village Declaration:

> We, the Indigenous Peoples, maintain our inherent rights to self-determination. We have always had the right to decide our own forms of government, to use our own laws, to raise and educate our children, to our own cultural identity without interference. (Kari-Oca Village Declaration, 1992)

Valid and degenerate forms of participation

However these contrasting forms of consciousness arose in the history of human consciousness – and we can imagine that this took place through several diverse pathways – I find it helpful to see them as exhibiting particularly valid and degenerate forms in contemporary life. By valid forms I mean those which elaborate and develop, multiplying possibilities of human experience, which encourage self-directedness and self-articulation; and which support communication and communion (here I am using as criteria of quality Swimme and Berry's characteristics of the creative cosmos: differentiation, autopoiesis, and communion). In contrast degenerate forms are those which in some sense rigidify, distort and close down possibilities. In making this distinction it is important to watch out for an almost inevitable tendency to stereotype and idealize.

Original participation honours humanity's embeddedness in the wholeness, the seamless web of the world. It allows us to resonate with being, to experience our presence in the world, to encounter directly other presences in the world and presence of the world as a whole. This capacity for resonating with being is the foundation of all experience, it is the source from which emerges the imagery in which we clothe this world of presence – the imagery of the senses and of dream and story, myth and archetype. Here I am following Heron's argument that the human capacity for directly encountering the presence of the world, and the imagery that cascades from this, is prior to language, categories and concepts, and is the bedrock experiential knowing on which all else is built (Heron, 1992).

So a valid form of original participation means that the individual, with soft and permeable character structure, will feel in alignment and community with the 'other', including the human, animal, plant and mineral worlds, and would experience these as infused with sacred presence. Awareness will be immediate rather than reflective, emphasizing experience – physically and kinaesthetically – and imagination – in myth, dream, song and story. Individual permeability will be reflected in the culture, with no harsh boundaries dividing cultural groups (gender, class, race, sexual preference, etc.).

That this authentic form of deep participation has been highly developed can be seen from accounts of indigenous people's experience world-wide – and in particular the accounts of healers and shamanic experience (Black Elk and Lyon, 1990). In the West we may see it in the life work of mystics such as Meister Eckhart (Fox, 1983), and some artists and poets. Barfield turned to the Romantic movement for 'a kind of instinctive impulse towards iconoclasm'

(1957: 137) which might topple the idols of reification; in particular he explored Goethe's scientific work, which he sees as containing 'the germ of a systematic investigation of phenomena by way of participation' (1957: 137–8; see also Bortoft, 1986; Goodwin, 1992). However Heron (1992) argues that this kind of direct experience of the presence of the world is available to each one of us, and clearly can be enhanced through the exercises he describes, those offered by Houston (1982), and through disciplines such as meditation and martial arts.

In degenerate forms of original participation consciousness is buried rather than immersed, flooded by context so that boundaries are lost or destroyed rather than permeable. Mythologies degenerate into superstition; playfulness becomes mere entertainment. Individuals disappear and societies stagnate, caught unawarely in recursive cycles. This is the ever-present danger of original participation: the notion of karma may be apt to describe some aspects of this.

I have already explored in Chapter 1 the degenerate form of unconscious participation, in which individual experience is isolated and cut off, fragile and brittle, wounded and distressed; and the structures of society are similarly rigid. I have argued in the present chapter that it was not the *differentiation* of consciousness that was the problem – that was necessary for the articulation of diverse forms of being; rather it was the *repression* and *denial* of participation, and the domination of one form of consciousness over another.

What is important for our time is to articulate a valid form of this differentiated consciousness. The essence of this is expressed by Martin Buber in his essay 'Distance and Relation' (1965). Human life, he writes, is based on a twofold movement, the first of which he calls 'the primal setting at a distance' and the second 'entering into relation': 'That the first movement is the pre-supposition of the other is plain from the fact that one can enter into relation only with being which has been set at a distance' (1965: 60). The setting at a distance supposes a boundary to the self, but one through which one can reach to Other, so that knower and known are distinct (but not separate) centres of being. Consciousness can become purposive and rational, and as Bookchin (1991) points out can range beyond the immediate situation to encompass the universal human and the wider process of the planet: notions of justice, freedom and human rights are possible from this consciousness. It is a world-view based on concepts and practice, on the development of the human mind as the primary way of being in the world.

A major pitfall for autonomous differentiated consciousness as it remains unconscious of participation is that it will get caught in one belief system, taking words and concepts to be the things in themselves, mistaking the map for the territory and not realizing the many visions of the world which are possible – the essence of idolatry, as Barfield points out. It may also mistake the process of map-making for the exploration of the territory, so that knowledge becomes bound up in intellectual structures rather than in cycles of experience, imagery, practice and reflection. Once intellect escapes the discipline of deep participative experience it quite literally creates all manner of worlds and can be quite ungrounded and out of touch. A second major pitfall is the tendency to cut through and attempt to control, through straight line purposive thinking, the complex ecological webs that constitute the natural world, and in doing so cut through essential feedback loops that maintain balance and prevent runaway escalation (Bateson, 1972).

There is a world of difference between a consciousness that fragments and rips apart, and a consciousness which separates in order to look back and behold with awe and love (Bakan, 1966). According to Susan Griffin, Bacon stated that 'we must put nature on the rack and wrest her secrets from her'; she catalogues the way in which modern science emerged in historical parallel with the burning of witches in Europe (Griffin, 1984). Separated consciousness, it seems, is an appalling danger unless based on a genuine experience of love, because love returns us to a sense of connectedness with that from which we are separate. Thus the true naturalist literally loves what he or she studies, and from a place of difference beholds and celebrates its beauty and its difference; similarly the true hunter knows intimately and loves that which he hunts. This quality of consciousness recognizes the sacredness of the other, and thus opens the space for inquiry from a state of grace (Skolimowski, 1992; Reason, 1993). Martin Buber shows us how distance and relation are intertwined, and that the essence of relation is confirmation, the acknowledgement, recognition, of the other in their own uniqueness – another way of speaking of deep love. As we have seen from Bookchin, it is this quality that constitutes humanity: 'That this capacity lies so immeasurably fallow constitutes the real weakness and questionableness of the human race: actual humanity exists only where this capacity unfolds' (Buber, 1965: 68). The highest form of this consciousness has brought us remarkable gifts, as we can see from the great achievements of civilization – scientific, artistic, moral and cultural. I have already given one account of the dangers of fragmentation.

The difficulty with both deep and separated consciousness standing alone is that the degenerate form is always close at hand, haunting the valid form and ready to engulf it. Original participation denies differentiation just as unconscious participation denies communion: neither of these forms of consciousness are sufficient unto themselves. As I have hinted already and will explore further in the next chapter, a future reflexive participation must be essentially dialectical, always in movement, formed moment to moment in creative resolutions of the paradox between deep participation and separated consciousness.

3

Future Participation

Peter Reason

Having explored original participation and the development of unconscious participation, what can be said about future participation? It is here that Barfield's framework of original participation, the loss of participation in modern consciousness and final participation, which was a useful starting point, presents problems, in particular its emphasis on a linear developmental sequence. The proposition that human consciousness moves from original participation through a loss of participation to final participation cannot be sustained. As we have seen from feminist and indigenous accounts, this is only a part of the whole story, since a sense of deep participation has always been carried in muted fashion as an undercurrent to the Western patriarchal consciousness; as Polanyi and Heron argue, participation must continually underlie any differentiated and articulated form of consciousness however much we try to shut it out; and as Swimme and Berry point out, all humans continue to participate in the great mystery of creation as a centre of consciousness within the cosmos.

The linear account also tempts us to idealize original participation and deprecate the potential of autonomous discriminating human consciousness. So the question arises whether it is possible to envision a form of consciousness based on future participation without idealizing and thus trivializing? And is it possible to *evoke* the experience of future participation rather than simply conceptualize it, for as Barfield writes, 'merely grasping the concept will not take mankind very far' (1957: 137) – although articulating a new vision with imaginative passion may help us take the first steps into new possibilities. In this chapter I attempt to do this, and to show how collaborative human inquiry can be seen as a practice or discipline through which the consciousness of future participation can be developed.

Rather than define future participation as one form of consciousness, I find it more helpful to see it as a range of possible moments within a dialectic, emerging from the contradiction of original participation and unconscious participation. Dialectical thinking is based on the realization that contradiction is inseparable from human consciousness, and that this contradiction has the curious and paradoxical quality that it encompasses both opposition and unity. We may experience love as the opposite of hate, yet when we look a little deeper we realize that there is often a little love in the middle of our hate – and if we are honest a little hatred in the middle of our love. It is also evident that love and hate come together as aspects of fiercely passionate relationship. Opposites co-define each other, stand against each other, yet also coexist as two sides of the same coin. Original participation and future participation are clearly oppositional, in that the qualities of the one deny the qualities of the other. Yet in the very manner in which they are in opposition they are deeply similar: two forms of consciousness that absorb the human mind in one perspective, with minimal reflexivity or capacity to establish a self-reflexive 'meta' position.

In a dialectical perspective, future participation moves beyond the polarization of original participation and alienated unconscious participation, of masculine and feminine consciousness, into the dance between them. Every thesis calls forth in some sense its antithesis, and the play between these is a flowing, changing, interactive pattern that arises, moment to moment, as a dynamic process that grows out of the tension of contradiction. This 'in between' is usually much more interesting and important than the static structures of polarized extremes (Watts, 1963).

Hampden-Turner borrows from ancient myth to illustrate this point:

> In early Greek mythology those sailors who tried to navigate the straits of Messina were said to encounter a rock and a whirlpool. If you were too intent upon avoiding the rock you could be sucked into the whirlpool. If you skirted the whirlpool by too wide a margin you could strike the rock. These twin perils had markedly contrasting natures: the first was hard, solid, static, visible, definite, asymmetrical and an object; the second was soft, liquid, dynamic, hidden, indefinite, symmetrical and a process. (Hampden-Turner, 1990: 24)

Anyone steering the boat with a bias to seeing either peril as more important puts the ship into danger. If they see the rock as the main danger because it is so hard and solid, they are likely to steer too close to the whirlpool; if they are fearful of the insidious pull of the whirlpool they may steer too close to the rock. The 'correct' course to steer is not predetermined, but rather continually adjusts to the wind and waves. This is a self-correcting cybernetic process: to be 'right' you have to take action which, if carried to an extreme, will be 'wrong'; every action brings forth a reaction and thus corrective feedback. As Hampden-Turner shows, steering the ship involves *leading* in order to *learn* and *learning* in order to *lead*; the ship is *erring* so that it must be *corrected*, and steering the ship involves maintaining *continuity* in the midst of *change* (1990: 16–17). Similarly, in the process of developing human inquiry, too much concern for participative identity among co-researchers will lead to loss of perspective; too much concern for perspective will leave co-researchers alienated from each other and from their experience. The dialectic involves both a movement between the two poles and a simultaneous articulation of the two poles.

Future participation arises as a possibility from the contradiction between the immersion of original participation and the alienation of unconscious participation – if humankind were not deeply familiar with both, the emergence of this third possibility would not be possible (and in this sense future participation is a part of a developmental evolution). As I have shown in

Chapter 2, original participation, with its deep sense of identity between self and other, prevents the development of a distinctly human consciousness, a development that takes place through differentiation and discrimination. While it would appear that the project to gain the freedom of a discriminating human consciousness has resulted not simply in the development of perspective, but in a loss of participation and an alarming alienation, this has created a most powerful dialectic. As Colgrave writes, the loss of identity with the Great Mother that arose with the development of human consciousness is followed by 'a struggle between the desire for freedom and the knowledge and longing for wholeness and peace' (1979: 198). She argues that this peace can be discovered through androgynous consciousness, a harmony arising from an integration of the masculine and feminine principles within the human psyche. While Colgrave's argument is at the level of the individual psyche, Tarnas has recently taken the argument onto a wider stage, portraying the whole history of Western mind and spirit as a masculine project driven by a heroic impulse to forge an autonomous rational human self. This gives rise to a longing for reunion with that which has been lost, and at the same time, Tarnas argues, prepares the ground for that reunion, in what is essentially one side of a vast dialectical process:

> the West's restless inner development and incessantly innovative masculine ordering of reality has been gradually leading, in an immensely long dialectical movement, toward a reconciliation with the lost feminine unity, toward a profound and many-levelled marriage of masculine and feminine, a triumphant and healing reunion. (1991: 444)

So it may well be that future participation will take many forms, according to the route through which it is reached. A future participation which has evolved from an indigenous tribal perspective (Colorado, 1988) may continue to emphasize the living interconnectedness of all beings; one emerging through feminism will continue to honour muted voices; while one that has evolved through the cauldron of the Western heroic adventure may carry more critical questioning. It will be through a dialectical dance between many different ways of knowing, rather than as one new story, that a new quality of epistemological robustness will emerge. Different aspects of participation may then coexist in an individual and in a culture, dancing together in different patterns at different times and in different places. Certainly in modern cultures the specialization of gender roles has led to a situation in which women are more likely to hold the experience of deep participation and communion while men articulate agency and separateness (Marshall, 1984). The problem has been not so much that we have separated gender roles but that we have devalued the feminine qualities and interpreted them solely in terms of the masculine. Similarly within an individual, different subpersonalities (Rowan, 1989) can be expected to hold different consciousness.

Another way of seeing the different aspects of participation is as phases of a cycle. In shorter cycles of experience we might, for example, be drawn through the window in direct experience of liquid sound; label the sound as the song of a thrush; notice the labelling; and choose to allow ourselves to sink back down into identity with the immediate experience. Something akin to this happens in meditation, as we learn to notice the mind drawn away into thoughts, and gently draw it back to our breath, to the sitting, to the immediate present.

Longer cycles can be seen in the development of a human life as the individual emphasizes individualistic and participative aspects of being in turn, developing more subtle syntheses as life progresses. And the development phases of a group can be seen in terms of a dialectic between seeking membership and asserting individual identity. Even longer cycles can be seen in human cultures. We might very schematically sketch the development of European civilization as starting from the deep participation of early Greek culture immersed in a participative and mythological experience of the world. At some point a more reflective consciousness emerged in the glory of Classical Greece which first flowered, and was later taken over, developed and to some extent brutalized in the Roman Empire. This over-reached itself and was overwhelmed by the so-called Dark Ages, a period of coexistence of deep participation in a shamanic world-view (Bates, 1983) and a culture devoted to the glorification of God on earth. The Renaissance then emerged as a time of new illumination, a new perspective (literally, see Romanyshyn, 1989) which was developed and over-reached itself in the modern age (Skolimowski, 1986, 1994).

Qualities of a future participation

So future participation may take many forms in the process of emerging dialectically from the tension between original and unconscious participation. However, I suggest that there will be a unity within this diversity and that all forms of future participation will share certain qualities, albeit expressed in different ways. In this section I reach towards an articulation of these qualities, covering a lot of ground rather fast, sketching some possibilities. As I see future participation it is a form of consciousness rooted in concrete experience and grounded in the body; characterized by self-awareness and self-reflection; experience is ordered through a sense of pattern and form rather than by discrete objects; there is a much deeper appreciation of the alienating power of conceptual language and more active and aware use of imagination and metaphor.

First of all, future participation will be self-aware and self-reflective. Neither submerged in unaware union with other nor seduced by the brilliant promise of a completely autonomous rational consciousness, the mind in future participation will learn to attend to its own processes. Torbert has shown how in earlier stages of ego development the mind is preoccupied by particular aspects of internal or external reality, seeing the world entirely through the limited perspective of personal needs, social conditioning, or technical competence. In this sense the mind is trapped in its frames. At later stages of ego development a *reframing* mind emerges: rather than allowing experience to be framed, and so limited, by any particular attentional warp, the person actively exercises

attention to the process of framing itself: 'A reframing mind continually over-
comes itself, divesting itself of its own presuppositions . . . [engaging in]
ongoing jousting, at one and the same time, with one's attention and with the
outside world' (Torbert, 1987: 211–13). It is difficult for an individual to
develop such a reframing mind alone, or indeed in a culture which encourages
only the development of autonomy; it is more likely to emerge in a community
setting designed to encourage such a development. As I shall argue, an inquiry
community may be one such setting.

Of course, this is not new. Perhaps the most ancient and intensive study of
the way the human mind attaches itself to constricting frameworks, and the
most developed processes for developing a reflective, re-framing mind, comes
to us through Buddhist practice. Buddhist teaching holds that behind the
everyday mind which creates a sense of duality, which gets attached to its
desires, its plans, its perspectives, is a mind which is able to see through this
attachment and is open to the ways in which we create ourselves and our
world moment to moment (Spretnak, 1991; Sogyal Rinpoche, 1992). This
mind becomes available to us through the disciplines of meditation practice.

A second quality of future participation is that the mind will move beyond
the world in which all is immersed in a seamless web, and beyond the world of
separate objects, into a world of pattern and form, of relationships within an
interdependent whole. Gregory Bateson's work in developing an 'ecology of
mind' takes us towards an understanding of 'the pattern which connects'. He
uses the example of a man cutting down a tree to illustrate his point. From a
materialist perspective we would understand this in terms of the physical
impacts and forces of the axe on the tree. The action is seen as causal and linear; the tree is a thing to be acted upon. But as Berman points out in his
review of Bateson's thought, if the tree is reified, so is the mind, 'for since the
self acted upon the axe, which then acted upon the tree . . . the self must also
be a thing' (1981: 244–5).

But if we enter Bateson's cybernetic world of mind, effects are brought
about not by forces but by information, by differences travelling in a circuit. As
he points out, the letter that you fail to write can carry as much information as
one you do write – and can result in grievous consequences. So to explain the
man-axe-tree:

> we shall be concerned with differences in the cut face of the tree, differences in the
> retina of the man, differences in his central nervous system, differences in his effer-
> ent neural messages, differences in the behaviour of his muscles, differences in the
> way the axe flies, to the differences which the axe then makes on the face of the tree.
> (Bateson, 1972: 459)

Bateson asks us to look not so much at what is in the mind but at *how* things
are held in the mind. He is concerned to point out the gross errors that emerge
from a materialist epistemology: as he points out, there are no cows, pigs, or
other objects in the mind, only patterns of difference. This makes for difficulties in the way we usually describe experience, for

> while I can know nothing about any individual thing by itself, I *can* know something
> about *relations between things* . . . I can only know something about relations

between things. If I say the table is 'hard', I am going beyond what my experience would testify. What I know is that the interaction or relationship between the table and some sense organ or instruments has a differential hardness for which I have no ordinary vocabulary, alas, but which I distort by referring the special character of the relationship entirely to one of the components of it. I distort what I *could* know about the relationship into a statement about a 'thing' which I *cannot* know. (Bateson and Bateson, 1987: 157; emphasis in original)

What, Bateson asks, is the pattern which connects all living creatures, and how do we know this pattern? He asserts that this is an aesthetic question, since the pattern emerges as we encounter experience, not through measurement and quantity, but through *recognition* and *empathy* with repetition, modulation, rhythm and form (Bateson, 1979: 8–10).

Another illuminating expression of understanding based on pattern comes from Chinese medicine (Kaptchuk, 1983). While Western medicine seeks explanations in terms of cause and effect,

> Oriental diagnostic technique renders an almost poetic, yet workable, description of the whole person. The question of cause and effect is always secondary to the over-all pattern . . . The Chinese are interested in discerning the relationships among bodily events occurring at the same time . . . The total configurations, the patterns of disharmony, provide the framework for treatment. (Kaptchuk, 1983: 4)

A third quality of future participation is the active and conscious use of imagination. Heron argues that the human psyche, through its imaginative capacity, creates a world of form out of our original experience of embeddedness and deep participation. This imaginative world evolves through sensation, image, dream, story (Heron, 1992), and is one of immense possibilities. One of the tragedies of the fundamentalism of unconscious participation and the positivist mindset is that this multiplicity is cut down to one empirical reality, one truth, one way of seeing things. The world defined by conceptual language, categorizing, pruning and pinning down, reduces this vast range of imaginative possibility to a world of fixed things. Among those who have helped us revalue the imaginal world are the archetypal psychologists, telling us again that 'imagination is reality' (Avens, 1980). They suggest that what we tell ourselves about reality, our concepts and theories, are 'guiding fictions' that we can learn to 'see through'. For example:

> One beauty of mythic metaphors is that they elude literalism. We know at the outset that they are impossible truths. Like metaphor itself, the power of which cannot be satisfactorily explained, a myth also speaks with two tongues at once, amusing yet terrifying, serious and ironic, sublimely imaginative and yet with the scattered detail of ridiculous fantasy. (Hillman, 1975: 155)

This process of seeing through, of relativizing, leads us to a central aspect of future participation, that it is less attached to conceptual language and to paradigmatic knowing than is consciousness based on unconscious participation. Since the process of classifying and labelling separates us from our experience, conceptual language can be a powerful source of alienation from awareness of participation: we become subjects in an alienated world of objects. Maurice Ash argues that through this process of reification we make

'things with words where otherwise nothing is . . . fabricating things of which
the senses have no experience' (1992: 24). Drawing on Wittgenstein and the
Buddhist philosopher Nagarjuna (second century CE) he asserts that the task
is 'to struggle against the bewitchment of our intelligence by language' (Ash,
1992: 24). In particular, Ash rejects the notion of a substantive self which
inevitably becomes placed over and above environment, leading to all the
problems of loss of participation which we have explored above.

Of course the deconstructive school of postmodernism makes a similar
point, drawing attention to the way in which language constructs reality.
However, the deconstructive solution takes us further into loss of
participation:

> It overcomes the modern worldview through an anti-worldview: it deconstructs or
> eliminates the ingredients necessary for a worldview, such as God, self, purpose,
> meaning, a real world, and truth as correspondence. While motivated in some cases
> by the ethical concern to forestall totalitarian systems, this type of postmodern
> thought issues in relativism, even nihilism. It could be called *ultramodernism*, in that
> its eliminations result from carrying modern premises to their logical conclusions.
> (Griffin, 1989: xii; emphasis in original)

The perspective I am developing here is more congruent with 'constructive'
postmodernism which is equally critical of the modernity with its loss of participation. The deconstructive position in the end is nihilistic because it argues
that there is *no* ground on which we can stand to construct a world-view; in
contrast the constructive perspective urges us to continually inquire into what
that ground might be. As Berman points out, the problem of radical rela-
tivism disappears once participation is acknowledged as a component of all
perception and all knowledge (1981: 136). Constructive postmodernism
requires the kind of developed, self-reflexive consciousness that is one hall-
mark of future participation (Griffin et al., 1989; Spretnak, 1991; Falk, 1992).

Ash suggests that we might cultivate the ability to see objects as 'but con-
veniences of speech' (1992: 38). Heron goes further, arguing the possibility of
developing a 'post-linguistic' use of concepts and language which attempts to
heal the splitting effects of the ordinary use of language. He argues that once
we allow ourselves to return to a direct experience of feeling the presence of the
world, we can re-vision our way of thinking and thus change our experience of
perception. To do this we need to implant in our minds a 'new conceptual
layer' which continually reminds us that what we see has no ultimate independent reality, but arises out of a dance between the primal process of the
cosmos and the forms projected out of the depths of the imaginal mind. In
other words, we learn to stop confusing the map of our language and concepts
with the territory of experience (Berman, 1981: 141). So future participation
will use language and concepts as a way of re-visioning our experience without
setting it in a new concrete form. One very down-to-earth way of accomplish-
ing this is used by my colleague Judi Marshall who often encourages students
to 'hold an idea lightly' – in other words as a potential, a possibility, a play-
thing which if permitted will illuminate experience without rigidifying it.

If in future participation we are less attached to a reality created by language we will also be less attached to cognitive, paradigmatic knowing. In his exploration of logical categories of learning, Bateson (1972) differentiates between learning how to operate *within* a conceptual structure, which he calls Learning I; and learning to move *between* conceptual structures, or paradigm change, which he calls Learning II. But beyond Learning II, he suggests the possibility of Learning III, in which the mind, not dependent on any one world-view, is able to peer over the edges of different frameworks, to reflect on and choose the premises of understanding and action. The reframing mind is able to leap between mindsets (with greater or lesser agility) in a manner that confuses minds firmly attached to rational frameworks.

Berman (1989) makes a brave attempt to explore a way of knowing beyond paradigms in his book *Coming to our Senses*. He explores our socialization in the West, suggesting that a yawning gap develops in experience as we create an identity that divorces us from our physical selves: we lose our somatic anchoring. Alienation arises when a constructed identity and way of knowing is imposed upon an immediately felt one. The history of the West is characterized by the emergence of ideologies and world-views that promise to fill this gap and heal the alienation; they attract passionate adherents because of the power of this promise. But of course these ideologies always fail to fulfil their promise because the alienation is somatic, prior to language and concept. He argues that far more important than developing a 'new paradigm' is learning to live without one, since all paradigms and belief systems do no more than fill the yearning gap of our alienation:

> The minute anything – science, feminism, Buddhism, holism, whatever – starts to take on the characteristics of a cosmology it should be discarded. *How* things are held in the mind is infinitely more important than *what* is held in the mind. An idea is something you have; an ideology, something that has *you*. (Berman, 1989: 312; emphasis in original)

Rather than the certainty of a new world-view, which will fade, we need the vulnerability of openness, self-remembering, in my terms, experiential inquiry. This requires a return to experience as the fundamental base for inquiry, a return to the concrete and kinaesthetic knowing of the body, and also to the conscious use of imagination in inquiry. Learning to live without paradigms means learning to reclaim the body, to live in the body rather than using it as a tool to carry around the mind. It means learning to use words and concepts as tools of consciousness, rather than as consciousness themselves. Reclaiming the body means that research will need to be based on physical discipline – T'ai Chi, yoga, breathing, Reichian exercises, and so on – as well as on spoken and written word.

Finally, I have several times suggested that a future participation will mean a very different experience of the self, an ecological self distinct yet not separate, a self rooted in environment and in community. Bookchin also offers us a vision of future participation in an 'ecological society', based on the argument that human nature arises out of participation: 'what we call "human nature" is a biologically rooted process of consociation, a process in which co-operation, mutual support, and love are natural as well as cultural attributes'

(1991: 317) This is most strongly argued: co-operation is not merely an actual or potential attribute of human nature, but *constitutes* human nature; we are not human without the extended socialization of the young and the mother–child relationship. Strangely, to grow 'up' in our culture is to grow away from this original socialization into civilization and into the loss of participation. What differentiates Bookchin's vision of a future ecological society from the earlier organic societies he describes is the notion of a universal *humanitas*; strong emphasis on human autonomy rooted in community; and the replacement of hierarchy by interdependence.

The organic society is so immersed in itself that it does not have the perspective required to be self-critical, and is thus vulnerable. The development of notions of justice and freedom provide the possibility of a more reflective relationship to humanity as a whole: Bookchin argues that 'civilization' has given us – 'in spite of itself' – the recognition that the ancient values of deep complementarity, the 'equality of non-equals', must be extended from the kin group to the whole of humanity.

The notion of the independent individual is essential for the development of this ethic of freedom, but Bookchin goes to great lengths to contrast the individual strongly rooted in a community with 'the self in the form of *homo economicus*, a wriggling and struggling monad, literally possessed by egotism and an amoral commitment to survival' (1991: 161). Bookchin describes this as decadent individualism, whose 'roots have begun to wither and the community base by which it is truly nourished has begun to disappear' (1991: 164) – we may be reminded of Margaret Thatcher's infamous remark that there is no such thing as society. In contrast Bookchin notes that 'The great individuals of history are rooted psychologically in viable and vibrant communities' (1991: 164 footnote).

Civilization has tragically associated the strong self with control, domination, and hierarchy; Bookchin argues that it can more appropriately be associated with imagination and creativity and with service to the community, just as Torbert (nd) more recently has argued the need for transforming leadership in creating communities of inquiry. Thus Bookchin's perspective again is one in which a more developed form of participative consciousness may arise out of the estrangement of civilization:

> Mutualism, self-organization, freedom, and subjectivity, cohered by . . . principles of unity in diversity, spontaneity, and non-hierarchical relationships, are thus ends in themselves. Aside from the ecological responsibilities they confer on our species as the self-reflexive voice of nature, they literally define us. (Bookchin, 1991: 365–6)

In this chapter I have touched, often all too briefly, on some of the writers who have pointed towards world-views based on a radically different consciousness. My intention has been to offer some hints, some directions, to indicate some potential openings. Those readers wishing to pursue these ideas in more detail need to engage directly with the authors involved. While many good ideas carry an immediate sense of validity, they also merit dwelling with and exploring in depth. Bateson, Hillman, Ash and the others point towards a very different presence in the world. I have also argued that the emergence of future participation is not simply cognitive, that it will draw on meditation practice, on a return to the physical self, and on the cultivation of imagination. This book is not the place to explore the educational processes and developmental disciplines required for this, for many specialist resources are now available. Rather I wish to turn to the main topic of this book, the practice of participative human inquiry, and show how it can be seen as a discipline for the cultivation of future participation.

4

Human Inquiry as Discipline and Practice

Peter Reason

I argued in the previous chapter that future participation can be seen as a process of knowing and doing that emerges from the dialectic of original participation and unconscious participation; and I touched on some of the qualities that I believe will characterize this process of knowing. I now wish to show how the process of human inquiry can be seen as a discipline through which forms of future participation can emerge.

A discipline is a method or a training, a set of rules, exercises or procedures which educate a person towards particular ways of being and doing. As I engage with a discipline I freely consent to abide by its practice rules as a process of inquiry into both the discipline and its teachings. In doing this I commit myself to a process of liberation.

A discipline in this sense is in some ways similar to a paradigm as described by Kuhn (1962); 'paradigm cases' exemplify a way of seeing and a method of investigation, and are a means by which students are initiated into the perspective of a world-view. But usually a paradigm is taken as a primarily intellectual structure; it is a set of agreed ideas and practices to which members of the scientific community conform. The notion of discipline has a wider connotation. It is a practice that develops mind, body and spirit: it draws attention to intuitive or spiritual questions of purpose and meaning; to intellectual questions of understanding; and to practise questions of behaviour; and it places these in the context of the practitioner's physical and social environment. Further, a discipline is necessarily self-transcending: while the initiate may productively 'follow the rules', the mature practitioner uses rules in order to develop a quality of attention and behaviour which, while born out of and nurtured by the practice and its rules, moves beyond them.

While a discipline can be an individual matter it is also the shared practice of a community. Most of us need the support of a community in order to follow a discipline, to receive both the wisdom of those more experienced than ourselves and the support of peers. Thus neonate scientists have to be trained to 'see' the world through the perspective of their science, not just in conceptual terms, but quite literally. For example, student microbiologists have to learn how to 'see' patterns on a microscope slide which to the untrained eye are invisible. An acupuncturist learns to diagnose the pattern of the patient's well-being by taking the pulses, which in the community of Western medicine do not exist. And Buddhists seek guidance and support from the *sanga* as they train the mind through disciplines of meditation, and may be able to develop states of consciousness particular to their practice.

The shadow of community lies in the possibility that the community norms will insist on a rigid conformity to both rules and world-view, so that the practice degenerates into a tyranny, rather than a means of inquiry which liberates both individual and community. For a discipline at best holds open the tension between individual and community and contributes to the development of both.

The methodologies of human inquiry can be seen as disciplines which can train the individual and develop the community towards a consciousness of future participation. In particular the iteration through cycles of action and reflection, and the various ways of bringing attention to bear in the midst of action are practices which at their best can contribute to a liberation of the individual and the inquiry community. In my work as an inquirer and a teacher I have drawn on three approaches to collaborative experiential inquiry which I see as clearly articulated and exemplified in practice: *co-operative inquiry, participatory action research* and *action inquiry* (Reason, 1994). I shall briefly introduce each of these to the reader and show how each can be seen as a discipline which can reach towards a form of future participation.

Co-operative inquiry

The idea of co-operative experiential inquiry was first presented in 1971 by John Heron, who later set out a full account of the philosophical case for the method and described its systematic practice (Heron, 1971, 1981a, 1981b). This has been extended and developed over the past 12 years (particularly in Reason, 1988; Heron, 1992; Reason and Heron, 1995).

Co-operative inquiry is based first on the assumption that persons are self-determining. A person is a fundamental spiritual entity, a distinct presence in the world, who has the potential to be the cause of his or her own actions. To actualize this capacity and become fully a person is an achievement of education and self-development. It involves learning to integrate individualizing characteristics with a deeper communion with others and the world (see Heron, 1992: Ch. 3).

A person's intentions and intelligent choices are causes of their behaviour; they are self-determining. If the behaviour of those being researched is directed and determined by the researcher, the research is being done on them and they are not present in the research as persons. One can only do research with persons in the true and fullest sense, if what they do and what they experience as part of the research is to some significant degree directed by them. So persons can only properly study persons when they are in active relationship with each other, where the behaviour being researched is self-generated by the researchers in a context of co-operation.

This means that all those involved in the research are both co-researchers, who generate ideas about its focus, design and manage it, and draw conclusions from it; and also co-subjects, participating with awareness in the activity that is being researched. One of the critical differences between co-operative experiential inquiry and orthodox research is that for the former the primary source of knowing, and thus the primary 'instrument' of research, is the self-directing person within a community of inquiry, and method is a secondary expression of this; whereas for the latter, method is primary and the subjects are subordinate to it.

The second important starting point for co-operative inquiry is an extended epistemology including at least three kinds of knowledge: first, *experiential knowledge* gained through direct encounter face-to-face with persons, places, or things; second, *practical knowledge* gained through practice, knowing 'how to' do something, demonstrated in a skill or competence; and third, *propositional knowledge*, knowledge 'about' something, expressed in statements and theories. In research on persons the propositional knowledge stated in the research conclusions needs to be grounded in the experiential and practical knowledge of the subjects in the inquiry. If the concluding propositions are generated exclusively by a researcher who is not involved in the experience being researched, and are imposed without consultation on the practical and experiential knowledge of the subjects, we have findings which directly reflect the experience neither of the researcher nor of the subjects.

Recently Heron (1992) has clarified the additional notion of *presentational knowledge* by which we first order our tacit experiential knowledge of the world into spatio-temporal patterns of imagery, and then symbolize our sense of their meaning in movement, sound, colour, shape, line, poetry, drama and story. The development of presentational knowledge is an important, and often neglected, bridge between experiential knowledge and propositional knowledge.

These two principles – the person as agent and the extended epistemology – are realized in the process of co-operative inquiry. In traditional research, the roles of researcher and subject are mutually exclusive: the researcher alone contributes the thinking that goes into the project, and the subjects contribute the action to be studied. In co-operative inquiry these mutually exclusive roles are replaced by a relationship based on reciprocal initiative and control, so that all those involved work together as co-researchers and as co-subjects. Of course it takes time, skill and hard work to establish full, authentic reciprocity, as is demonstrated in the examples in Part II of this book.

Co-operative inquiry can be seen as cycling through four phases of reflection and action, although it should be noted that the actual process is not as straightforward as the model suggests: there are usually mini cycles within major cycles; some cycles will emphasize one phase more than others.

In Phase 1 a group of co-researchers come together to explore an agreed area of human activity. They may be professionals who wish to develop their understanding and skill in a particular area of practice; women or members of a minority group who wish to articulate an aspect of their experience which has been muted by the dominant culture; they may wish to explore in depth their experience of certain states of consciousness; to assess the impact on their well-being of particular healing practices; and so on. In this first phase they agree on the focus of their inquiry, and develop together a set of questions or propositions they wish to explore. They agree to undertake some action, some practice, which will contribute to this exploration, and agree to a set of procedures by which they will observe and record their own and each other's experience.

Phase 1 is primarily in the mode of propositional knowing, although it will also contain important elements of presentational knowing as group members use their imagination in story, fantasy and graphics to help them articulate their interests and to focus on their purpose in the inquiry. Once the focal idea – what the inquiry is about – is agreed, Phase 1 will conclude with planning a method for exploring the idea in action, and with devising ways of gathering and recording data from this experience.

In Phase 2 the co-researchers now also become co-subjects: they engage in the actions agreed and observe and record the process and outcomes of their own and each other's experience. In particular, they are careful to notice the subtleties of experience, to hold lightly the propositional frame from which they started so that they are able to notice how practice does and does not conform to their original ideas. This phase involves primarily practical knowledge: knowing how (and how not) to engage in appropriate action, to bracket off the starting idea, and to exercise relevant discrimination.

Phase 3 is in some ways the touchstone of the inquiry method: it is the stage in which the co-subjects become fully immersed in and engaged with their experience. They may develop a degree of openness to what is going on so free of preconceptions that they see it in a new way. They may deepen into the experience so that superficial understandings are elaborated and developed. Or they may be led away from the original ideas and proposals into new fields, unpredicted action and creative insights. It is also possible that they may get so involved in what they are doing that they lose the awareness that they are part of an inquiry group: there may be a crisis which demands all their attention, they may become enthralled, they may simply forget. Phase 3 involves mainly experiential knowing, although it will be richer if new experience is expressed, when recorded, in creative presentational form through graphics, colour, sound, movement, drama, story, poetry, and so on.

In Phase 4, after an agreed period engaged in phases 2 and 3, the co-researchers reassemble to consider their original propositions and questions in the light of their experience. As a result they may modify, develop or reframe them; or reject them and pose new questions. They may choose, for the next cycle of action, to focus on the same or on different aspects of the overall inquiry. The group may also choose to amend or develop its inquiry procedures – forms of action, ways of gathering data – in the light of experience. Phase 4 is primarily the stage of propositional knowing, although presentational forms of knowing will form an important bridge with the experiential and practical phases.

This cycle between action and reflection, between propositional knowing, practical knowing, presentational knowing and experiential knowing, is then repeated several times. Ideas and discoveries tentatively reached in early phases can be checked and developed; investigation of one aspect of the inquiry can be related to exploration of other parts; new skills can be acquired and monitored; experiential competencies are realized; the group itself becomes more cohesive and self-critical, more skilled in its work. Ideally the inquiry is finished when the initial questions are fully answered in practice, when there is a new congruence between the four kinds of knowing. It is of course rare for a group to complete an inquiry so fully.

The cycling can really start at any point. It is usual for groups to get together formally at the propositional stage often as the result of a proposal from an initiating facilitator. However, such a proposal is usually birthed in experiential knowing, at the moment that curiosity is aroused or incongruity noticed. And the proposal to form an inquiry group needs to be presented in such a way as to appeal to the experience of potential co-researchers.

This sequence of phases can be shown in what has become known as the 'snowpersons' diagram (Figure 4.1) which was originally drawn by John Heron before presentational knowing was fully articulated (Heron, 1981b). An alternative diagram is shown in Figure 4.2. A group of people engaged in co-operative inquiry work together through these cycles of action and reflection. In the early stages the cycle may be relatively superficial: the ideas brought to the inquiry may be commonplace, taken-for-granted assumptions, borrowed from elsewhere as it were, and the experience relatively habitual. The group is unformed, relationships are tentative and polite, with little authentic engagement, little challenge of self or each other.

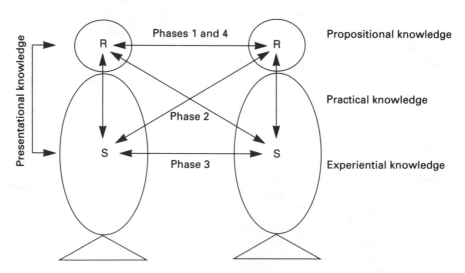

R indicates inquiry group members in co-researcher mode
S indicates inquiry group members in co-subject mode

Figure 4.1   *(after Heron, 1981b)*

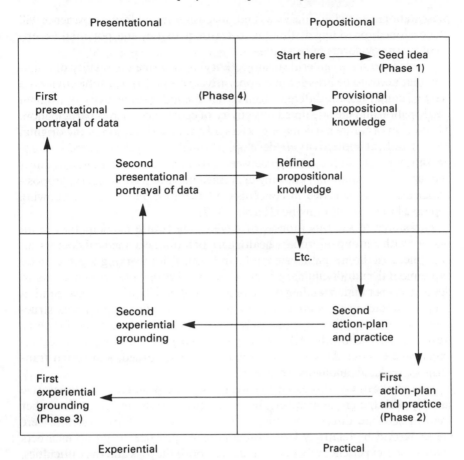

Figure 4.2 *(after Heron, 1992)*

It is quite possible that the inquiry will remain at this level: if the participants do not wish to explore their experience in depth, if they do not experience the group as evolving into a space with sufficient safety for them to begin to challenge themselves or each other, their process may remain superficial. But as the inquiry develops there is also the possibility that the group will deepen into a critical and risk-taking exploration of their experience. As the co-researchers take an attitude of inquiry into their practice they begin to notice experiences which had been previously tacit, at some level below full consciousness; as they bring these back to the inquiry group, stand back to discuss and compare experience with their colleagues, they may discover both that they are not alone, and that others have uncovered different issues in their experience. So the field of inquiry is enriched, experience both deepened and further differentiated. Further, through this process of discussion – supported perhaps by drawing, fantasy, story-telling (Reason and Hawkins, 1988), psychodrama (Hawkins, 1988) or movement, all of which can stimulate presentational knowing – the ideas and propositions that frame experience will be developed, providing a stimulus to future activities and potential experiments with new forms of behaviour.

I have used the term 'critical subjectivity' to describe the quality of attention that needs to be brought to co-operative inquiry. Critical subjectivity is a state of consciousness different from either the naïve subjectivity of original participation and the attempted objectivity of egoic unconscious participation. The notion of future participation offers a further articulation of the original idea of critical subjectivity. It develops through the cyclical process of co-operative inquiry, in the iteration between experiential knowing through direct encounter; presentational knowing expressed in patterns of imagery; propositional knowing expressed in concepts and theories; and practical knowing expressed in the skills of living (Heron, 1992).

I was able to see this process of developing future participation in an inquiry with a group of primary health care practitioners: medical doctors, an acupuncturist, homeopath, osteopath, and counsellor working together in an experimental multidisciplinary clinic (Reason, 1991a). Our purpose was to develop deeper understanding of the process and possibilities of collaboration between doctors and complementary practitioners. The inquiry was structured so that the clinic sessions were held one afternoon a week for three weeks, and in the fourth week the time was devoted to a meeting to reflect on experience to date. All group sessions were tape-recorded, and edited transcripts circulated among the co-researchers.

I had, of course, discussed the ideas and the practice of co-operative inquiry with the group members, but when the process started no one other than myself had direct experience of such an inquiry. Early sessions were characterized by relatively loose discussions of practice, as group members shared their experience of working together, both the joys and the difficulties, and offered their different perspectives on what was going on in the clinic. As I circulated transcripts of the sessions, attention was focused, sometimes all too painfully, on the interaction between the co-researchers, and helped people attend more closely to what was going on. I suspect that my presence in the clinic, and the questioning I stimulated, helped to remind people that we were engaged in an inquiry project as well as treating patients. And in the reflection sessions, as facilitator of the group process I continually summarized and fed back the issues that arose, helping to keep an account of the developing agenda. After two or three cycles of inquiry, I proposed that we devote some time to identifying the important issues that had arisen in our work together. It was about this time when one of the group members made a comment to the effect, 'Ah, now I see! It is out of these discussions that we are having, almost like free association, that we can begin to see what issues are important to us!'

On reflection, I believe it is reasonable to say that as the inquiry developed, the co-researchers moved into deeper awareness of their experience and behaviour of the clinic, and paid closer attention to their experience of each other. The reflection sessions helped them articulate the problems and opportunities of multidisciplinary work. On several occasions we experimented with different ways to work together in the clinic in the light of the discussions. One of the group members later wrote that the inquiry project 'greatly improved the team's ability to make sense of itself, to unravel and describe its own internal processes and manage its work better'; it was a 'lifeline as well as a thread through the maze' in their exploration of interdisciplinary collaboration (Peters, 1994).

In contrast to the loose and unfocused quality of early discussions, towards the end of the inquiry the group was able to develop theory and descriptions of its practice that remained rooted in their experience together. I remember one particular session. I had circulated a draft paper on multidisciplinary practice to the group, a paper I had written which was faithful, as I thought, to the group's reflections. At first, discussion of the paper was polite, but with an underlying tone of dissatisfaction: clearly I had not expressed the group's experience. Then one of the group took up a pen and stood by the white board. 'I wonder if we put it like this . . .', he mused, sketching a diagram and some words on the board. Another person stood up, took the pen, and added some further ideas. Soon the whole group was standing by the board, deep in collaborative development of a framework for understanding their work together.

The paper almost wrote itself (Reason et al., 1992). But more important than this, the process of inquiry helped the group move towards a practice of future participation: while deeply engaged in their work together, they were at the same time considerably more aware of the range of theoretical perspectives which guided their practice. They were more imaginative and playful in their work together and more flexible in their behaviour. This process appears to have continued in the years after the inquiry proper, as evidenced in a later paper reflecting on their practice together (Peters, 1994). I make no claim that we had travelled the whole road to a future participation – and there were many difficulties that I have not reported in this sketch – simply that we made some significant first steps. A similar process of emerging self-reflective consciousness can be seen in the examples in Part II of this book.

Participatory action research

Participatory action research (PAR) is probably the most widely practised collaborative research approach. It is important because it emphasizes the political aspects of knowledge production and is firmly within the tradition of liberationist movements. PAR draws strongly on Paulo Freire's ethos of *Pedagogy of the Oppressed* (1970), and its practitioners usually work with disadvantaged people, initially in Third World countries, but increasingly among the disadvantaged in developed countries. Key references to participatory action research include Fernandes and Tandon (1981); Hall et al. (1982); Tandon (1989); Fals-Borda and Rahman (1991); Hall (1993); Park et al. (1993). For a comprehensive bibliography see Cancian and Armstead (1993).

PAR has a double objective. One aim is to produce knowledge and action directly useful to a community – through research, through adult education, and through sociopolitical action. The second aim is consciousness raising or *conscientization*, to use a term popularized by Paulo Freire (1970): to empower people through the process of constructing and using their own knowledge, so that they learn to 'see through' the ways in which the established interests monopolize the production and use of knowledge for their own benefit. PAR aims to help people move beyond immersion in a parochial world-view and a culture of silence, and also beyond the adoption of a scientific or technical view imported from the dominant culture, and towards the creation of knowledge systems based on people's needs. Bessa Whitmore's work in Chapter 6 draws on the spirit of participatory action research.

It is easier to describe the ideology of PAR than its methodologies, because it aims to develop an alternative system of knowledge production based on the people's role of setting the agendas, participating in data gathering and analysis, and controlling the use of outcomes. In addition, PAR places emphasis on the emergent processes of collaboration and dialogue which empower, motivate, increase the self-esteem and develop community solidarity. So participatory action research is characterized by diverse methods, many of which will derive from vernacular and oral traditions: a PAR project may include community meetings, song, drama, as well as group discussion and more orthodox forms of data gathering.

Comstock and Fox (1993) provide an account of the experience of the citizens of North Bonneville in the US state of Washington, which shows how knowledge production can develop as a participatory community process. The town was about to be destroyed by the location of a dam built by the Corps of Engineers. The people of the town resisted when told that they would all have to move to other cities, because this would destroy their community, and proposed instead that the whole town be relocated on a new site. The account tells how, in collaboration with students and staff from Evergreen State College, the various 'complex external and political social forces' in opposition to this proposal were overcome, how a proposal for relocation was developed through a process of participatory inquiry with the people of the town into their needs and aspirations, how the social and political organization of the town developed in a participatory fashion. In the end not only was the relocation itself accomplished, but citizens became more aware of the value they placed on their community and the community as a whole developed an increased self-awareness and capacity for learning about itself.

PAR practitioners use the term dialogue for the process through which this was accomplished. In the case of North Bonneville, dialogue involved gathering the information needed to plan the relocation of the city and at the same time engaging in ongoing discussions with residents so that they could create and discover their own understanding, expression and use of the information: 'The data with which to make decisions, an awareness of external forces affecting decisions in their lives, and the self-confidence and capacity to make their own decisions all needed to be developed simultaneously' (Comstock and Fox, 1993: 115). The outcome was not only the development of a plan to relocate the city, but a new level of awareness and competence:

> As residents reflected and talked about what they knew about their community, they began to realize the discrepancy between their knowledge of who they were and the very different perspective of the Corps of Engineers and the politicians who wrote relocation laws. They began to define their community as a complex network of social, natural and spiritual relationships. They discovered that the government defined their community as abstract individuals and a quantifiable number of physical artefacts, such as a firetruck and so many lampposts . . . They realized that the Corps planning was a meticulously designed and carefully controlled critical path for technical efficiency . . . To the contrary the town's 'planning process' was the creation of knowledge about themselves . . . . They discovered that their goal – survival of the social relationships that defined their community – was quite different from the government's goal – to build a powerhouse as quickly as possible. (Comstock and Fox, 1993: 116)

The residents of North Bonneville were thrust by circumstances into the contradiction between their own experience of the worth of their community and their wish that it continue, and the external view that their city was a shack town destined to be destroyed in the interests of efficient electrical power. Out of this contradiction emerged not only a new city, but a new level of understanding and political competence. The discipline of PAR operated at a community level, the process of dialogue helping the residents take some steps towards future participation.

Action inquiry

Action inquiry is concerned with the transformation of organizations and communities towards greater effectiveness and greater justice. It has been developed as both a theory and a life practice over many years by Bill Torbert (see especially Torbert, 1981, 1987, 1991). Torbert's work develops Argyris and Schon's idea of action science (Argyris and Schon, 1974, 1978; Schon, 1983; Argyris et al., l985); but his articulation of action inquiry departs from this in significant ways. Action *science* focuses on the way practitioners construe their behaviour, their implicit cognitive models, and their actual behaviour. Action *inquiry*, while addressing these, in addition addresses outcomes (measured empirically), and the quality of one's own attention (monitored by meditative exercises as one acts). Further, action inquiry addresses the question of how to transform organizations and communities into collaborative, self-reflective communities of inquiry.

Torbert argues that for an individual, community or organization to practise action inquiry they require valid knowledge of four 'territories' of human experience. First, knowledge about the system's own *purposes* – an intuitive or spiritual knowledge of what goals are worthy of pursuit and what demands attention at any point in time (and thus also the knowledge of when another purpose becomes more urgent and pressing). Second, knowledge about its *strategy*, an intellectual or cognitive knowledge of the theories underlying its choices. Third, a knowledge of the *behavioural* choices open to it – essentially a practical knowledge, resting in an awareness of oneself and on behavioural skill. Finally, knowledge of the *outside world*, in particular an empirical knowledge of the consequences of its behaviour. Thus:

> The vision of action inquiry is an attention that spans and integrates the four territories of human experience. This attention is what sees, embraces, and corrects incongruities among mission, strategy, operations, and outcomes. It is the source of the 'true sanity of natural awareness of the whole'. (Torbert, 1991: 219)

Torbert's emphasis is on a form of inquiry conducted moment to moment in everyday life. It is primarily concerned with heightening awareness of the possibilities of this moment, here and now, and thus can be seen as 'consciousness in the midst of action' (Torbert, 1991: 221). Such consciousness presents the would-be practitioner with tremendous challenges to personal development; and in parallel requires for its full articulation a developed community of inquiry. In exploring this issue of personal development further Torbert draws on the ancient tradition of search for an integrative quality of awareness and on modern theories of ego development, particularly the work of Loevinger (1976) and Kegan (1980), arguing that only those at the later stages of ego development will be able to consistently practise action inquiry.

Thus, while co-operative inquiry emphasizes a cyclical dialectic of action and reflection, Torbert proposes a consciousness in which action and reflection interpenetrate. The process of action inquiry sets the practitioner right in the contradiction between deep engagement, participation and commitment to the moment; and simultaneous reflection, standing back, self-awareness. Thus action inquiry is a discipline relevant to those most deeply committed to participatory approaches to inquiry, and persons who wish to play leadership roles in cultivating this process with others.

To the extent that I have internalized the process of action inquiry it is part of my everyday life, including both personal and professional arenas. In the following paragraphs I offer my reflection of the quality of attention which I bring to my work with collaborative groups.

Purpose

Collaboration and participation are central values in my life. My intent is to act in ways that actualize them in all my relationships, with family, friends, in teaching and in research. This means seeking to create circumstances that initiate and nurture collaboration, which are genuinely educational for all those involved as well as highly effective; and behaving so as to invite others to reciprocate. I recognize that this is not a purpose I can hold blithely, but rather that it has the quality of a lifelong quest, both an inspiration and a struggle. I experience this intention as having a spiritual dimension, as providing a sense of meaning and inspiration to my life. I believe that if I announce this intent to my fellows and to the wider reality of the cosmos, I will be offered both opportunities and challenges to practise what I preach and to learn from that practice. In its most extended form this purpose is impossible to realize; thus I need also to learn to be reasonably gentle with myself, to forgive the shortcomings of my practice.

A purpose or intention cannot be seen as unitary: rather different purposes will nest within each other. Thus within this general intention to behave in a fashion which will develop participative relationships I will hold at times more specific purposes – to listen carefully or to assert a position; to allow equal time for all participants or to protect the space of one; and so on – according to what I perceive the situation calls for. These more immediate purposes will be derived from the theories I hold and the strategies that I adopt, and they will emerge as I monitor my behaviour and notice what is happening in the external world and the other people with whom I engage. Thus the four levels of attention are interdependent, it is not possible to describe one without the others; and my purpose may change, moment to moment as new needs emerge.

Holding sense of purpose is quite different from establishing an objective or setting a target, both of which I associate with alienated consciousness and unconscious participation. Within a material world-view our sense of purpose degenerates so it is narrowed down to the material and economic interests. Purpose is far more immediate and organic. Developing the capacity to hold and review intuitive purpose lifts consciousness out of both original participation and unconscious participation. Purpose interpenetrates strategy and behaviour, as it is simultaneously influenced by them.

There are certain disciplines which may help us evolve a purposive attitude. Essential are the basic ways of being centred and calming the mind, of freeing attention from internal concerns and preoccupations. In my own practice the cathartic discipline of co-counselling has provided a degree of emotional competence, and the physical discipline of T'ai Chi much sense of grounding and centredness. Developing the habit of asking oneself, 'What is my purpose?' at regular times of the day has been helpful, as can starting any group session by inviting all present to state their intention for the meeting. More specific disciplines help focus on particular purposes: for example anchoring a purpose in something you wear, an object which is kept on the desk or carried in pocket or purse, so that its presence is a continual reminder. One of my friends sets the hourly time signal on her digital watch so it regularly asks her, 'Are you awake?'.

Strategy

My intent to behave in collaborative fashion is guided by several theoretical perspectives, many of which I have used for so many years that I experience them as a part of me. I find I use theories which are quite simple to express, usually having no more than four fundamental categories or dimensions, but which I experience as unfolding in complex patterns within those dimensions. One of the theories I hold close to experience is the dialectical approach I have advocated in the previous chapter, and I suspect that all the theories I use have a dialectical quality about them which illuminates process and development rather than static entities.

Thus Torbert's model of action inquiry based on the four 'territories' – purpose, strategy, behaviour and the outside world – is at one level very simple. But it can be used to explore stages of ego development (1987), showing how at early stages of ego development attention is framed by just one of the four territories, while at later stages the person can develop an attention capable of interpenetrating all four territories, a reframing mind. The four territories also suggest an extended epistemology: we develop purpose through intuitive and spiritual knowing what is worthy of our attention; strategy through conceptual knowing which creates frameworks for understanding guiding action; behaviour through sensory kinaesthetic knowing, the knowing in our muscles and blood which help us develop skill; and we know the outside world through our external attention, through the empirical process of collecting, analysing, and feeding back information. And the four territories provide a guide for moment to moment action, as they are translated into parts of speech: I express my purposes by framing my contributions, making explicit the perspective I adopt; I can advocate strategies as I suggest in broad terms my plans and proposals; I can illustrate these with examples and stories, or more powerfully and analogically through my behaviour; and I can gather data from my colleagues by inquiring how they respond to my proposals, by behaving in such a way that others will join my action inquiry process (Fisher and Torbert, 1995).

Another theoretical perspective I have internalized is John Heron's approach to the politics of participative groups (Heron, 1989, 1992, 1993):

> Participation . . . honours the basic right of people to have a say in forms of decision-making. In our view, institutions need to enhance human association by an appropriate balance of the principles of hierarchy, collaboration, and autonomy: deciding for others, with others, and for oneself . . . Authentic hierarchy provides appropriate direction by those with greater vision, skill and experience . . . Collaboration roots the individual within a community of peers, offering basic support and the creative and corrective feedback of other views and possibilities . . . . Autonomy expresses the self-creating and self-transfiguring potential of the person . . . The shadow face of authority is authoritarianism; that of collaboration peer pressure and conformity; that of autonomy narcissism, wilfulness and isolation. The challenge is to design institutions which manifest valid forms of these principles; and to find ways in which they can be maintained in self-correcting and creative tension. (Reason and Heron, 1995)

Again, the balance between the principles of authority, collaboration and autonomy is conceptually simple, yet in experience provides a profound basis for understanding the process of group development and a helpful guide for intervention and facilitation.

A third example of theories which frame and guide participative relationship is Randall and Southgate's description of the creative orgasmic group (1980). This describes a creative group process as starting with a phase of nurturing in which the group members are brought together and the task prepared; developing into a phase of energizing during which the group engages actively with the task; a peak of accomplishment; and moving to a final phase of relaxing, during which the group winds down from its energetic peak and puts the finishing touches on its work. This cycle is a life cycle and parallels the human energetic cycle which is expressed in sexuality, in pregnancy and birth, in preparing, eating and clearing away meals, as well as in the task-orientated group. Again, this framework is quite simple, yet it is rich in its descriptive potential. It is also grounded in other sophisticated theories of group and human process, notably Bion's theory of groups (1959), and Reich's approach to the sexual biodynamics of human life processes (1972).

All these theoretical perspectives reach in two directions: they help me develop my sense of purpose and they guide my behaviour. Thus as people come together at the beginning of a group project I know they need nurturing, and that a degree of authentic authority will help contain anxiety; I also know that too much authority may create dependence and counterdependence, and certainly will not develop collaborative relationships in the longer term, so I must at the same time be paying careful attention to the emergence of a new phase and new needs.

Behaviour

The development of participative relationships requires, as Torbert has it, 'movements, tones, words, and silence – sufficiently supple, attuned, and crafty to create scenes of questionable taste' and to demonstrate the 'good taste of collaboration' (Torbert, 1981: 149). Such behaviour is both authoritative and democratic, centred and reaching out, charismatic and radically democratic; it is based on a profound self-knowing, on emotional competence and behavioural flexibility. To the extent that I have developed such crafty behaviour it is through the disciplines of experiential groupwork – everything from behavioural feedback, role play and psychodrama through to T-groups and encounter groups; through personal work on psychological distress which brings about rigidities in behaviour – personal development groups, and psychotherapy; and through spiritual work which helps develop a sense of connection with our presence in the world beyond the limitations of a 'skin-encapsulated ego' – meditation, prayer, retreat. I have applied these disciplines to everyday life with the help of self-observation, using audio and video tape recording and the feedback of friends and enemies.

At the time of writing I find myself content with much of my behaviour, but also seeking to extend my repertoire to encompass a lighter and more ironic touch at moments of challenge and difficulty.

Outside world

Knowledge of the outside world comes in part from our senses, our ability to notice what is going on as we attend simultaneously to our internal processes. This attention can be enhanced by empirical means such as audio and video tape recordings and systematic information gathering through questionnaires. But perhaps the most important external information is hidden from us, since we can never know others' experience directly. I need to know from others how they experience me, and how they respond to me emotionally, and I can only know this if they are willing to tell me – hence the importance of interpersonal feedback. In collaborative groups I try to ensure that the agenda for meetings is devised together so all can influence the intent of the group; I regularly ask, 'How are we doing . . . is this making sense . . . is this helpful?' I find myself frustrated and upset in groups where I cannot find out what is going on with others present, such as large teaching groups and formal settings such as Academic Boards. In such settings I feel that I am behaving like a machine with no regulator. Lacking feedback as a means of monitoring my behaviour I either over-react or fall into silence. I notice others behave in similar fashion.

This reflection on my current awareness of the four territories of experience paradoxically takes me deeper into a review of my behaviour. Since writing the first draft of the last few paragraphs I have noticed my own deeper questioning in the midst of action, and my increased tendency to articulate this questioning in public. The process of reflection draws attention to practice, which again informs reflection building a consciousness in the midst of action. The discipline of action inquiry is in this process of paying attention to all four territories, initially as a reflection after action, but increasingly in the process of action itself. As Torbert points out, action inquiry can only take place in its fullest sense within a community of inquiry in a community of action, a community of like-minded souls who also encompass enough diversity to offer each other both support and challenge in the development of knowledge in action. Such a community can move towards the establishment of organizational structures and process to provide relevant information concerning the consequence of different courses of action.

Participative contexts for human inquiry

What does this exploration of the nature of participation, and of an emergent participative world-view, have to say about the practice of participative forms of inquiry? In part, it points to the potential radical difference between inquiry conducted in a participative manner and orthodox objective research: we are not just amending the traditional approach to research so as to treat people better or to more effectively include their experience; we are contributing to the forging of a new consciousness and a new experiential epistemology.

So I suggest that co-operative forms of inquiry conducted in the 1990s and into the foreseeable future hang in a paradoxical situation: they both *require* the emergence of a future participation for their full realization; and at the same time are *part of* the secular shift (in Western societies) towards forms of future participation. In *Human Inquiry in Action* I discussed the way that co-operative inquiry is an *emergent* process (Reason, 1988: 19), meaning that it takes time, skill and patience for full co-operation to develop in an inquiry group. We can now see a wider meaning to that comment: co-operation, participation, is emergent over time in the development of a new societal consciousness.

The framework developed above provides a perspective on the participative context in which we are working. We may be seeking to conduct participative inquiry in a culture characterized by valid or degenerate forms of original participation or unconscious participation. The process of human inquiry will introduce a dialectical tension through which a form of future participation may emerge.

If the inquiry is located in a context of *original participation*, group members will be closely identified with their experience, may tell rich stories with unconscious symbolic content, and will need facilitative help to develop a capacity for critical self-reflection. In degenerate forms of original participation some form of consciousness raising may be needed to draw participants out of their deeply unconscious patterns: this is often one aspect of the participatory action research approach, since disadvantaged peoples often need to be coaxed out of their learned culture of silence (Fals-Borda and Rahman, 1991). Inquiry based on original participation will offer rich clarity, tell stories with resonance, drawing on metaphor and allegory to evoke in the reader or listener as far as possible the experience of participation. We may imagine that the process of participative human inquiry will call forth a deeply grounded reflection, and awareness of form and pattern, an artistry so that stories are told with a greater conscious sense of purpose and impact.

If the inquiry is based in a context of unconscious participation, group members may be strong in analysis and conceptual understanding, able to manipulate abstract concepts and handle quantitative data while relatively out of touch with emotional, imaginal and intuitive experience. They may hunger for participation and may express this in a non-reflective return to original participation, or they may be unaware of their alienation from participation and thus resist its power. They will need help to honour connectedness, intuition, experiential knowing and to integrate these with critical reflective consciousness. The process of human inquiry is likely to enable participants to see through, to deconstruct, their theories, and to enrich and ground them with experiential content.

Only if the inquiry is located in the context of future participation, or if the community of inquiry has evolved towards a form of future participation, will a full flowering of collaborative inquiry be possible. We can imagine that such a community would be able to integrate inquiry with everyday life, to reflect continually on how their actions fulfil their purposes, to create myth and build ceremony which enrich their intellectual understanding and support their life activities, to integrate an appreciation of wilderness with cultural artistic and intellectual creativity.

Thus those who wish to take the path of collaborative research be warned: this is no easy way forward. You and your co-researchers may be attracted to the rhetoric of participation; you may think you are deeply committed to the values of participative relationships. Yet for those of us encultured to unconscious participation the leap to a future reflexive participation is immense:

there will be doubt and mistrust, there will be disagreement and conflict, there will be failures as well as success. For the birth of a new more integrated consciousness means the death of the old. Future participation means the loss of the myth of certainty, the loss of control, the tempering of the rational mind. It means learning to trust the wisdom of the unknown other. The disappointments along the way to future participation will test us all.

Part II
The Practice of Participatory Research

Knowledge of one subject by another is love.

(Eckman, 1986: 95)

Love proper exists only between living beings who are alike in power
and thus in another's eyes living beings from every point of view.

(Hegel, trans. 1948)

5

Confronting Hidden Agendas: Co-operative Inquiry with Health Visitors

Hilary Traylen

This chapter tells the story of one part of my exploration of the nature of health visiting practice in the British National Health Service (Traylen, 1989). I began my work by interviewing a number of health visitors and by attending a workshop on the health visitor's role. One theme which emerged from this was the considerable level of stress experienced by health visitors in the course of their work. As I reflected on what I was doing I became increasingly unhappy with my research approach.

As I became more skilled in conducting the interviews I began to pay more attention to the interview process and to the way I was reacting. I began to feel very confused and uncertain about what I was trying to do, and realized how difficult it was to probe into the nature of this relationship between the health visitor and her client. The more I talked to health visitors the more I came to realize that what I was trying to understand was extremely complex. The health visitors themselves were not very articulate in describing their relationships with their clients. There were some similarities in their accounts but they seemed to me to be superficial. There were layers in the relationship. If I tried to probe further, some health visitors seemed to be saying that their relationship was something they could experience but could not fully express. If they were unable to describe the relationship, how on earth was I the researcher going to explain it?

I felt confused not only because I was unable to get much clarity but also because it was an issue for me. I wanted a nice neat definable answer. The experience aroused a whole host of anxieties about me as a researcher. I felt doubt about my own ability to see the research through feeling anxious and powerless in my confusion, my inability to pin down, tie up, package this 'thing' called relationships. I felt isolated, as if I was interviewing the health visitors in a vacuum, just two people struggling to articulate and make sense of issues that were beyond resolution.

These issues were not just of academic interest, they were important to me in a very personal way. I began to realize why I had chosen this research topic. When I first started out I had presented myself with all sorts of very reasonable explanations as to why this was the appropriate research to undertake. I had not really taken into account the emotional and psychological implications. In other words I had been pretty naïve at the outset. On the positive side the undertaking of such a research project has provided me with an opportunity to grow and develop. Questions have been raised about my own self-worth and have made me look much more closely at 'who I am'. These deep inner questions of identity, relationship, of facing my own doubts, needs and resistances has helped me to experience a new understanding of myself and I think of others. This personal process in turn contributed to the research because of my increased awareness and sensitivity.

Living with my anxiety about the impact of my questions on the health visitors was more difficult. The essence of my inquiry felt at times like 'twisting the knife' in what was already a raw wound. I felt unhappy about using a method which left these issues unresolved, and it seemed to me that I might be resurfacing issues for the interviewees. I was for them 'here today and gone tomorrow'. They were still faced with the day-to-day task of practising their profession, still tussling with unresolved dilemmas about their practice. I found myself sharing the pain, confusion and dilemmas the health visitors were expressing about their practice, and I was concerned that I might be raising similar doubts and anxieties in them. All the interviews seemed to achieve was an identification of some of the issues about health visiting practice, leaving the health visitors with these issues unresolved. I felt guilty. I was perhaps resurfacing these issues for them and then just leaving them in a mess. The issues which have emerged from the interview data and the workshop represented, in my view, serious problems. I wanted to explore a methodology which might reveal a deeper analysis of these problems. From the workshop and the interviews has come a strong impression of the health visitors' isolation, of their need for mutual support and the need to discuss professional practice issues. The health visitors were noticeably anxious about the management structure; they felt there was lack of support from their managers. What I wanted was to look for a different methodology which would be more orientated towards action research. A method that might go some way towards exploring these issues in greater depth.

The co-operative inquiry which followed the interviews provided a significantly different perspective on the issues. It enabled greater insight into the problems and it also led into action research to explore ways to change and develop health visiting practice. This research method was more powerful because I was no longer exploring these issues in isolation, but undertaking the inquiry with a group of health visitors as co-researchers.

The methodology of co-operative inquiry has been described elsewhere (Reason and Rowan, 1981; Reason, 1988). The advantage of this kind of inquiry is that the approach is not simply restricted to my asking the health visitors to describe their interactions with others, but focuses on their reciprocal interaction with myself, so that we become both co-researchers and co-subjects.

Another key factor in co-operative inquiry is that it is person centred; it recognizes the potential self-determination of those involved. The experience of exploring together in this kind of inquiry would hopefully lead to our own personal growth and development, and to some deeper insight or resolution of the issues of health visiting practice. In addition, co-operative inquiry purported to be a method which could be used by ordinary people, in seeking to change their lives, so that 'research' was not just the prerogative of professional researchers (Reason, 1988).

From the literature on co-operative inquiry I gained two strong impressions: first, any individual proposing to use such a method required considerable skills. Peter Reason and John Rowan (1981) emphasize the need for 'high quality awareness'; Heron (1981b) suggests that 'the discipline and rigour involved in this sort of research is formidable'. And Torbert writes 'that a person must undergo a to-him unimaginable scale of self development before he becomes capable of rationally valid action' (1976: 167). Reason and Heron stress that in order for the researcher to develop and maintain this 'high quality awareness' they needed to engage in some therapeutic disciplines or systematic method of personal and interpersonal development such as co-counselling (1981: 245–6).

Emphasis was also given to the likely effects such an inquiry can have upon individuals. Peter Reason makes this point when he talks about distress facilitation.

> Co-operative inquiry is an exciting business; it can also be an upsetting business. It is my experience that research which authentically challenges the way those involved conduct their lives raises all kinds of emotional issues which are ignored or denied by conventional research doctrine. It is an essential aspect of co-operative inquiry that these emotional issues are addressed. . . . It is therefore a clear advantage if an inquiry group has available to it a degree of emotional competence so that personal distress can be appropriately managed. (Reason, 1988: 28–9)

I felt relatively inexperienced as a researcher and I had little experience of therapeutic disciplines. There would not be time to fit in any kind of co-counselling course or develop the skills which the literature was suggesting I ought to have in using such an experiential method. So the literature really scared me off. Yet co-operative inquiry according to Peter Reason (1988: Ch. 1) was supposed to be a method which ordinary people like me could use.

I also found the literature very heavy going. I had to learn a whole new language. I struggled through torrid chapters heavily laced with such terms as *ontological assumptions, epistemological assumptions* and *axiological assumptions* (Lincoln and Guba, 1985), thinking to myself 'I don't even understand what they are trying to say half the time'. This reinforced any foreboding I had about my capability to understand the method, let alone how I could explain it simply to a group of health visitors.

I found John Heron's chapter describing the philosophical basis for a new paradigm (1981a) useful – the literature at the time was very thin on practical guidance on how to use a co-operative inquiry approach. (This was before Peter Reason, to some extent at my instigation, wrote Chapter 1 in *Human Inquiry In Action* (1988) which provides a more practical guide to the co-operative inquiry group.)

To help clarify my mind and identify what I needed to prepare for such an inquiry, I picked out from the literature all the practical hints I could find. I then translated these points into a simple form I felt I could work with and produced an outline of how I might proceed with such an inquiry.

First I sketched out an aim for the co-operative inquiry: To carry out research into our own health visiting practice and to share that experience with our co-researchers. This would lead to a discussion about which aspects of health visiting practice should be investigated. Such an investigation might, for example, focus upon the health visitors' relationship with their clients. Alternatively the discussion might develop into areas outside of my immediate research concern and this made me think through how I might handle this situation if it arose.

Just suppose the group decided to undertake an inquiry which was not important in my research, how would I deal with this situation? Peter Reason sees this difficulty. He suggests that the research initiator ask

> 'Who is this research *really* for?', and 'Is there a genuine possibility for co-operative endeavour?' If there *is* an inquiry task around which a group of people can genuinely join to explore, then any problems of initiation, ownership, and power can be resolved through authentic negotiation and confrontation. But if there is no such possibility of a shared inquiry task, then, the group will have been set up on a phoney basis. (Reason, 1988: 20–1; emphasis in original)

I was concerned that I needed to provide a forum in which the health visitors could genuinely contribute. I wanted to avoid getting into a position in which the health visitors might only be collaborating to help me in my research. The issue under investigation had to be a matter which was vitally important for the health visitors. One way round this was to set up an introductory seminar in which I could talk about my research and the issues I was interested in investigating further. The participants could then decide for themselves, whether they were interested in the issues and the idea of a co-operative inquiry approach.

The introductory seminar

I decided to invite the health visitors whom I had met at a workshop on health visitor practice. These health visitors had already built up a degree of trust with each other and myself, and from the participants' involvement in the workshop it seemed natural for them to now move towards researching into their own practice. I also contacted some of the health visitors I had previously interviewed and invited them to come along, and I spoke to a number of the managers so that they could pass on the information to those health visitors who they thought might be interested.

I decided that the seminar would need to be structured and mapped out for the participants. The health visitors would probably be feeling uneasy about the idea of research, especially with the idea that they could 'do research'. I needed to tailor the seminar to meet my own and the group's needs, so I drew up an agenda and made a list of points I wanted to cover.

1 *Getting to know each other*: Some of the participants might not know each other, so time would need to be set aside for introductions.

2 *Hilary's research*: I would outline the main areas of my research and discuss with them the work undertaken so far. I intended at this stage to share with them the emergent themes and declare my intention of wanting to explore these in greater depth by using a new research method.

3 *Expectation*: Time would be given for general discussion in order to elicit why they were interested. I also hoped that it might draw from the participants any burning issues they may want to explore further.

4 *What does co-operative inquiry mean?*: I would explain in simple terms how we might use this method together. I was not very confident about my ability to do this so I also wrote up a handout for the participants to take and think about afterwards. This would tell them about the method again and the implications of becoming involved in such an inquiry.

5 *What am I getting into?*: This would allow for some discussion about the implications of undertaking such an inquiry. This kind of inquiry would have a direct and personal effect upon the participants. The participants would be probing into, and asking questions of themselves about matters which they cared about and this was likely to cause some anxiety. I was particularly concerned that they should be aware of the likely consequences of research in terms of their own personal distress and how it was intended the group should handle that distress. I would also emphasize that these experiences would bring rewards such as elation, creativity and personal growth.

6 *What's next (contracting)*: I intended to outline some ground rules for an inquiry group: for example, confidentiality, giving permission for individuals to say 'no' if they felt they were getting into issues they were not interested in; time to talk about how individuals were feeling, and roles within the group. I also wanted, if time allowed, to map out how an inquiry might progress, and to end this with a session of brainstorming how they viewed health visiting practice. Participants would then be free to go away and contact me individually if they were interested in setting up an inquiry group.

Of the eight health visitors who wanted to come for various reasons only five were able to attend. I saw the other three health visitors individually, briefed them about the seminar, and about what co-operative inquiry might involve for them.

The seminar was held in the morning and lasted for two hours. I would have preferred longer but the time had to be restricted due to the health visitors' work commitments. We started the morning with introductions, each participant telling the others a little about their previous work experience and where they were presently based. Next we moved on to some flip charts I had prepared and I gave the group a brief outline of my research to date and the reasons why I was proposing an inquiry group. After this session I asked permission to use the tape recorder because I did not want to forget any of their ideas.

Using the flip charts again I started to describe the co-operative inquiry approach. They seemed enthusiastic about the idea of action research and the philosophy of research with people rather than on people. One of the participants was quite taken by the idea of a more holistic approach.

I then showed the participants an example of what we might do by putting up the aim of the inquiry I had previously outlined in my plan, and showing how they might decide on which aspect to inquire into and how they might put this into practice. I could feel at this point they were a bit lost, so tried out a little mapping exercise to see if this would help. This seemed to fit into their culture of 'being up and doing'. I took 'health visitors' relationship' and got them to brainstorm their ideas. I encouraged them to share ideas and these were put onto a flip chart.

Someone offered the idea that the relationship was affected by their 'expertness'. I was not sure what they meant and after a long silence, bit by bit we made a list of what they thought they meant and through discussion it emerged that all this knowledge was not necessarily known to the families they visited. They suspected that perhaps only four areas of their 'expertness' might be known to the people they visited. These were child development, nutrition, immunization and child behaviour problems. This realization that families might not know what the health visitor has to offer provoked considerable discussion about how much they were prepared to communicate with their families. Participants varied in how they described their role and their reason for visiting their families. This discussion also revealed that the health visitors varied in how much they would communicate to their clients about their role and reason for visiting. Several other issues linked to the health visitors' relationship were mentioned, and gradually we began to draw various concepts together.

This exercise seemed to work extremely well as it helped to get everyone involved and yielded a lot of rich data which had not emerged earlier in the research. For example, it was the first time I had heard the health visitors talking about manipulating their clients, of being devious and having hidden agendas (by this they meant that they did not give the client the real reason behind why they were visiting them).

After this exercise I moved on to describe the processes involved in this kind of inquiry. I introduced them to the idea of cycles of inquiry. This would involve taking an aspect of health visiting practice and deciding what method would be appropriate to explore it, for example, questions and discussion. Then trying this out and coming back to the group to re-examine their original ideas in the light of their experience. This might result in changes being made, and new ideas tried out. This recycling may occur several times.

Briefly I covered some of the ground rules an inquiry group should consider – issues of confidentiality, permission to say 'no' and time to be given for checking out how people felt. However, when I started to mention validity procedures I could see that individuals were looking a bit lost; one or two people looked puzzled. When I checked this out, one of the group confirmed she felt confused. The group, I felt, were not all that interested in the process of inquiry; rather they were much more keen on 'doing something', never mind the processes involved. This experience was to be repeated several times in the course of the co-operative inquiry.

I returned to the brainstorming exercise and more issues were raised. Doubts were expressed about their role such as 'Why do I visit?'; 'Who am I now? So many things to so many people'; 'What am I doing?'; 'How well am I doing?'. These problems of feedback about themselves and their practice were a recurring theme already raised by the interview respondents and in the workshop.

After the two hours were up several of the health visitors wanted to meet again as soon as possible and another date was arranged.

Co-operative inquiry in action

The inquiry itself spanned a period of eight months and during this period went through a number of different phases:

Phase 1: Identification of the issues to be explored.
Phase 2: Convergent cycles of inquiry in action.
Phase 3: Engaging in chaos.
Phase 4: Communicating the research.

Phase 1: Identification of the issues to be explored

Over the period June to September the group met twice and settled to a core group of five health visitors with myself making the sixth participant. All the sessions were tape recorded and many of the ideas explored by the group recorded on flip charts. Many of the themes and issues about relationships, support, role conflict and evaluation had already been raised in the interviews and workshop. In this account of the co-operative inquiry I intend to recount only those themes which the inquiry explored through action research, and to explain the inquiry process the group undertook.

My role within group   In these first two sessions I worried quite a lot about my role within the group. I saw myself initially needing to help facilitate the group but I did not want to get caught in this role. I was concerned that the facilitator's role might become that of leader with the group no longer authentic co-researchers. I hoped it would be possible for this role to be shared, so that others within the group would also act as facilitators.

This did not happen in the early stages of the inquiry and on reflection this was inevitable. The group members were new to each other, we needed time to get to know each other and to feel safe with each other. In my role I realized that I needed to nurture and educate participants in using a method they were unfamiliar with. Whether I liked it or not in these early stages I was seen as some sort of expert in co-operative inquiry.

The first meeting   The group spent the first session getting to know each other, sharing views about health visiting practice and identifying possible areas for the inquiry. From these discussions we began to focus on three key issues which the group found difficult to manage in their practice. Through discussion we came to realize that these issues were interrelated. These we called feedback, hidden agendas and confrontation.

Feedback concerned evaluation: How do you find out whether you have been effective? Are there any methods or techniques you can use that can give you this feedback? From this exploration came the link with *hidden agendas*: How much do we discuss with our clients particularly highly sensitive issues such as child abuse, incest, drug and alcohol abuse and poor relationships? One participant recalled a visit in which she felt the mother had a poor understanding of what to expect of her children. The health visitor was finding it difficult, saying, 'I can be open about some things, but it is actually quite difficult to confront her and say, "Look you are having some difficulty in relating to your child"'.

Thus feedback and hidden agendas linked with *confrontation*: several found confronting clients a big problem. Some described themselves as skirting around the issue rather than being directly honest.

We all recognized that some of the visits were superficial, not tackling the fundamental concerns we held about some families. If we were to be effective as health visitors these sensitive areas needed to be explored further. The group concluded that in order to assess how they were doing with families, they needed to be more open and honest, to confront them with the real reasons for visiting: 'no hidden agendas'. They also needed to seek families' views about their visits to them to gain feedback.

Was this an issue the group wanted to inquire into? It seemed at first that the answer was, 'no', and we all slid away and 'skirted around the issue'. Just as we had identified a core problem with visits, the group moved away from this sensitive question and started to explore around about the issues again.

This second exploration led us to probe into why feedback, hidden agendas and confrontation were such problematic areas for us. This discussion unearthed a lot of underlying anxieties. Some of the group felt they did not have the courage or the strength to get into these issues in their day-to-day practice. Some described themselves as having 'chickened out'. One explained how she felt: 'I have this big dread about that day I have to visit a certain family, and all you do is bury it. You think "I will visit them and get it over with" and you know there is a whole host of problems, but you don't go searching for them'.

Others worried about whether they could cope if they 'unearthed' families' needs. Questions arose such as 'How do I cope with the consequences of that confrontation, do I have the skills?' Issues were raised about 'How much are you responsible for actually digging around for what's going on?' All this imagery of burying, digging and unearthing conjured up in my mind images of graveyards in the dead of night and childhood stories of unimaginable goings on. We were all fearful of what might happen, of getting out of our depth, of making things worse.

One group member got angry, she felt so frustrated:

Here we are talking about something we all feel quite passionately about I think. This is something we need help with. It's the first time it's [she was referring to the problems about confrontation and feedback] been discussed with me . . . this is still a big problem with me, but this is the nitty gritty of health visiting I feel . . . I just feel that somebody up there [she meant managers] should be looking at what I am doing and asking why I find health visiting difficult. 'Why haven't you visited this family?' I need help with that.

It was in circumstances like these that I saw that the help would come from the group, from sharing these experiences together and by exploring together how we might manage these issues.

The second meeting   The group spent a lot of time in the second session circling around these problems and others in health visiting practice. I think this was because we were feeling at a loss about how to tackle the issues and in particular the issue of confrontation. The group continually sought sanctuary in talking about *content* rather than tackle the problem of *process*. In other words, how are we going to deal with this issue? At this stage I felt the need to help move the group on. We were all hovering on the brink. All that was needed was just a little nudge to get us into trying to work out together the processes involved in confrontation.

The breakthrough came when I asked each of the participants to describe a hidden agenda, a problem which they felt unable to discuss openly with the mother of a family they visited. Each problem was explored in depth, and we found that often the individual participant felt unclear about what was going on, and the joint discussion enabled us to be clear about the area of concern and to get some idea of the possible reasons why the health visitor thought her client was behaving in a particular way.

From these discussions various suggestions were explored with the individual health visitor until an outline strategy was worked out. For one participant the suggestion was that she should make a clear offer of counselling to one of her mothers which would be absolutely confidential, just between the two of them and no records made. Another idea involved rehearsing how the health visitor might confront the mother: what sort of language should be used? How direct should the confrontation be? Is this the right time and in the right circumstances? What do you do if having confronted you get a complete denial or you 'open up a can of worms'? The group explored each question in depth and tried out various actual words and sentences.

By the end of this second session a contract was agreed. Each of the co-researchers would try out various ways of confronting the problems we had discussed. They would experiment with ways which would help them to achieve a more open and honest relationship with their families. They would try to explore ways in which they could begin to probe into the more sensitive areas and share those concerns with their families. The methods to be used in recording progress was only very lightly touched upon and was left to each individual to decide. All the group felt anxious about the decision but at the same time they were determined to try out some of the ideas we had discussed.

Reflecting afterwards on this second meeting I was quite frightened by what the group had agreed. What they were proposing to do meant confronting themselves, their fears about their skills, of the danger of causing damage and getting it wrong. This was a highly risky undertaking for them and their families. The group might experience adverse reactions which could destroy their newly found confidence. Perhaps we had taken on too difficult an issue for the first cycle of inquiry. I was so worried I telephoned each of the members and shared my concerns. I thought it was important that individuals should feel free to go at their own pace. One of the members I talked to did feel she needed more time before she could handle some of the issues. Others were more confident and seemed determined to pursue some of the ideas.

Phase 2: Convergent cycles of inquiry in action

Over the period October to mid-November the group met three more times. During this time the group was deeply immersed in the action of the inquiry, each session being spent on hearing each other's experiences, refining the research methods and going back into action again. The third meeting was tense and full of expectation. Each of the group gave an account of how they had tried various ways of being more 'open' during their visits to families.

One of the participants had followed the group's suggestion and offered counselling to one of her mothers. The offer had been made on the under-standing that there would be absolute confidentiality. This had been accepted with alacrity, which both pleased the health visitor but scared her too: 'Oh my God what do I do! Do I have to read up something, do I have to sit passively? . . . Are you going to help me or not?' (meaning the group).

We spent a long time talking through the next steps of how she might manage the first counselling session. Much of the facilitation came from the group member who was undertaking a counselling course. Key counselling concepts were explored with suggestions being made such as 'Go at the pace of the client, let them tell you what they want to tell you . . . There are ways of letting them know you are there, you are following what they are saying, reflecting back or summarizing what they have said'.

Time was spent encouraging, supporting and helping the group member come to terms with guilt feelings she was now experiencing about this particular mother. She had visited this mother over several years and was feeling bad at not having picked up signs, not having realized what this mother might have been going through. Offers of support were made so that as the group member moved into the next cycle with this mother she would feel supported.

Another member gave an account of a visit to a mother who had recently given birth to her first baby. Her hidden agenda was that she suspected there was something going on and it was connected to the episiotomy the mother had sustained during the birth. The health visitor suspected the mother was anxious, but was uncertain how to raise the problem. She described to us her previous visits: 'I was going in to do my weekly visit, thinking "I am not absolutely sure where we are getting here" because she talks an awful lot, and she's always very jolly, and I felt useless there. As if I wasn't getting anywhere'.

The key which opened up the underlying problem was the health visitor's decision to ask a direct question about how the mother felt about her episiotomy scar. This opened up a 'whole load of stuff'. The mother started talking about how she had frantically been doing exercises to 'get it right', her fear of being examined post-natally and how 'she would happily leave her sex life for another two years'. She complained of feeling tight and uncomfortable. Other issues emerged about how long they had tried to have a baby and how her previous pregnancies had ended in miscarriages.

Reflecting back on this visit the health visitor felt quite brave at having tackled the problem. She had felt that she might have got out of her depth and could have easily avoided the underlying problem. The group reflected on this experience and various suggestions were made about how the next visit should be managed.

The next participant described what happened to her on the very day we had all decided on the contract. She explained

> I was really spent by four o'clock and someone came into the clinic, one of my priority families and I thought I just don't want to see this lady. So I avoided her because I really couldn't cope. But she heard my voice and had me out. 'Can you come round?' I said, 'No I can't'. She burst into tears on me, so I went round [to her house] and I was there for two hours, and it was the best two hours I have ever spent with them.
>
> The first thing I said when I walked in (because my temper was short) was, 'I have nothing to offer you, I am here to listen, I can give you no money. The only support I can give you is for the next hour'. I put a time limit on it. I was really very very cross and they could see I was. So they made me a cup of tea and made me sit down and they just talked to me for two hours. They were so *honest* because I had been very honest with them. It was *great*. It *really worked*. I just felt very strong from the morning. My honesty just produced a lot of honesty with them. We had no hidden agendas. We talked all about child abuse and wife battering and his illegal drugs and how many times he breaks into the meter, and it was *incredible*. It had been a *great relief* and it's really really *reduced my stress*. That was my main thought when she came into the clinic, 'I cannot cope with them because my stress would be too high'. So that was very very useful.

Another health visitor concerned about a mother's relationship with her new born baby tried a more direct approach too: 'I can't quite remember the exact words but I think I said something like "Am I right to think you don't feel close to your baby?" I had been dreading this question'. She got a very honest answer to this question which confirmed her assessment. The mother openly admitted she did not love very small babies.

One of the group had kept notes on six visits where she had tried this more direct confrontational approach. She found the responses very positive. In her experience she found she had made far greater progress in getting someone to change. For example, one of her mothers kept failing her appointments and when she challenged her, she was able to get at the underlying problem. The result was that she was able eventually to get the mother to keep her appointments.

She found too that she had been worrying unnecessarily about some families and this greatly reduced her stress. In some incidences she had also saved herself some work by checking out with families whether she needed to continue to visit them. Another time where she had been visiting weekly and feeling she 'wasn't getting anywhere' she had asked 'What do you expect from my visits?' and she actually got some feedback:

> She gave me lots of positive things about how much she valued what I had said. When I went back this week, she had a whole list of questions for me. She had actually thought out what she wanted to ask and I felt she had changed a bit of emphasis there. Instead of me questioning her, I had made her think, so she could then ask me things and that it was alright for her to do that.

Another family where the child was possibly at risk from abuse was challenged by this health visitor. She said '"I feel you resent me visiting you". I said that as soon as I got over the doorstep because I was in a fighting mood. She was taken aback. She said "No, it gives me status", that's more or less what she said, "You are seen to be doing your job." She explained that on the council estate where this mother was living, there were frequent allegations of child abuse made against her. The fact that the health visitor visited tended to stop the allegations. So 'She does not resent me visiting, she likes me going in fact!' She admitted later to the group that the mother was moving and it was this fact which had given her the courage to confront. She knew that if it went wrong it would not matter as she would be no longer responsible for visiting her.

On one occasion things did go wrong. She had gone to visit an elderly person and her daughter. She had suggested to the daughter that she felt she was very very burdened by her mother.

> 'That was a big mistake . . . she was really angry with me and she was quite abusive . . . she said she did not want anyone interfering with her mother, and, yes, she was a burden, but what could I do about it? [The daughter went on to vent her feelings] I don't know anything about the family background, I don't know anything about the family feuds that go on. How can I make statements like that when I have only been two times. I have talked more to her mother than to her . . . I write all these things down and then I go off and *do good*. How do I know how she feels when she is stuck at home and her mother is moaning all the time.

This incident had caused the health visitor a lot of stress. She had felt very uncomfortable and she felt what she had done was dangerous. On further questioning it felt dangerous because she was getting quite upset and stressed to the extent that she knew she could not handle it. She did not feel strong enough to stay and talk through the daughter's anger. The group spent some time in giving support and encouragement which ended in the health visitor agreeing to go back, to which she replied 'Oh well I will try and follow her up then at our next meeting. If I come in a heap you know what's happened . . . or if I don't arrive!'

Reflections upon the inquiry process   Looking back over this time the group went through three cycles of inquiry. Each session would start with each of us checking out how individuals were feeling and spending time on those issues. Each member gave an account of the progress they had made since the last meeting and these were discussed in detail, ideas refined and developed for the next cycle of research.

During this period the group members were almost solely preoccupied with action and were not the least bit interested in the process of the research. This need to make progress was a powerful influence and its parallel can be seen with the health visitors wanting their families to move on too. Reflecting back over this period, not to progress might have represented failure to the group. Although I raised the question several times that perhaps we should spend some time reflecting on the research method, the group were much more interested in exploring and reflecting back on the research material.

Quite early on one of the group members had asked 'Where is the research part going to come in?' What was being proposed did not fit in with her ideas about research. She had been on a research appreciation course and she had never heard of a research method such as co-operative inquiry. How could this be research? There seemed to be a considerable culture gap. They were more familiar with traditional methods and felt unclear about this new method. In some way too this discussion was connected to what I suspected were doubts about their ability to undertake research in their own right. The group during this time tended to avoid the issue of identifying how we did it.

My role within the group underwent a number of changes. Earlier on in the inquiry I had worried that I might have got stuck in the leadership or facilitator's role. This in itself raised questions about whether this could be a full blown co-operative inquiry. If I got stuck in these roles, how could I be a participating member of the inquiry group? In the early part of the inquiry it was important that I should undertake these two roles. The group members needed to get to know each other and to feel safe before they could move on into deciding what they wanted to do.

I shared with the group my concerns about my role. I was different from other members of the group. I was not a practising health visitor, so how could I become an equal participating member of the inquiry group if I was not going out with them to explore these issues? Paradoxically the answer came to this question when I found myself exploring these issues in relation to my relationship with the participants.

This happened during the first feedback session, when they were giving an account of their experiences. I was worried that one of the group members might have gone into the inquiry overenthusiastically. I felt uneasy; as she talked I could feel aggression. I felt uneasy about how outspoken she had been with the families. She was making statements like 'I was in a fighting mood'. I felt puzzled as to how I could broach this with her. So my 'hidden agenda' was 'concern that this member had gone off at full steam and needed to slow down and reflect a bit more on her experiences'. I found myself preoccupied with the question of 'how do I confront her without causing distress?' Another group member needed to be challenged about something she had said. All through this period I found that I was conducting the same inquiry as the group, but in parallel.

During this phase of the co-operative inquiry the group experienced intense excitement. We were focusing on an aspect of practice which we were particularly anxious about. There was a lot of risk-taking involved for all of us and despite the fears, each member of the group had succeeded in breaking through into a deeper understanding of their practice. These personal accounts were full of life and energy, almost effervescent, and it gave everyone a tremendous feeling of confidence. There was general acknowledgement that these experiences were helping them to feel stronger and more confident, not only with their families but in their personal lives too. I became deeply immersed in the research to the extent that I started to have dreams. One morning I had woken early from a dream which had a nightmarish heavy quality about it. The dream had centred upon the group member who had offered counselling to one of her mothers.

There was a lot of noise in the dream which prevented me from hearing what was said properly. (This probably represented my fears of not understanding the research material.) People were hovering out of sight in the wings. I think they were the 'managers'. (I saw them as being a possible threat to myself and the group.) The group member in the dream was very upset because she had been faced with something indescribable, mad and out of control. I recognized that in the corner of my left eye lurked something equally as nasty and was connected to the group member's distress.

Reflecting back on this dream it made me think again about the issue of distress which is involved in this kind of inquiry. In the heat of the inquiry, with the group so fully committed to action, the group's anxiety may not have been sufficiently explored in the sessions. I decided to check this out with the group in the next series of meetings.

Phase 3: Engaging in chaos

From the end of November to mid-February the group met another three times. By this time the group had been through a number of cycles of the research. We had first tested out ways in which group members could confront their clients in order to facilitate and open up underlying issues, and experimented with ideas which would help achieve a more open and honest relationship with clients. These research cycles involved the group taking these ideas several times round the cycle of reflection and action. However, the balance between action and reflection tended at this time to be much more weighted towards action. The group realized that the inquiry would be coming to an end since two of the members were due to leave in February. So in the last three meetings the group concentrated much more upon reflection, sense making and evaluation in order to create a better balance between action and reflection.

In the first of these three meetings I proposed to the group that we should spend some of the time hearing from each other about our experiences and part of the time discussing the research, defining and recording what we had achieved so far. There was general agreement and a time agreed for feedback and time to deal with the process of the research.

The group member who had offered counselling to her mother now recounted her first counselling session. The meeting took place in the mother's home. She had arranged for the husband to take the children out for the afternoon so they would not be interrupted. Significantly the mother had suggested they should talk in the dining room, a room she had never been in before having always talked to the mother in the lounge. She realized the symbolic reason for this suggestion. The use of this room made the distinction between her former relationship with this mother as her health visitor and her new relationship as her counsellor.

The mother poured out her feelings of resentment she had held against her third male child. Taking the health visitor back to the beginning of the pregnancy and how desperately she had wanted a girl, she explained how she had felt, from hugging the child in desperation, to losing control and hating the child. She talked about an incident with the child screaming so much, that she started shaking him, and shaking, and shaking him. The husband came in. She was screaming, the baby was screaming, and he hit her to stop her from doing it. In retrospect she knew that something terrible could have happened.

The mother could not talk to anyone about these feelings for fear of being labelled as a child abuser. This was why she had not taken up the health visitor's previous suggestion to seek help from a private counsellor, and why she could not talk to the health visitor about these feelings. It was not until the health visitor made the offer of absolute confidentiality and no records kept, that she could feel safe to reveal this burden she had carried for so long.

The health visitor was aghast. She had no idea in the many months she had visited, that this mother was suffering in this way. On reflection there were signs which she had failed to recognize and this made her feel guilty. Before the session ended the mother checked again and asked 'Are you recording this?' The health visitor replied, 'No, that was part of our agreement, there is no record of it at all.' They agreed to meet again.

This incident provides a different insight into the issue of child abuse for parents. Here was a mother who desperately needed to talk through her feelings and dared not, because she was haunted with the fear of being labelled a child abuser.

Other group members fed back their experiences. One of the members had experimented with being more assertive and more open with one of her mothers. This mother did not attend clinic despite repeated invitations. There was a history of cot death and some evidence of a poor mother–child relationship with the eldest child, now aged five. The health visitor had received a copy of a report recommending that all babies should be weighed regularly if there had been a cot death in the family.

The health visitor was getting fed up with going in to weigh the baby when the mother could come to the clinic: 'I told her quite bluntly why I wanted him weighed'. What happened next amazed the health visitor. She was taken into another room and out came the photograph album and she was shown pictures of a ten-month-old baby who had died (cot death syndrome) six years ago. The five-year-old child had very similar looks to those of the dead child and from this discussion the mother was able to talk about why she felt so ambivalent towards the child that replaced her dead baby. This simple direct explanation on the part of the health visitor seemed to be the key in moving towards a more open relationship which allowed these issues to be explored.

Out of this discussion one consequence of labelling families was revealed: the health visitor had held a strongly preconceived idea, reinforced by other health visitors, that the family was hopeless. Statements like 'You can never do anything with this family' had been made. The health visitor was highly amused to think that she may have succeeded where previous health visitors had failed.

The last member of the group to feed back had some tragic news and was clearly upset. The news concerned the mother who had recently given birth to her first baby and had revealed she was worried about the episiotomy scar. The health visitor had been back several times and gradually it became apparent there were sexual problems. On the last occasion they had talked about miscarriages and death: 'I spent a long time there and she was able to talk about how she couldn't believe the baby was there. Yes couldn't believe the baby was actually there and then the baby died. Sudden Infant Death.'

Everyone in the group was shocked to hear this news. The health visitor had visited the day after the baby died and had subsequently spent a lot of time listening and supporting. She was thankful for her earlier frank discussions. She felt this had helped deepen the relationship and provide support through the parents' bereavement. The experience had upset her because she felt helpless, she had experienced the feeling of wanting to 'make it better' and she knew she could not. This incident reminded us all of similar feelings when faced with dying patients and the group spent some time dealing with this distress.

Reflections and sense making   After the feedback session the group moved on to start to identify the processes involved so far in the research. We started by focusing first on what the experience had been like and these collective statements were recorded on flip charts. Reflecting back on these statements we came to realize that the main method of inquiry had evolved from storytelling, from telling the story of their experience with particular families, or by recounting a visit which enabled us to analyse and understand what was happening. Except for one group member who kept a diary of the visits where she had experimented, the remaining group members recalled from memory. From these statements came a clear message of 'what it felt like' and I shall call this 'personal process'.

Personal process   All of the group at the start of the inquiry had felt anxious and talked about 'needing to feel good', 'getting the time right', 'feeling strong' and 'having the courage' to go and try out new ways of developing a more open and honest relationship with their families.

Given these initial feelings the group work prior to each inquiry cycle was seen as essential: the group was seen as an empowering agent. One member told us this story.

I was quite assertive, far more than I have ever been in a case conference . . . I felt good about it and my clinical nurse specialist was quite amazed at my reaction. I then had to explain, 'I have just come from this meeting [meaning the co-operative inquiry group] and power is coming out of my ears'!!

Having experimented with being more open with families the group members experienced increasing confidence. They found out that they had worried about situations quite needlessly and so experienced considerable relief. Their stress levels reduced and they found they could work more effectively. They found themselves tackling problems they had shied away from in the past. For example, one group member got fed up with the way she was being manipulated by social workers, so she told them how she felt. Another group member experienced changes for the better in her personal life. Others had found they had had an effect on work colleagues, one of whom had confided to a group member that she felt she was not coping with her case load; the group member talked to her about the work of the co-operative inquiry group and now the colleague too was trying to be more assertive and open with clients and finding it worked for her.

Next the group moved on to consider the original contract. At the beginning the group had concluded that in order to assess how well they were doing with families they needed to inquire into a number of areas: They needed to be more open and honest. To confront clients/families with the real reason for visiting, have no hidden agendas. They needed to seek clients'/families' views about their visits to them, to get feedback. The group's next task was to see if we could identify the process which enabled us to explore these issues.

This identification went relatively well at first. The group had found the most helpful method was to get each other to talk about particular families. This was because we were uncertain of what was happening within the family or we were perplexed about how to manage the situation. Then through discussion and mutual support we ended up with different strategies to suit particular situations.

These discussions helped in a number of ways:

- Increased our knowledge of the particular families we discussed.
- Increased each other's knowledge about our practice.
- Helped us in deciding how we would manage our next visit to this particular family.
- Explored various key words or sentences to help facilitate a more open and honest discussion with our families.
- Helped us to come to terms with our anxieties and through mutual support give us the confidence to go out and explore.

This process was repeated at each group meeting.

From these discussions we began to learn that a number of strategies seemed to work. Direct questions which focused on the area of concern were a good way of getting feedback. For example the health visitor who asked one of her mothers what she expected from the visits; and another who asked a direct question about how the mother felt about her episiotomy scar. These direct

questions seemed to be a key factor in moving towards a more open relationship which allowed these issues to be explored. Health visitors experienced
what they called 'a better quality, deeper, closer, more equal relationship' with
their families.

Another strategy which appeared to help involved the individual becoming
more assertive and being more open about how they felt about a situation or
a particular client. For example, the health visitor who told one of her mothers
that she felt she resented her visits. The same health visitor made it clear to one
of the social workers that she felt she had been manipulated. Another health
visitor who pointed out to her client that her failure to attend for her appointment resulted in her missing her lunch. She received an apology from the
client.

Others made it more clear to some clients the work they were prepared to
undertake with them. For example the health visitor who offered counselling
to one of her mothers. Others made it clear what work they would not undertake, such as lend them money or deal with their rent arrears.

Chaos   While identification of these particular strategies was successful, when
we came to link this with what we were trying to do as health visitors, the
group started to get confused. The same old issues came up again: what are
health visitors' aims? What are we doing as health visitors and what is our role?
The group struggled with the formal statements which are made about health
visiting aims, such as 'prevention of ill health and promotion of good health',
trying to see how such a broad concept can be applied meaningfully to actual
health visiting practice. One member described her feelings: 'I am quoting aims
that have been quoted at us, and I no longer believe in them . . . Sometimes I go
in and waffle on about preventative health, but what the hell does that mean?
They look baffled and I feel baffled, it doesn't mean anything really.'

Just when we were feeling so confident the group was thrown into confusion, uncertainty and depression. In a way we had been deceiving ourselves
that we were doing all right: this discussion stopped us in our tracks. Everyone
knew intuitively that the group had to address this more fundamental issue
about our practice. We were swamped by the enormity of the task and scared
about whether we would be able to make sense of it all. This first session in
which we had set aside some time for reflection proved to be the most dis-
tressing period the group went through. The group had found that once they
had got up the courage to move away from doing the research, identifying the
process we had used had gone reasonably well. But the group's pre-occupation
with action had, I think, something to do with avoiding the key issue of our
lack of clarity about the health visitor's role, which had always been present
hovering in the wings. I had no idea how we were going to address this. All I
could hang onto at this stage was the thought that if the group could hold this
chaos for long enough perhaps something would emerge. We agreed to do
some thinking and writing before we next met.

At the second reflection session we spent quite a lot of time dealing with
how badly we felt after the last session, dealing with feelings about adequacy,

competence and articulation. Despite these feelings each of the group had done some thinking or writing as agreed. Everyone had experienced some difficulty, mainly because they found themselves getting stuck every time on the issue 'What am I doing and why am I doing it'. We shared what we had and gradually we began to identify factors which seemed to cause us the most difficulty and these we called our sticky areas.

We needed first to sort out what we meant by 'health visiting aims', and we found a typical formal statement from the Council for Education and Training of Health Visitors: 'planned activities aimed at the promotion of health and prevention of ill health' (CETHV, 1977). From here we were able to identify why we felt stuck.

This aim was too big for us to handle. One member put it this way

> It's all-encompassing, we delve into so many areas of life. Not just the healthy parts of people's lives, it impinges on the social, the physical, the mental welfare, everything . . . Perhaps that is the problem, it's not specific enough; it's all too general, we can't define it and it needs to be more specific.

This aim was too broad, too enormous for us to put into practice as a health visiting aim, and we felt this lay behind the group's inability to answer the questions 'What am I doing?' and 'Why am I doing it?'

To help us to move on we brainstormed on flip charts what we thought were the specific sticky areas of practice. This helped, because we were able to focus much more sharply on the health visitor's aim, our role and how this related to the people we visited. After lengthy discussion the group experienced a breakthrough. We had struggled with this idea about health and we asked ourselves 'What does this mean to the families we visit?' Gradually we began to talk about the idea of health as being a sense of 'well-being'. The role of the health visitor was to help families maintain an equilibrium and quality of life which contributed to this sense of well-being. One of the group began to see the implications of this idea and how she could relate to this concept.

> If people feel better, then isn't that linked into feeling stronger, confident and in control. Isn't that what we are trying to get families to be? If you are feeling ok, you can tackle the more important problems in your life. If you don't feel ok, you never get round to dealing with it because you don't feel strong enough or confident enough.

The group began to see the parallel of this idea to the work they had been doing earlier with some of their families. Had we not talked about needing to feel good before we could go out and try out new ways of developing our relationship with our families? The health visitors realized they could act as a catalyst in helping families to cope or to move on in their lives.

A new cycle of research began to be formulated around the idea of how we could communicate this health visitors' aim of 'well-being'. How to explain to clients what we were trying to do and the kind of service which was available for them to use in achieving this aim. We began to identify factors which were likely to influence client families' equilibrium, such as the birth of a new baby or illness or death. The role of the health visitor in these circumstances would be to help explore these potentially stressful areas with their clients. The antenatal visit was seen as an ideal opportunity to start exploring possible issues which might surround the birth of a baby. For example, the physical, emotional and psychological impact of a new baby, as well as the practical problems of infant management and feeding.

Key questions such as 'What do you think?' and 'How do you feel?' were seen as helping to facilitate this exploration and at the same time inform clients about how the health visitor could be of use to them. One member started to laugh with relief at the idea of asking such a simple question. She explained 'It applies to everything, when you do a bereavement visit, you say "How do you feel?" . . . The child playing up, "How do you feel!"' Another member reflected about the mother who for three years had hidden her negative feelings towards her third baby: 'Maybe if someone had asked her very early on "How do you feel?" that might have opened that up for her'.

This discussion seemed to clarify some of the sticky areas which had got everyone so blocked. Somehow the idea of well-being seemed tangible to us. We experienced an *intuitive knowing* even though someone outside of the group might well interpret this concept as being just as broad as the standard health visiting aim mentioned earlier.

These discussions also partly answered other sticky areas concerning the role of the health visitor and feedback. The job seemed less broad because we would be focusing in on how client families wanted to use the service. This in turn would determine to some extent priorities, because it would be family-led demand for the health visiting service rather than the other way round. 'Not what we want, or what we think they ought to have. It has to be directed and led by families' was the way one group member put it. Feedback was improving as the group became more practised at asking the right questions and being more open about the issues which concerned them.

At the end of this session the group had contracted to explore ways in which they could communicate this aim of 'maintaining and enhancing individuals' well-being' and at the same time inform individuals about how the health visitor could be of use to them in achieving this aim.

For my part I agreed that I would draft a paper which would begin to draw together an account of our research. We all agreed it was important to try to record the work we had undertaken in order that it could be shared with colleagues and their managers. We hoped that by presenting a paper this would be more influential than just talking about the inquiry.

Phase 4: Communicating the research

Prior to the third reflection session, I sent a draft paper to group members which started to give a brief account of the group's research. This session was entirely taken up with discussion of the paper which had been circulated and there was no time to explore the last cycle of inquiry and how they had got on with our idea of health as well-being. The group was coming to an end and communicating the research now was a more important priority for us.

My paper was discussed in detail, with the group feeling that the language needed to be made more simple and straightforward if the paper was aimed at other health visitors. After a lot of debate I agreed to redraft the paper for our last meeting at which I presented the group with a rewritten draft of the work which included the changes agreed. The extracts from the transcripts were the same as those I have used throughout this chapter. They were chosen to illustrate the various methods the group explored in trying to achieve a more open relationship with their families. It was left to individuals to decide how to use the report with their colleagues.

Ending

At the final meeting the group reflected back on their personal experiences and concluded they had experienced changes in their personal and professional practice. They were continuing to explore and develop the issues we had identified. Some of the members were sharing these experiences with their work colleagues, or in peer support groups, much in the same way as we had done in the co-operative inquiry.

My main regret in looking back through the inquiry was that the group ran out of time at what I think was an important breakthrough in our thinking about health visiting practice. Towards the end of the inquiry we had been confronted with chaos, confronted with the issue of what is the role of the health visitor. From having struggled through our own anxiety and confusion, we had generated for ourselves some sense out of the vagueness of the health visitor's role. Health as 'well-being' gave a much sharper focus than the rather vague definition of 'prevention of ill health and promotion of health'. 'Well-being' felt like completion of the project; it seemed to pull everything together for us but unfortunately we had no time to really test out the idea.

So what did this inquiry achieve and to what extent did it adhere to the key features of co-operative inquiry?

In my opinion the experience of exploring together did lead to personal growth and development. The group members found themselves growing in confidence and able to be more assertive, particularly in situations where they felt they were being manipulated or devalued.

The group did I think achieve considerable autonomy and the choices made about the directions of the inquiry were reached on a co-operative basis. The inquiry very much developed as we went along and roles within the group were constantly changing. There was some tendency to collude over getting into the action rather than reflecting on the processes of the research and the meaning of our work.

We got excited, depressed and distressed at various times. We argued and disagreed, we used the devil's advocate role (Heron, 1989) to confront, especially when we were trying to escape from coming face to face with health visitor aims. If we had not been able to confront each other, but only our clients, then there would have been something very wrong with the validity of the research. We supported each other and gained strength to carry on. The group itself became an empowering agent.

There was full and authentic participation in all stages of the inquiry except in the writing up of the inquiry. I initiated this development and did most of the writing. Although I checked out with the group about the content, I suppose it could be argued that I shaped the final account of the inquiry and therefore deviated from the idea of full participation. Ideally there should be co-operative reporting. In practical terms the group members did not feel able to write and looked to me to act as their scribe and to write on their behalf a collective account of what we did. They shaped the account and made sure that it would resonate with their culture. The group were tough critics and made sure that what I had written was valid.

The process of the research as experienced by the group did, I think, lead to gaining valid practical and experiential knowledge. At the beginning the research method was challenged by one of the members when she asked 'Is this really research?' I think we progressed from this point to learning about how to do experiential research. At first this was intuitive and then gradually the group began to identify the processes involved. The group undertook a number of convergent cycles of research; each cycle added to and deepened the ideas we were developing. At one stage the group members were too much into action and it took some time to get a balance of action and reflection. When we started to review our work and ask the question 'We know how we did the research but what does it mean to our practice?' we descended into chaos and were faced with the dark side of health visiting, the key issue about the role of the health visitor. This was a major challenge to the validity of the research: the group could have colluded and avoided the issue, but managed to stay with the confusion and out of that experience we created the idea of well-being.

We began to develop some propositional knowledge. For example, simple direct explanations from the health visitor about why she was visiting or what she wanted seemed to be a key factor in moving towards a more open therapeutic relationship in which important issues for the individuals concerned could be explored. Confrontation, feedback and contracting with their clients helped the group members move towards greater autonomy with their clients/families.

We also learned that practising health visiting was a frightening and confused experience. The co-operative inquiry had created some degree of support and structure about how to tackle the issues mentioned above, but there still remained the fundamental issue of uncertainty about their role and the enormity of the job they were expected to do.

Conclusion

At the beginning of my research I was looking for a way which would enable me to develop a sensitive and revealing method of inquiry. As my first research tool I interviewed a number of health visitors and this revealed that there were major problems facing the respondents including stress and lack of support within their organization. These issues were to weave their way through all of the subsequent research: the key issue to emerge over and over again was the dilemma and ambiguity the respondents experienced about their role as health visitors.

The co-operative inquiry proved to be the most significant of the three research methods I had used. The inquiry enabled me to evolve questions and answers as a shared experience with a group of health visitors as co-researchers. The group discussions facilitated self-awareness and greater articulation of the key issues in a way which had not been possible earlier. Not only did the inquiry enable greater insight into the problems but it also led to action research which specifically focused on some of those professional issues. The group had a unique opportunity to explore, and experiment with ideas which might resolve some of the problems for themselves. The action research helped the health visitors not only to express what they felt about their real problems but also to move towards a more open and constructive relationship with their clients, with each other, with other agencies, and with their managers. It provided the health visitors with a means of finding a better and more effective way of practising as health visitors.

6

To Tell the Truth:
Working with Oppressed Groups
in Participatory Approaches to Inquiry

Elizabeth Whitmore

In a recent evaluation of a pre-natal programme for single expectant mothers, conducted by a group of programme participants, we discussed why they felt they could obtain better information than I, a university trained evaluator. One of the mothers explained:

> 'You're dealing with a lot of people on social assistance and welfare. You're dealing with real hard to reach low self esteem people. And when they see anybody coming in that they think is high class or has anything to do with welfare and you working with them, they are scared to death that you're going to squeal on them. . . . They [the respondents] are just scared that you work with those people [social workers], you deal with them, you're high up there so that they can't trust you cuz you're right in with them. But we're not in with them [social workers] and we're not in there to tear them apart. And I think they really know that.'

This says a great deal about oppression and about 'truth'. It highlights what I learned in working with this team of co-evaluators about participation and power, about trust and class barriers, about language and meaning and their relationship to the quality of research or evaluation. By class, I am referring to oppressed groups of people in our society who have internalized a view of themselves as worthless, as less intelligent, and as somehow undeserving of the privileges which others assume as given. These groups have less education and fewer opportunities, are poor and/or dependent on social assistance. Many are single parent women or members of marginalized racial or ethnic groups in a predominantly white society.

In this discussion, I would like to explore the gap which exists between university trained researchers and evaluators and members of oppressed groups from whom we collect data and interpret its meaning. This has profound implications for how we define and identify what is 'good' research or evaluation, and how we know when we see it, especially as it relates to participation and to working with people who are marginalized. I use the term quality rather than validity. As Reason suggests, the term validity is too ideologically laden, whereas 'quality' allows more space for us to formulate new standards and to draw on widely different fields of thought' (Reason, 1991b: 3)

The pre-natal education programme

In the mid-1980s, a community resident (who later became programme Coordinator) approached the Director of the Community Services Association, to inquire about assistance in implementing a pre-natal programme for single women. Over 20 per cent of the households in the community were headed by single women, many of whom received social assistance as their primary source of income. This group often experienced serious health, social and financial problems during their pregnancies. For the most part, they did not attend pre-natal classes sponsored by the Department of Health or at the local hospital. These traditional pre-natal programmes usually assume a (male) partner, are held in a downtown hospital or health unit, do not provide transportation and do not address personal or social concerns of participants. Public health nurses reported that the most under-represented groups in their pre-natal classes were teens, single parents, low income women and working women.

Local social workers, public health nurses, nutritionists, librarians and church officials held a series of meetings about supporting such a programme and as a result a Pre-natal Advisory Committee was formed. This group drafted a proposal to Health and Welfare Canada and in early 1986, the Committee received funding for three years to develop a prototype pre-natal programme. Later, two programme participants were added to the Committee. The Coordinator researched, designed and implemented the programme with the support and advice of the Advisory Committee.

This pre-natal education programme reached out to single mothers in a variety of ways. Classes, held at the local Single Parent Centre, were small and informal, boyfriends, parents and relatives were welcome, the Coordinator wore casual clothes (a very important signal to participants that she wasn't 'putting on airs'). Participants were encouraged to share their experiences with each other and ask questions. A wide variety of personal and social topics of interest to participants (including abuse) were raised, along with the immediate physical concerns of labour and delivery.

Recruitment was done with sensitivity and patience. Initially, women were referred by public health nurses and nutritionists who worked in the community and were well known. The Coordinator then contacted each potential participant personally and visited her in her home. She told the mother-to-be about the programme, answered questions and reassured her that no one would pressure her or tell her what to do. There was also provision for concrete needs and incentives (the Coordinator provided transportation for anyone needing it, which was most of the participants; child care was provided for those who had other children; nutritious snacks were served; the Centre often had used clothing to give away). Since many women came into the programme very late in their pregnancy and would deliver before the eight-week programme was completed, the Coordinator developed a crash course (of one to three weeks) so that everyone could participate, even if only briefly.

Advocacy was formally recognized as an important aspect of the programme and was structured into the Coordinator's role. She spent many hours assisting the women negotiate their way through the welfare bureaucracy, for example. She played the role of adviser, confidante and even mother, responding to individual needs as they arose. For many, she was the only person they could count on in times of crisis. The Coordinator also made a point of visiting each mother in the hospital and followed up afterwards, keeping track of their progress (and that of the new baby) as they struggled with the pressures of single motherhood.

The Coordinator hired one of the participants as an assistant; other participants were asked to lead discussions (on breast feeding, for example). The fact that their peers were an active part of the programme offered role models for women who are so often isolated and whose self-esteem is fragile. In discussions, everyone was encouraged to share their knowledge and experience; everyone's input was valued.

Once the programme had run for a year, the word had spread and young women themselves contacted the Single Parent Centre to sign up. The Coordinator was, by then, well known and liked by the women. Participants brought their friends, who were welcome to try out a class or two. Classes were soon overflowing and the programme was reaching women earlier in their pregnancy. Within two years of operation, the programme had attracted 97 participants. Most of these women were single, and about half were in their teens. Of these, 81 per cent received social assistance as their primary source of income.

The Single Parent Centre also developed postpartum classes and a follow up parenting programme, both in close collaboration with the Coordinator.

The evaluation

In 1988, the programme was nearing the end of its three-year grant. The Community Advisory Committee issued a call for evaluation proposals, specifically requesting designs in keeping with the informal nature of the programme and also sensitive to the needs and vulnerability of such a marginalized group. The Advisory Committee stated up front in its evaluation plan, for example, that 'overzealous testing of these women for the sake of evaluation will defeat its entire objective. Since many of these women have limited skills in reading and writing, extensive questionnaires and testing will only prove threatening.' Those representing the funder locally were very supportive of a community based approach, both for the programme itself and for the evaluation.

In response to their call for proposals, I suggested a participatory approach in which I would hire a group of programme participants as co-evaluators and train them to do the evaluation. This approach was based on assumptions inherent in the participatory research and evaluation (PR/PE) model. These include the assumption that experts are not the only ones who can create valid knowledge. Ordinary people are capable of generating knowledge which is as important and as valid as that produced by more highly structured and scientific processes. This model also recognizes that science is a cultural product and both the process and results reflect a historical and cultural context.

The proposal was accepted and together with the Advisory Committee, we worked out a recruiting procedure which resulted in four of the women who had taken the programme being hired. Four Committee members agreed to serve as an evaluation subcommittee which worked closely with us throughout the process.

Recruitment

We began by drafting a letter to all programme participants describing the evaluation and inviting them to apply. The teaching assistant then 'translated' it into language which would be easily understood and accepted by the women. We included a simple application form, asking for basic information (age, schooling, etc.), one reference, and a brief statement on why they were interested in the job. These letters were sent to all women who had participated in the programme over the three years (at least all those we had current addresses for). We also posted notices at the Single Parent Centre, a place where many of them gathered for a variety of activities.

This was followed up with personal contact (with those women still living in the area) by the nutritionists and others (the Director of the Single Parent Centre, for example) who knew most of the women personally and were trusted by them. They encouraged the women to apply and supported them in following through. Some women already had jobs; others did not want to work while their children were infants. A number, however, welcomed part-time work as a chance to get out of the house, to earn some money and to have the challenge of an interesting job.

A nutritionist, specifically one known to the applicants (which we hoped would make them feel more comfortable) and I formed an interviewing team. We interviewed all six who applied. We were interested primarily in determining whether the applicant would be reliable (Were there obstacles to her attending regularly and sticking with it? Did she have back up supports in time of crisis? Was she planning to move? Had she moved frequently over the past few years?, etc.). We also tried to assess how comfortable she would be contacting strangers, how well she could explain the evaluation to interviewees and take down notes of what was said. We reassured her that she would not be penalized on her social assistance because she was working and that we would provide for transportation and child care.

Of the six, one was eliminated when she seemed only marginally interested in doing the work. We decided to hire the other five (even though the budget allowed for four) on the assumption that there would probably be at least one drop out. This actually happened in the first week and we ended up with four, as planned. (I will call them Jane, Sue, Nancy and Rhonda.)

The evaluation team (the four programme participants and myself) worked together for six months (September to March), first designing the evaluation, then collecting the data, analysing the information and finally, reporting it. We met regularly two mornings a week as a group, doing other tasks individually in between, such as interviewing or analysing specific data.

One day at a time

I knew that we needed to begin slowly, for they needed to get to know me and each other and they also needed to build some confidence that they could, in fact, do this. I knew it would take time for them to trust me, for as a university professor I lived in another world. They had a long history of negative experiences with social workers and as far as they were concerned, I was 'one of them'. Somehow I had to become a real person to them and this was not going to happen overnight.

We began by getting to know each other and sharing a lot of experiences with the programme and information about our lives as single mothers. We also did some group exercises, learning how to give feedback and just having fun together. We learned what an evaluation was all about and different ways we could go about doing it. Each got a brightly coloured binder for notes and information. This was a concrete representation of our work, reinforcing not only the teamwork, but also the importance of the task at hand. I tried to build task and process into each meeting so that we got on with our work, but we also had space to share feelings and concerns. At the beginning, I took responsibility for facilitating each meeting, setting out the next tasks to be done and offering ideas of how to do them. As time went on, we decided this more as a team.

For data collection, we decided on a mixed method approach, gathering both qualitative and quantitative information from a variety of sources. This included interviewing as many programme participants as possible, at least the ones we could get hold of. (Over the three-year period of the programme, many had moved and we had no way of contacting them.) Other sources of information included a mailed survey of professionals in the community who were likely to have contact with programme participants (health professionals, nutritionists, social workers, etc.), a survey of all members of the Advisory Committee, and in-depth interviews with the Coordinator and her assistant.

We began designing the participant questionnaire by first taking the original goals of the programme and developing categories of questions related to them. So, for example, one goal was to provide a support system during childbearing and the immediate postnatal period; another, to give programme participants the tools (information, skills, confidence) to help them deal effectively with social service and other systems (hospital, other health services, etc.). In responding, they could draw on their own experience in the programme. We brainstormed possible questions (Did you make friends with anyone in the class? Did the classes help you know your rights as a mother in the hospital? Please explain) and spent several weeks refining them and wording them so that they were clear and easily understood. We wanted it to be down to earth, not full of big words.

We also formulated the questionnaire so that it would be easy to write down their answers and to show them that no names (only an ID number) would be used. Confidentiality was very important, for we knew that they would be very reluctant to talk to strangers and fearful that what they said might be used against them, especially in relation to welfare. Before we actually began contacting the women, we practised listening and did some interviewing with each other. They each did two pre-test interviews with people they knew and we made final revisions to the questionnaire on the basis of their feedback.

For the next six to eight weeks, the women conducted interviews with programme participants. I interviewed the Coordinator and her assistant. We met once a week during that period, sharing our adventures and noting preliminary impressions. They found that the interviews took many hours, for the respondents wanted to talk. From my reflexive log:

> All reported that the respondents want to *talk* and *talk*. That's a real characteristic of all their contacts. And they say, well, we just can't cut people off in the middle of a sentence and say we have to pay attention to the interview questions only. They are sensitive to the respondents' need to tell their stories and also to get information.

Jane reported that one respondent wanted to ask her a lot of questions about getting on welfare, the rights of a mother, etc. My log that day quotes Jane:

> 'I feel good them asking me [questions about welfare, etc.]. I guess I am kind of an expert since I have a child and have been on welfare.'

Rhonda reported that one of hers said she asked the nurse 'what are you doing?' (even though she knew) just to test the nurse. The respondent felt that the nurse ought to ask permission to do any medical procedure, even though she was prepared to give her consent. She also asked other questions and when the doctor asked 'where did you learn that?', she answered proudly, 'in the pre-natal classes!'

The women gained confidence as they exchanged stories about their interviews. They also supported each other. Jane, for example, felt quite comfortable going into the housing project, while others did not, so she did all the interviews with respondents living there. They knew the community and who was around. From my log:

> Nancy reported that one person's mother said she hadn't seen her daughter for months. Sue's response was, 'Bullshit. I seen her just the other day walking down the street!' Sue agreed she'd interview her and switched a name with Nancy.

Sometimes they had to make two or three visits before they found the respondent home and able to talk to them. A few refused to be interviewed. This was partly because they were scared of answering questions from a stranger, or perhaps because, at first, they told them that the evaluation was being funded by Health and Welfare and the respondents thought they were from welfare. Once they left that out of their introduction, they had very few refusals.

As we proceeded, I met regularly with the Evaluation Subcommittee, keeping them up to date on our progress. About halfway through the process, the Advisory Committee asked to meet with us, for they were intensely interested in the process and wanted to meet and talk with the women themselves. At first, the women were quite intimidated, and we prepared carefully. We put our information on flip charts (sample, timetable) so that they could talk from the information on the chart. I also urged them to talk about their experiences in their own words and reassured them that Committee members wanted to know what we were doing, not because they were 'checking up' but because they were interested. We agreed that I would begin and then divided up the rest of it. I recorded what happened in my log:

> They were quite scared at first, but then found their voices and took off. I started by presenting some of the material on the flip chart and gradually they began to fill in the gaps. Then [one committee member] asked them directly about their impressions so far. Sue is particularly good at speaking in front of a group and had no trouble finding her words. Her sense of humour is wonderful and she really projects personality as she described what she is doing. Jane also began to speak up, especially when asked a direct question. Nancy reported that one of the nutritionists was mentioned by name several times as especially helpful. They noted how verbal the respondents are and want to talk about their experience and also about welfare. . . .
>
> At the end, a committee member exclaimed: 'You are *really* on top of it. I'm impressed. You are proving that this kind of research can work, and it's very different from most evaluations.'

The group was elated! The meeting had been a big boost to their confidence and sense of purpose. We continued interviewing and recording our progress as we went along, and by early November, the interviews had been completed. (The other data – survey of professionals and of the Advisory Committee – were still in process but continuing apace.)

Once most of the interviews were done, we began the analysis. We did this by cutting up a copy of each completed questionnaire and putting the answers to each question in a separate envelope. We then divided up the envelopes, recorded all responses and developed preliminary categories. From my log:

> It's hard for them to deal with this new task. It's a difficult cognitive one and they need a lot of guidance on how to sort the answers into piles. But at the same time, they were the ones who developed clear ways to record the answers on a piece of paper so that it summarized everything but no information is lost. I'm impressed with how thorough and careful they are. They don't want to make any mistakes.

Each of us was responsible for 'presenting' a set of responses and then we would discuss it as a group. It was especially helpful to have the original interviewer present, for she could fill in the context when an answer was unclear. From my log:

> Slowly, we're reducing the data – first by recording on one sheet all information on the slips of paper, then categorizing or trying to get the essence of what is in the data. They still have to work on reflecting the data and not their own experience or opinions. In some cases, the response tells us something quite clear. In others, it's more a matter of interpretation. And here their own knowledge of the programme, the respondents and the context helps.

We had talked earlier about the importance of their asking the questions as we had framed them, recording the answers accurately, and not commenting (or making any non-verbal gestures) on anyone's responses. We had discussed their own opinions openly and the fact that other participants not only had a right to different ideas, but that the evaluation report would not be credible if we said that everyone loved the programme and it had no problems. We had practised how they would handle a respondent who had a different opinion from their own. As we analysed the data, all of us kept this in mind and would often check this out with each other. We all wanted very badly to produce a report which would be believed by others, for our credibility, theirs and mine, was on the line.

When we had a pretty good sense of what the participant interviews told us, we compared the themes with the information from other sources (which we had analysed in a similar way). Slowly, a set of conclusions and recommendations began to take shape.

About the time we were completing the analysis, we were asked to take part in a women's action research conference being held at a local university. The interviewers were intrigued, but very wary. At first, just as with the Advisory Committee, they said they would not talk. I reassured them that they could discuss their own experience and we agreed to set the whole next meeting aside to prepare for it. They had never been to a university before and were terrified at the prospect of speaking in front of such a group. My log recorded the action:

> They were very nervous and clung to their 'scripts' rather than let go with the spontaneity they showed at the Advisory Committee meeting. They were just beginning to open up when time ran out. The sea of strange faces was intimidating. This was their first time at a university, let alone speaking to women they perceive as 'above them'. The next speaker had us break into small groups, so they were forced to let go of each other and interact with others. Of course, they did just fine.

At lunch afterwards, they were on an incredible high: 'All those important people actually listened to us! They liked what we said!' Jane was tickled pink to see her name on the programme. Having her name in a 'book' made her feel so important. She took a handful of copies to take home. She just could not get over it.

As we developed our conclusions and recommendations I began to put all of it on my word processor. We listed the main points we wanted to make as a group and then I put it into sentences. I brought my computer to our meeting place and we worked together, editing and especially purging 'all them professor words'. My log notes: 'When I used big words, Sue said "This is supposed to be our report, too!" She keeps me honest.' They were also beginning to react to the fact that we were coming to the end of our work together. We had been working quite closely for six months now and our relationships had become intense. Leaving all this was going to be hard.

Over the last few weeks, we had spent increasing amounts of time discussing what each was planning to do after this project was finished. I quote Jane in my log:

> 'I like this kind of work. Any idea about jobs after this? I'm going to hate it when it ends. I look forward to coming to work. I wish it was full time. I love doing this stuff!'

Later, I comment:

They talked a lot today about what they could do after this project was finished and would very much like to find a way to use their new skills. They really enjoy what they are doing.

As we neared the finishing line, there was simply no time to teach them how to use the computer, so I did all the typing. The tension mounted as our time began to run out and we were scrambling to complete the final report. We got it done by the deadline, but it was close. My log notes were brief and to the point, reflecting my own lack of time and fatigue, too: 'Finished! Concentrated well. It's really going to be hard for all of us to let go.' The following week, they met with the Advisory Committee to give their final report. This time, they were much less intimidated. (Shortly thereafter, they were also asked to be speakers in a university class. By this time, our preparation consisted of a mere five minute huddle outside the classroom.)

The process of working together

As we proceeded with our task, the group dynamics proceeded apace. Already, by the third meeting, serious conflicts had arisen within the group. Three out of the four were on social assistance and were extremely sensitive to others' attitudes towards them. They had been irritated at Nancy, the fourth member of the group, who had reiterated several times that she was not on assistance (in the context of our discussions of the budget and of being careful not to jeopardize their welfare cheques). This was interpreted as snotty and a put-down by those who were. My log picks up on this:

> These meetings are both productive and tumultuous! . . . After we formulated some questions and tried them out on each other, Jane and Sue asked if they could inter-view in pairs. Nancy (and Rhonda) expressed some reservations, feeling the respondents might be intimidated by two people. This led to a heated discussion, with Nancy trying to explain why this might be the case and Sue and Jane becoming more and more upset. The issue was clearly not interviewing in pairs, but their anger at Nancy.

This issue would haunt us throughout the process. There were days when we simply adjourned to the local coffee shop to talk it out. I remind myself, in the log that these times are important:

> I must be flexible and allow time for personal issues to be discussed and to give sup-port when needed. Today we accomplished very little of the 'task' but a lot of process. Work gets done intermittently, but personal needs must be attended to.

At one point, Rhonda got a full-time job and dropped out and we discussed the possibility of replacing her. The group felt that it would be difficult for a new person to become part of the group: 'We've had all our fights and know each other now and how to get along. It would be hard for another person to understand that.' The remaining three decided to divide up the extra work and saw no problem. The women's very strong commitment to the task and their conviction of its importance kept them going, however, even when emotions were high.

Each of us also had many other pressures in our lives (particularly illness) which influenced not only how much time we could devote to the task, but also our moods and how well any one of us could tolerate frustration. But, as time went on, they had their own way of working things out, during smoke breaks and on the phone afterwards, which was usually far more effective than any intervention by me. We also built in some fun, going out to dinner to celebrate holidays for example. These are women who have little opportunity to go out alone (without their children) and just let loose.

One major mistake we made was to decide to contact the press. Giving the programme and this kind of evaluation some publicity seemed like a good idea at the time. We decided that our approach would be to talk with a reporter as a group.

Nancy agreed to contact the local newspaper to set up an interview. The reporter insisted that he could speak with only one person and demanded that she do the interview that very evening. Naïvely, she gave him her address as she tried to explain to him that we wanted to be interviewed as a group. He then showed up at her home and basically bullied her into telling him about the evaluation.

The next day, an article appeared in the local newspaper. Jane and Sue were furious, accusing Nancy of doing it on purpose because she wanted to be the only one in the paper. (To make matters worse, the article highlighted issues of drug and alcohol use by expectant mothers, which, though a concern, was only one small part of our report.) All the old feelings came to the surface again and there was much bitterness. Though we contacted the paper's editor and followed it up with a very sharp letter, we could not undo the damage to the group. An undercurrent of tension pervaded our remaining work together.

Our world is different from yours . . .

One day, as we were working on the questionnaire, the Programme Coordinator came into the room. At the time, she was doing a Master's degree and had recently interviewed two of the team members for her thesis. They commented on how difficult her questions had been. 'I really had to think a lot in answering those questions. They were hard!' one woman blurted. Yet, when I asked what her questions were, they were almost exactly the same as the questions we were going to ask. Something else was going on.

Over the next six months, as we worked together, I became more and more aware of the implications of this incident. Their reactions to the Coordinator's questions had to do with how they viewed themselves in relation to her (a university educated professional), what they thought they ought to say or not say, and, above all, protecting themselves from people they saw as having power to harm them. Even though they liked and trusted her very much, there was still a barrier. It could be that they did not want to hurt her feelings by being critical of the programme. Or perhaps, in spite of genuine feelings of friendship and caring, differences in class were indeed a major issue. This, in turn, had important implications for the question of the quality of data (both the gathering and analysis). These issues were evident in two ways: in our use of language and meaning, and in the question of trust.

Towards the end of the project, the women allowed me to tape a discussion pursuing these questions. We recalled that incident with the Coordinator and asked why they thought they could produce better information than I, a professional evaluator.

> 'Our world is different from yours. The fear is that people always want to humiliate you, put you down (for being on welfare) . . . We have a different lifestyle from you. We just don't trust people the way you do.'

> 'The girl I interviewed said she never would have answered all them questions if it hadn't been me.'

As we worked together, I became acutely aware of how different our worlds really were.

Trust

After the women had been hired, but before we began our work together, I interviewed them individually, pursuing my own research interest in participatory evaluation and the process of empowerment. I asked them about their expectations, what they hoped to get out of their participation in this process. I recorded my thoughts in a reflexive log:

> This interview is not only an opportunity for me to gather information on my topic . . . it's a chance to get to meet each person individually, in their own home. The atmosphere is informal and it's on their turf.

Later, I concluded in my log that

> the interviews went well. J. and S. were most talkative; N. was brief and to the point. R. talked about her feelings and asked me a lot of questions about social work.

Their recollections six months later were quite different. If I had not appreciated the barrier, they certainly did.

> 'But we didn't know you, OK? We had met you cuz we were applying for this job. We didn't know anything about you. We knew that you were a professor from the school of social work. That automatically says, "whoa, dude!"'

So they told me what they thought I wanted to hear, and assumed that there was a 'right' answer somewhere (in spite of my assurances to the contrary at the beginning): 'I was scared I'd answer the wrong way . . . I was trying to give you answers that you wanted to hear . . . that would make you feel that I was smart.'

In spite of all my professional training and attempts to put them at ease, then, it didn't work very well. What was the difference between what they did in the interviews (with respondents) and what I did?

> 'I went in there and told them I was nobody . . . so they were willing to give it [information]. It's people that are higher up that they're more scared of . . . they have a great fear of . . . being squealed on.'

'It comes from different lifestyles . . . Things are so different. It's the way people live and the way they act, the way they are. You can't help it. You can't change yourself just because you do something.'

They instinctively know 'one of their own' from outsiders, and one thing that is meant by outsider is someone with more power, more education, someone who is 'up there', as they put it. With such people, they use subtle but very effective survival skills, telling 'people up there' what they think they want to hear. Beyond that, however, is also a profound difference in style. They could share a space, a reality which I could not (no matter how nice, easy going, or 'cool' I might be). The team members knew how to approach the respondents, putting them at ease.

'You talk about their lives, make them feel comfortable . . . that's when you're going to start getting information from them . . . They knew you were on the same level, their wave length . . . We were participants in the programme, just the same as them.'

'We would just get them going, praise them a bit . . . When you ask a question, you [meaning this researcher] just stop . . . and wait for an answer. That's scary! You can't just do that. They need a little bit of encouragement.'

I asked for an example of how they made the respondents feel comfortable.

'[The respondent] didn't have a phone, so on a Sunday afternoon, I had to take my daughter with me cuz I didn't have a baby-sitter. I just went to her door . . . and I told her who I was and why I was there and if she had a few minutes . . . So she invited me in and gave me coffee and fed my kid . . . And we talked about an hour directly about the programme and I spent four and one half hours there. I almost couldn't get away. It took about two hours and she really started to loosen up . . . If I talked about my labour and delivery, she'd go right into hers. She told me things about her sister and her boyfriend and herself that I'm sure her best friend doesn't know.'

'I laughed and carried on and joked with them, made them feel comfortable. I told them stories about my labour . . . and they just wanted to get in there and tell me everything . . . They just started talking cuz they got so comfortable in what you were saying.'

From the beginning, I knew that we would have to spend time building trust. While they initially quite easily found things in common among themselves, my world was clearly different. They were polite but wary. They waited (and expected) me to say or do something which would confirm their worst suspicions. In many ways, I was the enemy until proven otherwise and I found myself walking on eggs much of the time. Again referring to my initial interview with each of them (in which I took notes as they talked):

'You didn't tell us what you were writing, why you were writing, what was in our interview. We didn't know you. You're in touch with welfare . . . Our personal life, you were in our home . . . You just didn't understand.'

All of these things (what, why, etc.), I had indeed explained to them. The issue was far more complex. Later, in my reflexive notes, I concluded that 'it's easier to teach these women the methodological/technical skills than it is to teach middle class people about another culture'.

The women felt enormously vulnerable. This sense of insecurity and being controlled by outsiders, especially those in authority, was pervasive (and not unjustified, in my view). Yet, they had their own ways of surviving. They told me, for example, that before applying for the job, they had checked me out pretty carefully. In explaining their own fears, one woman described the feelings of a respondent:

> 'It's people that are higher up that they're more scared of, and that's why . . . it's because they have a great fear [of] being squealed on . . . One woman was scared to light up a cigarette. She thought that if I was with them up there that she wasn't allowed to have that cigarette because she wasn't allowed to take enough money out of that budget they gave her to buy herself some smokes.'

Somehow they expected my life to be perfect and felt inadequate in comparison. My self-disclosure helped break down barriers. On one occasion, I drove one of the women downtown and on the way, she asked if we could stop by my house.

> 'I didn't want to get too personal, like do you make enough money to live. I'm interested to know how other people live. Other people like in your profession. You are a professional and I'm not. I'm, like, down here. I just wanted to know and I thought you wouldn't mind.'

In the course of conversation, she asked me about my daughter (who is the same age as she). I told her about some of the difficulties she had had. The fact that a child of a professor would drop out of school astounded her. A bubble had been burst and she began to see me, not as a fantasy, but as another human being.

> 'See, everybody's normal. Everybody makes mistakes! [I thought your kids would be] "eugenes", snobs.'
> 'What's a 'eugene?'' I asked (confirming her suspicion that I was pretty out of touch).
> 'Oh man, you don't know what a "eugene" is? Nerds, smart nerds.'

Gradually, we built up trust, so that in the end, they felt comfortable sharing their feelings with each other and with me. I could make mistakes and they were amused (and even gratified) rather than angry. With the respondents, however, there was almost instant trust, for the class barriers were not there. They understood each other and knew that they had a world in common. Consequently, information and feelings were shared which never would have been discussed with an outsider like me. But their interviews with programme participants were more than information gathering; this was a time, however brief, that they 'connected' with another person and were treated with respect.

One might wonder if our work together was not just a way of using the women to get information from the programme participants which I could not get. Part of my own research work was to look at what they got out of participating in this project, using a framework involving empowerment at an individual, a group and at a community or environmental level (see Whitmore, 1990). I conclude that the women did benefit, especially at the individual and group levels. As individuals, they gained a great deal of confidence, in addition to the specific skills and knowledge learned. The group experience helped overcome the isolation felt by single mothers trying to bring up children alone, giving them a chance to interact with others in an atmosphere of support. We learned to work with our conflicts rather than just walk away; we learned to get beyond the anger and recognize that our common commitment to the task was also a commitment to each other, whatever the disagreements. At the community or environmental level, the benefits were less clear, for this assumes collective action by a more or less cohesive group. The benefits noted – speaking to outside groups, educational and employment opportunities and challenging the social service system – were ultimately tied to each woman as an individual. The group was simply not cohesive enough to continue working together towards some kind of broader action.

So, while I would say that they were not simply 'used' for my research ends, it is an important question to keep in mind when people like myself seek to involve others in participatory work. Participants should benefit, of course. But the underlying principles of a participatory approach are much more profound than that and in this case 'empowerment' was limited to the individual and group levels.

Language and meaning

In spite of the fact that I was acutely aware of talking in 'academese' and tried hard not to use jargon or big words, my small words were often their big words. What I assumed was 'normal talk', they saw as 'professor words'. My choice of vocabulary, how I put my thoughts together, how I phrase a sentence – all reflect a level of education they did not have. My language was simply different from theirs, no matter how hard I tried to bridge the gap. In referring to the initial (hiring) interview with them, one assured me that 'you did good in the interview, but you just didn't know. You're not used to . . . talking with [us].' Our common vocabulary was limited.

Words are one thing, of course. Even more important, however, is who asks them and how they are asked. The meaning – what is understood and conveyed – is part and parcel of who and how, as well as what. Here is where their common ground with the respondents made such a huge difference.

> 'It doesn't matter how much you're trained. We were all brought up different and how to speak, and all these things. But you have to look at who you're talking to, not what you've been taught.'

The way we organized our thinking, how we expressed ourselves, both cognitively and emotionally, were different. The verbal and non-verbal meanings were simply not understood in the same way. They could insult or tease each other and laugh about it; the same things said by me were not funny. Other feelings (hurt, vulnerability, etc.) tended to be expressed non-verbally, not surprising when one realizes that being on welfare makes people feel so vulnerable. On one occasion, I built in a 'get it out on the table' exercise to try to get at some underlying conflicts that were interfering with our work. To social workers, this may be good 'communication skills', but they viewed it

with enormous suspicion and the barriers went back up. We spent hours undo-
ing the damage, which they did much more effectively by getting at the deeper
issues in their own way (over the telephone or during smoke breaks).

Another issue here is one of ownership. The words, both in the questionnaire and in the report, needed to be theirs. It was easier with the
questionnaire, for this was the tool for communicating with other programme
participants. The analysis was also theirs, for it was they who analysed and
interpreted what the respondents meant. With the final report, however, our
audience was the Advisory Committee and ultimately a funder. Of the four
women, only one had completed high school and the reality was they could
not write for such audiences. Such an expectation would be unfair and un-
realistic. In the report to the government, we had to use certain language and
for the most part, it could not be theirs. Our compromise was to decide as a
group what we wanted to say and then I would format it and put it into sentences. Predictably, my sentences and words were not theirs, however, and we
spent many hours purging 'them big professor words'. Even then, they felt the
final report was more mine than theirs. How to reconcile the need to write a
formal report for government departments and the importance of ownership
continues to be a dilemma for me.

The oral presentation to the Advisory Committee was theirs, however. This
was a place where they could discuss their experience in their own words and
they did it extremely well. The presentation at the action research conference
(and later to a university class) were enormously gratifying, as they realized
that 'they were really interested in what we had to say!' They also enjoyed listening to other presentations at the conference. Their confidence blossomed,
as they realized that they had connected with a world which otherwise intimidated and often disrespected them.

Conclusion

What have we learned about oppression, about participation and about quality from this experience? One thing is clear to me: as a middle class, university
educated researcher, I could never entirely share the meanings of those from
less privileged groups, especially those in the most marginalized sectors of
society. The verbal barriers are difficult enough. Beyond the verbal – affective,
sense-making, one's experience of the world – understanding is class based, as
it is also gender and race based. Our experience of the world is very very different.

The implications of this are being felt in the women's movement, for
example. Until recently, the discourse has been dominated primarily by white
middle class women, who have just assumed that their experience and priorities reflect that of all women. Working class women, women of colour and
Native women are forcefully challenging this, for their reality is certainly not
the same.

The barriers are real and very high, even if seemingly invisible on the surface. Passivity or quiescence is often mistaken for apathy; resistance is subtle

but well understood by those without power, however. One well known example is the song 'Steal away', sung by slaves in America to let others know when the coast was clear to escape. John Gaventa, when asked in 1985 what he would change about his book *Power and Powerlessness: Rebellion and Quiescence in an Appalachian Valley* (1980), remarked that he would reinterpret what appeared to be quiescence. He later realized that the people had their own, very subtle ways of resisting, which were deliberately invisible to outsiders.

In addition, interpretations of phenomena reflect one's experience and understanding of behaviour and events, which is certainly bound by class, race, gender, culture, etc. While I might conclude that the lack of a birth partner (someone, usually a family member or friend, assisting during labour and delivery) indicated social isolation, the women quickly recognized it as a reluctance to acknowledge the presence of their boyfriends for fear of being cut off welfare.

We think that respondents are telling us the truth, that we are collecting information that is valid. We think that we know the 'true' meaning of what we hear and see. This is a sad illusion. The reality is that the economic, cultural, racial and gender differences among people are profound and extremely complex. To ignore these is to create knowledge which is deeply flawed. (Yet much of our social policy is based on just such knowledge.) Furthermore, it is a fallacy to think that gender alone can overcome these barriers, as Kohler Riessman's (1987) analysis certainly illustrates.

Though these barriers can never be entirely eliminated, they can be reduced/permeated through a participatory process, however. The question of control and ownership is fundamental, of course. Who benefits from the research? Who is in charge of decision making? Who is this really for? The role of the professional changes dramatically, with the focus on process as well as outcome. Such a process calls for skills well beyond the technical ones expected of traditional researchers and evaluators. These include first of all a commitment to the empowerment of others and a clarity of class, race and gender analysis (and age, ability/disability, and sexual orientation as well). It also involves communication skills, an understanding of individual and group dynamics, an ability and willingness to self-disclose and share personal feelings and experiences. Such skills are well known in many schools of social work.

This takes time, however, more time than traditional research. It involves a commitment not only to attend to the process but also includes a willingness to go beyond the immediate task in helping people cope with poverty. This means helping to provide such basics as transportation, child care and sometimes money. It means mediating with the welfare department on occasion. It often calls for hours spent listening to personal concerns and responding as best one can. In a nutshell, it means recognizing all participants as human beings, with all our attendant needs, concerns and joys. It also means working at a broader level, taking action to try to change the larger political, social and economic structures which oppress us.

What does this have to do with 'truth'? Truth here refers to 'somehow getting it right' (Reason and Rowan, 1981: 241) though I hasten to add that this must not imply that there is one 'right' way. More recently, Reason has indicated that

> we can no longer argue that our inquiry is in any sense a search for 'truth.' We can very clearly accept the post-modern statement that we are in a situation 'after truth.' So within this field of emerging practice, we need a methodological inquiry into the question of quality: what is good research. (Reason, 1991b: 3)

As Guba and Lincoln (1989) suggest, the real question is not 'is it true?' but rather, 'does it increase understanding?'

I would argue that the participatory process by itself is important but insufficient to enhance quality. A thorough analysis of the dynamics of oppression and attention to the issues raised here are key to that process if one is to 'somehow get it right'.

Acknowledgements

The author wishes to thank Karla Firth and Sharon Hollett for their contribution to the research as co-evaluators. The other two members of the evaluation team could not be reached personally, so their contribution must be acknowledged anonymously.

7

Supervising the Child Protection Process: a Multidisciplinary Inquiry

John Cosier and Sara Glennie

Our experience of training and facilitating improvements in industry and the public sector has convinced us that a key ingredient in catalysing change in large organizations lies in the notion of ownership. Other ingredients are also necessary, but without ownership firmly placed at the fulcrum, a high level of resistance to change can be expected if not actually predicted.

We believe that ownership exists in its ideal state when an individual or group is empowered to give expression to their own sense of knowing about a situation. Such knowing may or may not be defined in terms of a 'problem', but in the contexts in which we work, it often is. Knowing must then be exercised and explored in ways that make sense to the individual; not subjected to remote, detached diagnosis by experts. Finally, if change is thought appropriate, the creation of alternative courses of action should be developed which have genuine relevance to the individuals concerned – conditions need to be such that they feel able to 'buy in' to understandings of cause and possible solutions. It follows that ownership cannot be *given* to anyone: it can only be elicited and developed through active participation in all stages of a planned change process.

The inquiry which forms the basis of our discussion gave us an opportunity to work towards this ideal of ownership through active participation. We are both experienced change agents but we are novice inquirers. We openly report our uneven progress and process towards the stated ideal for two reasons. First, we recognize that the discipline of a public report will continue to serve our own learning. With each review of the experience we eventually shared, we add another layer to our understanding of how powerful co-operative inquiry is in generating the conditions under which participation can flourish. Second, we are keen to contribute to the continuing process of co-operative knowing which this edited collection represents. Our experience may help to put some detail on the maps which others are drawing for themselves in this emerging field of research.

The inquiry context

The origins of the inquiry, if we are honest, can be traced to time spent in conversation on an oriental carpet at Hawkwood Conference Centre in

Gloucestershire. We went there as delegates to 'Emerging approaches to inquiry' in September 1990, were touched by the experience in similar ways, and left determined to find a way of giving practical expression to our hitherto cerebral exploration of the potential of co-operative inquiry as a tool for catalysing change in organizations.

The opportunity which emerged (or which we constructed?) was rather more complicated than our conference musings had allowed us to imagine. We eventually worked with six public sector organizations simultaneously.

Sara had been doing some Child Protection training in Northamptonshire. The county's Area Child Protection Committee (ACPC, a multi-agency committee which monitors and develops various aspects of child protection services) was interested in improving the quality of management, professional supervision and support available to workers who have face-to-face contact with children and families where abuse is a concern. Teachers, health visitors, social workers, police officers, probation officers and other specialist workers all have different roles to play in the process of protecting children from abuse. Whatever their role and organizational setting, all workers in this field need professional supervision and support. This is widely acknowledged because there are some characteristics of child protection work which set it apart from other professional tasks, specifically:

1   The high degree of personal and professional anxiety which the work generates in individuals *and* their organizations and
2   The complex and sensitive nature of inter-agency communication and co-operation which an effective child protection system demands.

The need for competent supervision and support had been acknowledged in Northamptonshire, but little was known, locally or nationally, about how (and if) such needs were being met within the major agencies involved in child protection. Clearly (or so it seemed to us), the situation presented an exciting opportunity to do some preliminary discovery research in an area which had not been well travelled and where there was an identified and agreed need. Furthermore, collaborative inquiry seemed a highly appropriate research tool to use for the purpose. We began to focus on the possibility of facilitating an inquiry group of first line managers from the agencies concerned with child protection locally to explore and describe the management, supervision and support of child protection practitioners. This seemed to be a sensible first step if improvement was on the ACPC's agenda. How could we make it happen?

The absence of an immediate answer focused our attention on the fact that most of our preparatory thought had actually been directed towards the management of the collaborative inquiry process *once* a group had emerged or had been identified. We were quickly confronted with our naïvety, and our accompanying uncertainty, about how to turn our good idea into a reality. We needed to find ways of sharing it with a group of as yet unidentified people who, from our perspective, lay deep inside a complex and possibly impenetrable system. Our recognition of an opportunity for inquiry turned out to be only a first small step in a long and complicated process of negotiation during which ownership of the idea and the initiative required to progress it passed among a number of key individuals and groups. We now recognize that collaborative inquiry, when it does not emerge spontaneously from an existing group experience, falls into two major phases, each with its own process and dynamic, each requiring very different skills.

1 Phase 1: Enabling it to happen.
2 Phase 2: Facilitating the happening.

We also recognize that the issue of ownership and participation can be particularly problematic during Phase 1. We discuss this more fully below.

In retrospect, one sees a pattern so clearly! At the time, the first phase felt like pushing a great weight up a very long hill while the weight itself obscured the view ahead. Planning for uncertainties and unknowns, a very imprecise process, seemed all we could do. We now see that our journey closely mirrored that described by Bate and Mangham (1981). Our own derivative model of the planned change process which was eventually initiated provides a useful framework for our subsequent discussion (see Table 7.1)

Table 7.1   *Steps in the planned change process*

Dis-ease	Identification of the opportunity for inquiry
Negotiation	Widening ownership of the idea
Access	Identifying appropriate inquirers
Entry	Forming a co-operative group
Boundary setting	Agreeing the territory and conditions for inquiry
Data collection	Cycling; doing, discussing, focusing, further doing
Analysis and reflection	Pulling out messages
Intervention	Widening ownership of inquiry outcomes
Exit	Withdrawal from the inquiry territory

Negotiation

Having formulated and developed our good idea a bit further, we found ourselves in the ideologically uncomfortable position of having to use any power and influence we could muster to sell an idea which is based on the principles of participation, power-sharing and peer relations! It felt odd and incongruent, but there did not seem to be any alternative. We started to push.

In order to test the temperature of the water, Sara initiated informal discussions with a Social Services Department Training Officer. She talked about the possibility of using collaborative inquiry to explore ways in which the managerial/supervisory task was currently experienced across agencies. The University of Nottingham's School of Social Studies, with which we were both consultants, agreed to provide the institutional home to the project. Sara met with enthusiastic support in principle and the promise of a facilitative link to the Chair of the ACPC, the potential commissioning body. This very easy first step in the negotiation process may not be common. We widened ownership to someone who already knew and respected the University's work in the multidisciplinary field and who was personally committed to improving the quality of supervision in the county. Our idea gave him a focus and launch pad to progress his own concerns. Our ideal ownership conditions were therefore met at this critical first step.

The subsequent stages were much more testing.

The promised facilitative link led to a meeting some two months later with the then Chair of the ACPC (an Assistant Director of Social Services) and a senior manager from the Social Services Department with special responsibility for child protection. On our way to the meeting we rehearsed how to introduce the concept of peer group inquiry across several totally different agencies, run by two people who, although experienced group facilitators, had never run an inquiry before, and furthermore, one of them had never set foot in the public sector. A contract did not seem very likely.

The meeting was gratifyingly informal and positively supportive of the ethos of action research which we outlined. The stumbling blocks came when we started to discuss the practicalities of engaging the interest, commitment and participation of a number of agencies with different organizational frameworks, supervisory structures and approaches to staff support and development. How could we convey the aims and intentions of the inquiry sufficiently clearly to find the 'right' participants? How could we ensure wide-ranging support for a project which might already be identified as a Social Services initiative? Would that lessen its potential impact? The unanswerable questions continued and we became more and more convinced that we had been too ambitious. The multidisciplinary approach which we had hoped to adopt, although potentially rich, seemed to be foundering in a sea of practical problems.

What is it that enables some people to take risks? We are still not sure what happened during the meeting to turn the tide of problem-focused discussion. We reflected afterwards that the atmosphere seemed to shift when we acknowledged that it was probably *too difficult* and started collecting our papers as if to withdraw. At that point, the senior manager appeared literally to grab the idea from us and proceeded systematically through the list of problems which he had just constructed to find a solution for each one. He agreed to take our proposal, with a strong recommendation to accept, to the next meeting of the ACPC. Had we transferred ownership? It felt like something significant had happened. We certainly felt that there were more than two of us pushing and our excitement as we left the meeting was tempered only by the realization that we might actually have to DO IT!

As it happened, we had several more months of negotiation ahead as the Social Services Department tried to establish wider commitment to the initiative. The ACPC meeting had not gone 'as smoothly as expected', there were natural concerns about costs, some doubts about whether or not anything useful would be achieved, and a suggestion that research questions could be built in which would suit the needs of the various organizations. An ad hoc group was to be convened by the senior Social Services Department manager who had enthusiastically championed the idea so far in order to discuss these and other concerns with us before making a decision.

Two months passed. The four person committee assembled as we arrived in a bare green and cream room with plastic stacking chairs. We sat around a central table with a chipped and peeling Formica top which was furnished with aluminium foil pie cases as ash-trays. The mood was tangibly solemn as our champion outlined the issues for discussion. The meeting developed into the first clear paradigm clash: the need to monitor budgets closely and get 'value for money' seemed to underscore an already existing preference held by at least two group members for research designs which aim to generate widely generalizable hard data. We could offer no such promises, and emphasized our belief in the usefulness of open peer group exploration of the issues. Outcomes could not be pre-empted. The discussion felt inconclusive and there seemed little detectable shift in attitudes or ownership as we withdrew to allow them to consider their decision.

A further two months of silence followed. We then heard that the ad hoc group, originally empowered to be decision-makers, had been called to report to the next full meeting of the ACPC. Another hurdle!

It is perhaps worth recording our feelings during this period. We have already noted our relative unpreparedness for the protracted Phase 1. As it went on, we recognized quite dramatic shifts in our mood and approach. When positive, we were unreservedly excited about the 'almost there' inquiry and optimistic about its potential. When negative, we acknowledged considerable anger at 'them' for being so apparently mistrusting of our motives and competence, and anger at the 'system' which exists primarily to protect children from abuse, but was finding it so achingly difficult to make even the most modest move towards a small piece of research which might yield improvement. Meanwhile our heads reminded us of the inevitable complications of negotiating indirectly with organizations which have differing priorities and complicated systems of communication. A wise colleague who has had much more experience of multi-professional work than either of us, cautioned against impatience. We should recognize how many frames of reference we were trying to encompass within a single project and not underestimate the inherent psychological threat of exposure which such a multidisciplinary venture risked. Eight months after we began negotiation, the phone rang. The ACPC had decided to commission the inquiry. Did we have any ideas about how a research group could be effectively recruited?

Access

Ideally we hoped for informal preliminary discussions with potential group members. That seemed to be the only way in which prospective participants could genuinely be enabled to develop an interest in and commitment to the inquiry subject and process. However, the very real difficulties in gaining access mentioned earlier made this impractical. We settled for second best: our link person took responsibility for contacting each agency to invite participation. We agreed that in order to try to communicate a consistent message it would be helpful if he used some 'advertising copy' to help sell the concept to all the prospective client organizations. This confronted us with the question: how can we succinctly communicate the information required to make rational choice of participants possible? Our answer was the summary document reproduced as on pp. 106–7.

It is interesting rereading this 'advert' after the event to see how close we were to reality in some dimensions and how far from it in others. Close in the sense that everything we wrote about the process and content of the inquiry was more or less to occur in the research group. Far because the initial expectations of the group members were very mixed, and the criteria by which they were ultimately selected made it far from the peer group of researchers we had hoped to convene, at least at the beginning of the group process. There are a number of issues to note which contributed to these discrepancies:

Temporary loss of ownership

We were at least four links removed from those who were being invited to work with us.

Link 1:   Us to champion.
Link 2:   Champion to point of contact in each organization.
Link 3:   Contact to line manager of prospective inquirer.
Link 4:   Line manager to potential inquirer.

The potential for mixing and missing messages in this process does not need elaboration! It felt like Collaborative Inquiry via Chinese Whispers! Having pushed for so long, all of a sudden we felt powerless, literally out of control. The very act of writing and handing over the 'advert' seemed to symbolize our loss of ownership at a critical scene setting stage.

This feeling was complicated by the news that our champion was to transfer to another job soon after sending out the 'advert'. We were therefore to be handed over to his successor who would act as link between the inquiry and the ACPC. Being handed over felt very uncomfortable and risky at this stage. We had no reason to believe that the new link person would be any less effective, but recognized that if this were to be guaranteed, we had further ownership transfers to effect.

Differential recruitment processes

We had hoped for two peer representatives from each participant organization in order to increase the sense of individual and professional safety within the research group. We also thought that if we were to explore an area of practice which we knew to be diverse, it would be useful to encompass as broad a range of experience as possible. Practically, we foresaw some sessions where there would not be full attendance and wanted to guarantee full agency representation for as many research meetings as possible.

Two agencies, Probation and the National Society for the Prevention of

Cruelty to Children (NSPCC), decided to send a single representative to the inquiry. We are not altogether clear whether this mattered *critically*, but insofar as it represents a deviation from our intention it is worth reporting.

Wide range of resulting expectations

Our distance from the recruitment process for an extended period led us seriously to underestimate the wide range of expectations which were being generated by it. From our perspective outside the system, we optimistically assumed that a potentially co-operative group was being formed, whereas in reality, co-option seemed to more closely represent the group's experience.

> 'I only heard I was coming the day before the inquiry started.'
> 'It's not as if we all got together and decided to do this.'
> 'I was sent.'
> 'I feel really second, possibly third, best, I'm here because X and Y couldn't come.'
> 'I was intending to send one of my staff; but he fell ill, so I came myself.'
> 'My manager was going to come, but had other pressing engagements, so sent me.'

The nature of these experiences was not to surface fully until the third meeting of the research group. Their impact, however, must have been immediate and conditioned the task we faced on entry. In retrospect, we feel that these problems could have been largely overcome by us meeting with participants individually before the event. However, because of time and cost constraints, this was not possible.

Entry

The inquiry was scheduled to meet for six half-day sessions over a four-month period. We were to be based in the professionally neutral territory of a quiet, convenient diocesan conference centre just outside Northampton. It was, we thought, a perfect setting for reflection.

We started the group forming process a month in advance of the first session by writing individually to the nominated participants. We spent a long time fine-tuning the detail of the letter, aiming for a combination of warmth, enthusiasm and clarity regarding dates, times and venue. We also enclosed a copy of the 'advert' thinking that in the protracted recruitment process some of them might not have had sight of it.

An issue which featured in our discussions at this stage was our respective roles within the inquiry – how to manage our own collaboration. We felt intuitively that our skills were complementary and well suited to the task in as far as it could be predicted. John had wide experience of facilitating the Improvement Process in industry and was well equipped with process tools. Sara's teaching and research experience in the field of child protection meant that she had a grasp of the issues that were likely to provide the focus of the inquiry. We loosely divided process tasks and content tasks accordingly. In practice this division seemed to be appropriate. Sara found herself up front to a large extent during the sessions where content issues were manifest. John was

The summary document

Northamptonshire Child Protection Committee
and
The School of Social Studies
University of Nottingham

The Management, Supervision and Support of Child Protection Practitioners

A Collaborative Inquiry

What?

The Area Child Protection Committee is seeking ways of understanding and improving the quality of management, supervision and support available to practitioners working in direct contact with children and families where abuse is a concern. Among other initiatives, the ACPC has commissioned the University of Nottingham's School of Social Studies to undertake a small-scale research project, a collaborative inquiry. The aim of the inquiry will be to explore and describe in as much detail as possible current management/supervisory practice in Northamptonshire's key child protection agencies and to develop discussion about the process of improvement.

Why?

All professionals involved in child protection, no matter what their professional or organizational base, are affected to a greater or lesser extent by:

1 The high degree of personal and professional anxiety which the work generates in individuals and their organizations.
2 The complex and sensitive nature of multidisciplinary communication and co-operation which effective protection demands.

These characteristics place particular demands on managers and supervisors but to date we know very little about how they are responding to and meeting such needs within the major agencies involved. We know even less about the way in which people feel such processes are hindered and how they might be improved. The aim of the collaborative inquiry is to begin the debate in a multidisciplinary forum where we can learn not only *about*, but *from* one another.

How?

Rather than interviewing people separately, or sending out question-naires, we will be using a research method which is especially helpful when people have considerable experience of a particular issue and can profit from sharing their knowledge and expertise.

The idea of collaborative inquiry as a research tool is simple: funda-mentally, it is that a group of people with a common concern, work together with a facilitator as co-researchers in exploring, describing and possibly changing their world. It is research *with* people not *on* or *about* people.

In this case, the aim is to invite two representatives from the following agencies to meet together for six sessions lasting two or three hours over a period of approximately three months.

Education	Police
Health	Probation
NSPCC	Social Services

The group will have the responsibility for defining the content of their project and shaping the research task so that it reflects local conditions and preoccupations with the overall aim of exploring and describing the managerial/supervisory task in child protection within each agency. We (John Cosier and Sara Glennie) will take responsibility for the research process.

Who?

The inquiry will take place in the Northampton Division and each par-ticipating agency is asked to nominate representatives who are currently involved in first line management/supervision of staff involved in child protection. The choice for some agencies, particularly Health, may be difficult given the range of staff involved. However, the only prescriptive criteria for inclusion is current involvement in the task and a keen com-mitment to participate in the inquiry.

When?

It is hoped that nominations will be complete in the autumn so that the inquiry can commence during November 1991.

most active and creative between sessions, analysing and steering the process.

We were incredibly eager to begin. The weeks leading up to the initial meeting dragged by as our file filled with notes for the first session which we worked and reworked. The end result of this 'worry work' was fairly predictable; we knew we *needed* to spend a significant part of the first session getting to know one another, establishing safe foundations for co-operative activity. We *needed* to be as clear as possible about the events which had led to the inquiry and help the group move towards an appreciation of the collaborative inquiry process. We *wanted* to enable active participation and share ownership!

In session one, a full group convened. Something had worked. Were they really interested, curious, keen – or just compliant? Again our own fluctuating confidence played games with our capacity for positive interpretation. But there they were, apparently ready to start. The full group is listed in Table 7.2

Table 7.2   *The full group*

Post	Agency
Senior Probation Officer	Probation Service
Head Teacher	Education
Principal Education Welfare Officer	Education
Patch Manager (health visitors)	Health
Patch Manager (health visitors)	Health
Sergeant (child abuse)	Police
Detective Inspector	Police
Deputy Team Manager	NSPCC
Principal Social Worker	Social Services
Unit Manager	Social Services
Training Officer (child protection)	Social Services

How to begin? We made efforts to maximize the safety and comfort of the physical environment by ensuring that everyone had coffee on arrival, comfortable easy chairs in a circle and a background of Baroque guitar music. The former were perhaps expected and common, the latter clearly surprised people. They later commented on how they came to value it as a means of easing the transition from one world to another; from a highly pressurized to a more reflective environment.

Generally, the first session of any group encounter represents a three-way tension between person focus, process focus and task focus. All three need attention in order to create a group which can work co-operatively and purposefully. Striking the appropriate balance in this context tested our intuition. Remember we had no direct inquiry experience to draw on. It also tested our capacity to understand each other's style and preferences as facilitators. We hoped we could read each other's messages accurately during the session when one of us shifted or felt the need to shift the balance.

Initially we chose to focus primarily on people. We started with a session almost entirely devoted to getting to know each other. After a brief introduction to the objectives of the inquiry, the meeting consisted of three main components:

1 Interviewing someone from a different agency and introducing them to the group.
2 In small groups, addressing the question 'What can we contribute to the inquiry, and what do we want from it?'
3 A plenary presentation from each group, which led to a general discussion about the common features of the management and supervisory role as the group was experiencing it *now*.

Although some group members said subsequently that they felt unclear about objectives and direction in the early phases of the inquiry, we feel that our intuitive choice of focus was appropriate. Enabling group members to explore one another in a number of different ways laid a solid foundation for the open and honest exchanges which were to follow and helped a focus to develop which was relevant to their concerns.

An important piece of group culture emerged during this session. John noticed that on several occasions, people, although using the same words as one another, were clearly endowing them with different meanings. He suggested that we start a 'glossary' of terms whose meanings needed clarification. The group never got round to filling in the definitions, but the process was invaluable in that it sensitized members to the use of jargon. It also served as an excellent barometer to the group's ownership of its process: it started with us writing words, then group members suggested words for us to write, then group members asked our permission to add words, and finally the group added items freely whether or not we were present in the room.

The group process by the end of the first session was totally divergent. Members ranged widely in their discussions, moving from details of child protection procedure to feelings generated by abuse, to the political and social context in which they operate. This was perhaps particularly important given the multidisciplinary nature of the group. Although ostensibly doing the same job, the widely differing organizational structures, functions and cultures which the inquiry embraced meant that the inquirers had a great deal of checking out to do with one another as professionals as well as people. This need became even more apparent as the focus of the inquiry began to sharpen.

Boundary setting

The exhilaration of starting gave way to a sense of rising panic in our gut after the first session, though we perhaps did not acknowledge it immediately at head level. The feelings seemed to be about how to facilitate rather than prescribe the move from the divergent early exploration of an incredibly wide territory to a path of inquiry that would be recognizably coherent and valuable for the group's purposes. The 'stuff' elicited in the first meeting was exciting and necessary but seemed overwhelmingly complex. We were particularly conscious of the very limited time-scale of the inquiry (six half days). We also

recognized the pressure under which group members were working and the difficulties they had in freeing themselves to attend the inquiry. Although we
knew they had to own the inquiry in order for it to become appropriately
focused, we felt we wanted to give them a tangible direction. As our link person cautioned us later, 'you can't go with the flow forever!' The 'doing culture'
from which each participant had emerged constantly (sometimes unhelpfully)
reinforced this message and we were not immune from its seductive influence.

Extracts from our taped post-session musings reflect our concern:

> the process is a tool which is not inherently important . . . it is a tool for helping
> them to do what they need to do. I think it is important that we shouldn't be
> attached to a particular technology of doing it. I think the fundamental thing is
> them admitting that they want to do it. 'Cause if it is *us* doing it with them, then it's
> never gonna work . . . we're not going to be effective in the doing of it and it's not
> going to be owned by them and the output isn't going to be used . . . maybe a pre-
> scriptive stand up in the front and manage the process is the way. I dunno, I
> wouldn't personally prescribe that process, on the other hand, I wouldn't *not* do it
> if it was going to be effective.
> . . .
> I wonder how guided, or misguided, we've been in being committed to having a mul-
> tidisciplinary group? I feel at one level it is the only way to begin to address the issue;
> on the other hand I am very aware that people come from very different cultures of
> learning and doing.

(Incidentally, we would prescribe that anyone facilitating an inquiry should
hold the meetings 50 miles from home. The drives to and from sessions with
the cassette recorder almost permanently on were an essential part of our
learning process.)

We continued musing and decided as a first step to try to make sense of the
group's wide ranging discussion (which we had taped) for ourselves by 'chunk-
ing and sorting' the transcription (Bell and Hardiman, 1989). We did so with
an oppressive sense of guilt about taking over the group's task, but from it we
distilled a very useful starting point from which the group could shape the next
stage of the inquiry. We posted the sorted and clustered 'chunks' for the group
to examine and reflect on as they gathered for the second session.

At this point John offered a more detailed outline of the collaborative
inquiry process as a research method. Intellectually it seemed late (with 17 per
cent of the meeting time over) but in practice it was ideally placed because he
could quote incidents from the group's experience in the first session to illustrate key points of action and reflection. Indeed, it became a meta-inquiry
within the main inquiry. This pattern of reflecting on the group experience
continued and John was later to introduce models of the improvement process
(Cosier, 1991a, 1991b) and experiential learning (Kolb et al., 1979).

The group split during this session to explore two main 'chunks': issues
relating to the *job* itself and issues relating to the *context* in which it is experienced. They asked themselves the question: 'What do we need to do to
progress these issues?'

More plenary discussion led to the beginnings of one of the most important
process tools of the inquiry: the inquiry map. With each week's session it was

amended and extended thereby bounding and directing the inquiry. In retrospect, it enabled us to see a quite distinct three part pattern to the group's life together. We dubbed these phases, *ascent, flight* and *descent*.

Ascent – the first two sessions – represented our coming together as a group and the generation of energy and direction. Flight, lasting three sessions, was full of 'doing'; information gathering, representing and sharing. Descent, the last and breathless formal session, contained the important next step's discussions which were to finally give shape to the inquiry's product (see Figure 7.1).

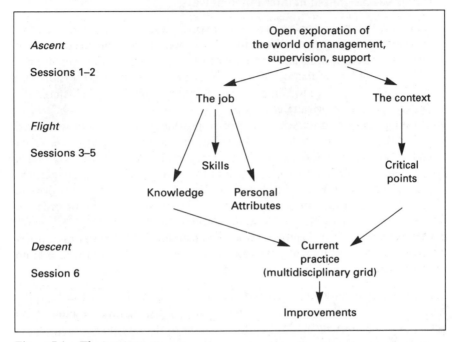

Figure 7.1   *The inquiry map*

The emerging sense of shape and direction during session two lifted our mood. Our post-session reflection was optimistic, light and clearly signified ascent:

> I think they have definitely changed gear . . . last week I felt that they were happy to be there but passive. At the end of today I feel that they are enthusiastic to contribute. I really do think that we have shared ownership.
>
> . . .
>
> there was a kind of intrigued suspicion on the edge last week . . . she wasn't ready to jump into the puddle yet. Now I feel that the inquiry has fully engaged her intellectual curiosity.

We moved more confidently into the data collection phase of the inquiry.

Data collection

The group chose to explore three major aspects of their role as supervisors each of which reflected the need for cross-agency learning and co-operation in the child protection field. Their exploration began with a detailed elaboration of the knowledge, skills and personal attributes thought to be required for efficient function in role. This focus helped to clarify thinking for individuals about the job they did, while providing a means of checking for similarities and differences across agency boundaries.

Knowledge, skills and personal attributes

The task was progressed in three different ways:

1   Initially, the group took away a homework question which had been formulated through general discussion: 'If you were to be replaced tomorrow, what knowledge, skills and personal attributes would your successor need to have in order to function effectively?' They came to the next session with comprehensive notes to compare. Small groups collated and clustered the products of their private reflection.
2   In the process of doing this piece of work, one group member wondered what the question would look like with another set of glasses on. That query sparked the next step in the exploration. Each supervisor went back to their organization to ask both practitioners and their own managers the same question: 'What knowledge, skills and personal attributes do you think a child protection supervisor's successor should have in order to function effectively?'
3   Finally, two group members took responsibility for formulating a questionnaire (asking basically the same question) which was introduced and distributed at a meeting of the ACPC.

The gradual widening and deepening of this part of the inquiry (perhaps the best illustration of the cyclic nature of the inquiry process) was fascinating to watch. It was a dramatic and validating example of the group's growing capacity to take charge of its own direction, test its sufficiency and then alter course to suit its own purpose. The learning for us at this stage was potent. It *does* happen, this elusive thing called ownership, we saw it, *moving*.

Post-session notes confirm this shift in confidence.

> Tremendous bit of initiative, enthusiasm and commitment!
> . . .
> my faith in this process has been totally justified today . . . my doubts completely wiped out. First of all M. mentioned the 'other set of glasses' and all I did was to underline that in the group discussion by saying 'that's an interesting question, you mean we could actually look at this in more than one way?' And then, three quarters of an hour later P. comes in with the perfect mechanism for getting at that! . . . and as you know I have been aching for them to ask the punters (practitioners). I was afraid I was going to have to prescribe it

This high carried us through the next month and the long Christmas period. Why did we not anticipate the trough ahead?

Session four was undoubtedly the lowest point for us. Excerpts from our post-session discussion illustrate this:

it started off like yesterday's rice pudding . . . Even before the session started! It developed a crust as soon as the first participant arrived with her doubts and anxieties about the value of the inquiry!

We had been concerned about post-Christmas attendance (having already received apologies from four participants) and had given quite a lot of thought about how to get the remainder back on board. Also (in retrospect) at this the half-way point our anxieties were flipping from how to continue to maintain ownership (the process) to what to put into the report to the client (the task). We had decided to address these issues directly with a review and clarification of the objectives of the inquiry and had just written the question on a flip chart ('We will know that we have succeeded in our task if . . .?') when the first member arrived. She had just been to a difficult and apparently unsatisfactory meeting at work and her distress was still wrapped tightly around her. She greeted us warmly but then went on to express genuine concern about the progress and direction of the inquiry. 'Is this what you wanted?' was one of her questions, restimulating obvious alarms in our minds about ownership. John reflected the question: 'Is this what *you* wanted from the inquiry?' This precipitated a lively internal debate with very little intervention from us during which she became convinced of its value and recommitted to the process. She concluded that it was useful to spend time reflecting on her role and particularly helpful to do so with colleagues from other agencies.

Meanwhile the smallish group had arrived and the subject opened up to all. They sat, unresponsive and clearly in another place. The turning point came when the member who had arrived earlier and had had time to start reviewing objectives contributed. She offered a clearly thought out case for the inquiry. Others slowly joined in.

The outcome of their debate was the following set of targets:

We will know we have succeeded in our task if:
1   We heighten our awareness of other people's roles and issues central to the management and supervision of child protection.
2   Our people receive better supervision.
3   We identify what we can do to make things better within existing resources.
4   We construct a report of our work which:
    (a)   is usable and friendly
    (b)   we all own and support.

Thus the nadir transcended to the zenith; a public and overt declaration of ownership, or at least the intention to own.

We reflected afterwards on the importance of this review and reconnection with objectives and its serendipitous emergence into the group's process.

That's one thing that has been the common theme through the whole inquiry . . . serendipity. Things have just fallen into place at exactly the right time. The thought of the right question, the thought of the right activity . . . exactly when it has been appropriate. Quite amazing.
I don't know what that stuff about serendipity means . . . I don't know whether you just begin to trust it will happen . . . or whether there is something else going on. But

it was a very profitable first half hour and they have a much better understanding of what they are doing.

Having literally re-formed around a commonly agreed intention, the group moved on to the next and quite natural phase of their exploration. They had identified relevant knowledge, skills and attributes; they now directed their attention to the context in which they worked and focused on what they called the critical points in the child protection process.

Critical points

Essentially the group was trying to generate an explicit understanding of 'who does what when' in each agency during the protracted processes which span suspicion of abuse through to treatment and recovery. The group decided to set itself some more homework. Each participant agreed to develop a map or flow chart of their supervisory/managerial activity which they would then present to the next meeting. They intended to design their map in such a way that it would demonstrate points in the child protection process within their agency which:

● required supervisors to be particularly active
● made particular demands on supervisors
● offered scope for greater multidisciplinary collaboration.

The maps were shared with the group and checked for clarity and under-standing. The critical points listed in Table 7.3 emerged as a consensus.

Table 7.3   *The critical points*

1	Prodromal
2	Incident
3	Referral/information gathering
4	Strategy meeting
5	Investigation
6	Case conference
7	Core group
8	Child protection plan/implementation
9	Review

This piece of work was valuable in the following ways:

● It helped individuals to see the different strands of their complex role with more clarity.
● It made it possible for people to identify the fact that they required different knowledge, skills and expertise at different stages of the process.
● It provided a tool for examining the differential contribution of individual agencies at different stages in the child protection process.
● It enabled a distinction to be made between reactive and proactive styles of management and supervision.

The work also laid the foundation for the group's next exploration – the description of current practice within each agency. This was the brainchild of one group member who envisaged the possibility of representing, in matrix form, the supervisory and managerial activity of each agency at each critical point in the child protection process. It was an ambitious task, and time was running out.

Our own anxiety at the prospect turned our post-session reflection towards the cynical and facetious.

> I hope he can pull his matrix off . . . I asked him to come up and draw the idea on the flip because I thought it was such an enormous task. With only half the group there, by the time we reconvene in a month, heaven knows how we actually *do* it!
>
> Don't you know how we do it? We struggle for six or nine months on the first column, the critical points that we have been eliciting today. It's all the functions of every possible referral. That's why you need a team of lawyers and practitioners and experts and professors working on that for six or nine months. Then you pin it up on a board and you say, OK, which bits do you get involved with?. And in 15 minutes you have a matrix of ticks. Quite easy really!

Current practice: a multi-agency representation

A matrix was in fact created at the next session, the fifth. The full grid was originally constructed on scraps of paper and posted, covering the majority of an oak panelled wall of the conference centre. In interim form it was transcribed, cut and pasted, filling an A1 flip chart. Ultimately it became a nine-page coloured section of the final inquiry report. As a courtesy to our readers, we do *not* include it as part of this chapter.

It showed each participant's account of current practice at each critical step in the child protection process. It proved effective in helping the group to gain a detailed cross-agency perspective, and served as a preliminary base line for the question: 'If this is what we do *now*, what do we need to do to improve?'

We were much relieved that this third and major group task had borne fruit which the group valued. By the end of the fifth session we were anxiously and almost exclusively focused on acceptable outcomes. It feels somehow invalid to admit to such a pragmatic concern, but we *were* under contract and were cognizant of the need for a product that had meaning for more than the inquiry group.

> session five was good because it generated data that is structured, shared and usable . . . it's a lot more comfortable when it comes out structured. I was very anxious before today; bloody hell, how are we going to process all this data with the group and come up with some conclusions when we've only got two sessions left!
> . . .
> that's interesting, in terms of our own process, the focus of our anxiety has totally shifted away from the group . . . they've gotta produce some data that someone else will recognize as being worth our fee! I think we have to acknowledge that.
> . . .
> I guess you can divide the six sessions into three twos . . . One was 'take off and climb', two was 'what a beautiful flight' and three is descent and landing.
> . . .
> the feelings associated with that are real anxiety about whether we will get to the desired altitude and will we crash? And in the middle it is really comfortable . . . nice metaphor.

Analysis and reflection

The final stage of the inquiry, reflecting on three months of working together, was difficult for the group and for us as a consequence. In the sixth and last session we had a very full agenda: we had to pull together some conclusions from the (by now) large mass of data, invent and agree a process for the group to own the final report and finally, we hoped to review the members' impressions of the process. Right from the start we knew we were on a loser! Whether it was deliberate prevarication, problem avoidance or blissful unawareness we were never to find out, but the discussion was rambling and endless. Reiterating the agenda failed to focus the group, as did reminding them of the time remaining. Our distress was clear in the post-session tape:

> I was in absolute panic half-way through . . . I just couldn't cope, with the mechanics of it or the content! . . . I was totally relying on the tape to pick up all that stuff that I simply couldn't understand and find attention for.
> . . .
> they kept losing their way . . . they couldn't keep focused on the task . . . they had worked well with the brainstorm that they chose initially . . . and then they came to a grinding halt!
> . . .
> and then B. and G. started their independent debate which went on and on and far away . . . there was a lot of discomfort in the group at that point.
> . . .
> none of them were being concise or crisp and they knew we only had today!
> B. said a couple of times 'I've lost the thread of what I was saying' – Well, *that* was an understatement: I don't think he ever had a thread!

The burden of ownership is evident from our transcript. We had considerable doubts about whether it was still willingly shared by the group. There seemed to be a lot of unfinished business about. Eventually we arrived at a list of items that the group clearly thought were areas for improvement and further research by extracting comments and highlights from the discussion onto a flip chart. With this we went away to write a draft report for them to consider.

The group met on one further occasion some six weeks later, having read the draft. (Two members who could not attend sent contributions by post.) At this meeting, there was, interestingly, much more focused attention on formulating conclusions and careful consideration of a strategy for moving the report back into the constituent organizations.

They felt it was important to distinguish between changes which were thought desirable as a result of their learning, and those which were *desirable* and *achievable* within existing resources. There was complete consensus on this issue. The group wanted to be heard outside the inquiry and wanted their voice to be thought pragmatic and reasonable. This concern demonstrated that they had managed to generate a healthy balance of attention: attention inwards to their mutual exploration and attention out to their clients (the practitioners they supervised and the ACPC). They too, felt under contract.

Mindful of that, the group confirmed specific areas for attention, discussion and action which clustered in the following way:

- Specialist characteristics of the managerial/supervisory task in child protection.
- The need for role clarity across agencies and possible mechanisms through which it could be enhanced.
- Specific issues of cross-agency communication and co-operation in practice.

In this final review meeting people became fully engaged in discussion about specific content issues that we raised. However, notable by its absence was any feedback from the group (either from those present or in writing by others) about the report as a whole: no comment about how good it was, or how bad; how long it was or how short; how well written or how badly; how representative of the group's work or how different. We became very anxious about the absence of affirmation of the report. We were in an uncomfortable position. After the lively and highly participative data collection phase we now felt a sense of uneven ownership of the final and now tangible group product. Without wishing to seek compliments we found ourselves giving people opportunities to make spontaneous general remarks. None came. 'Why?' we asked ourselves repeatedly. Had we got it exactly right? Was it precisely what people had anticipated? Was it so far adrift from their expectations that they dare not tell us? After the event, did they feel that they had been used as guinea pigs by the academics? Were the group in some way disclaiming ownership in the final moments of the project? Or had we usurped or offended the group in some way by offering to write the report on their behalf? Sadly, we were never to find out. We should have confronted the issue squarely but did not fully comprehend the nature of our dis-ease until the meeting had finished and we had had an opportunity to check out impressions with one another.

Also, during the final session we were keen to give the group an opportunity to consider and comment on their experience of collaborative inquiry as a research method. We were hopeful that both product and process would be recognized as valuable. We had prompted this reflection by sending an open set of questions for them to think about or write about before the final session. Time ran out on us and we were left, sadly, without the full thoughtful discussion we had planned. A paper picture of their impressions revealed that with one exception the group enjoyed the experience of working together co-operatively and some had very specific thoughts about how the method could be used effectively to explore particular issues within their own work settings. The only concern/criticism about method that was expressed had to do with clarity of objectives from the outset.

> 'We need clear objectives in the first session.'
> 'Keep us on track more rigorously.'
> 'Half way through I lost track of our aims.'

This raised a number of questions which we are still musing over:

1 How, in a relatively short inquiry, can one effectively convey the participatory ethos of the method particularly if it runs counter to the prevailing culture of the organization in which participants are working? As we were recently reminded in another context, empowerment takes time.

2 Was the lack of clarity a manifestation of the protracted and difficult process of access and entry which characterized this particular inquiry?
3 Does the criticism simply give voice to the inevitable tentativeness and anxiety associated with exploratory research methodologies? Should real attempts be made to solve the problem, or is it simply necessary to recognize and manage it?
4 Do the concerns reveal the early dependency which a group inevitably feels when convened by experts, in this case, academics from a distant (and distancing?) institution? Reason reminds us of the

> important tension at the contracting stage. If the initiators are already very clear about what they want to do and how they want to do it, there will be little room for negotiation . . . it is unlikely that a genuinely co-operative climate will flourish: the group will either form in a dependency mode, doing the inquiry *for* the initiators; or will be resistant and argumentative; or will simply not get off the ground at all. (Reason, 1988: 24–5; emphasis in original)

5 Were we just plain fuzzy? Reason again:

> if the initiators are completely open and flexible the forming group will have nothing to get its teeth into at this early tentative stage, and so may flounder around in ambiguity and confusion. (Reason, 1988: 25)

Intervention

There were very clear expectations from the client, the ACPC, that we would formally present the report of the inquiry's findings. This was communicated directly at the contracting stage and reconfirmed at a meeting with our ACPC link person as the inquiry drew to a close. We understood the origins of this expectation, and in many ways were sympathetic with it; you buy, you expect delivery. We were, however, concerned that if the report were seen publicly to belong exclusively to us, the outsiders, the force of its potential impact would be lessened. We tried therefore to continue to find ways of maintaining group ownership and participation at the intervention stage of the planned change process. This was attempted in two ways.

First, we invited our link person to meet with us and a member of the research group after session five. The purpose, ostensibly, was to report progress to date and to agree details of feedback into the organizations. An indirect purpose and outcome was actively to enable her appreciation and support of the method and likely products of the inquiry. The change in her attitude during our discussion was marked; she moved from expecting specific *prescriptions* to looking forward to a set of emergent *understandings* about the role of supervisor/manager in child protection which might then form the basis of a whole range of future actions. The meeting, in effect, re-created the role of champion.

Second, the formal presentation of the inquiry's report was made to a joint meeting of two ACPC Subcommittees (Procedures and Professional Practice). Serendipitously (again!) two active and keen members of the research group were also committee members. They sat supportively on either wing of the semi-circular audience offering confirmation and expanding points as the presentation and subsequent discussion progressed. Their presence helped us feel that the transfer of ownership that was going on was from the whole inquiry group to the ACPC. We concluded the session by symbolically handing over the overhead projector slides that we had prepared and used in the presentation to our champion.

The full inquiry report is at the time of writing being reviewed and sifted by a subgroup which has been convened by our champion and which contains two research group members. They have taken responsibility for making some specific recommendations for action to the next ACPC meeting. We have transferred ownership for the last time. We are no longer participants in the process and its products will be shaped, appropriately, by those who commissioned it and must use its learning.

Exit

Leaving the territory after having been resident for so long feels strange. We have not, if we are honest, even now divested ourselves of ownership (or its consequent manifestations). We listen to and tweak our network for news of developments. Nothing yet – too early to tell. What we do hear is that there is almost exclusive attention to the content outcomes of the inquiry. There is no evidence that the introduction of a new research methodology has had any impact beyond the research event. This saddens us because we felt that it proved to be a particularly powerful tool for such a complex exploration.

The group has stopped meeting; there are no more deadlines but it does not *feel* finished. Will anything change? Has it made a difference? Will children be better protected as a consequence of the inquiry? The answers to these questions matter *enormously*.

We have every confidence that the inquiry was valuable to those who participated directly. They actively enjoyed learning with and through one another. They dramatically lowered the unhelpful barriers which can exist between agencies and professionals who share a common, painful and difficult task. Their perception of their role and its potential has expanded. Their practice will be different. We celebrate that achievement and our part in it.

The possibility of wider learning is more difficult to anticipate. It seems critically dependent on the ability of those who have neither direct experience of collaborative inquiry, nor inherent sympathy with its paradigm, to trust in new ways of knowing. We wait and hope.

It's going to leave a huge hole when it's finished.

Yeh....................................

Long silence

8

Creating Collaborative Relationships in a Co-operative Inquiry Group

Moira De Venney-Tiernan, Annette Goldband, Lyn Rackham and Nancy Reilly

We are a group of youth workers with different roles in Merton Youth Service in South London, England. The purpose of our work is to empower young people, that is, to enable them to acquire the skills, knowledge and attitudes necessary for them to practise their right to self-determination. The Youth Service mainly operates in the social sphere of young people's lives, using the methodology of experiential learning (Kolb, 1984). This methodology also forms the basis of most of the training and staff development processes for youth service personnel.

While most youth services have a number of professionally trained full-time youth workers, the majority of youth workers are part-time and voluntary. People who wish to make the transition from part-time to full-time work (with a few exceptions) can only do this by undertaking professional training, usually by full-time attendance at an institute of higher education. This prevents a number of workers from making the transition, because they are unable to leave dependants or current employment in order to study full-time.

This led Annette, the second author, who is a full time Youth Officer with responsibility for training and staff development and who was undertaking a Master's degree, to initiate a project researching into Alternative Routes to Qualification (ARQ). She chose to use a full collaborative experiential inquiry method.

The co-researchers included eight part-time youth workers both paid and unpaid, from the maintained and voluntary sectors; one full-time youth worker and one freelance trainer/part-time youth worker (ex full-time youth worker). The group consisted of men and women: African, Caribbean, Asian and white people, as well as some workers with people with disabilities.

Writing this chapter

Annette was invited to contribute to this book, and in order to maintain as full a collaboration as possible she invited all co-researchers to participate. As the research group was still meeting, only four people were able to find the time to do this. In the event, one of these four (the only male volunteer!) was unable to join in.

The importance we attached to being as fully collaborative as possible determined our methodology for writing. First, we debated what aspects of our experience we would write about. We then brainstormed all the issues, incidents and accidents in the life of the research group which we perceived as significant and relevant to this story. We put these in a logical order and worked in pairs to write about them, using Annette's dissertation and the personal portfolios of Lyn, Moira and Nancy. Annette collated these and checked the finished article with the co-authors. When agreed by the whole writing group, the draft was sent to all co-researchers and the editor of this book simultaneously, who were all given the opportunity to challenge its content. This process was repeated until we arrived at the final article. This paper, therefore, while written by four members of the original project, has been validated by the whole research group. The first main section – 'Creating the group' – is from Annette's perspective as initiator of the project and so is written in the first person singular; the next section – 'Creating and maintaining collaborative relationships' – is written from the perspective of the group as a whole.

Creating the group – the initiator's perspective

It was my intention to invite the following individuals to join the research group, because they would have a vested interest in the provision of Alternative Routes to Qualification:

1 Part-time youth workers who are looking for an 'alternative route to qualification'.
2 Trainers who are looking to provide/access alternative routes.
3 Employers who wish to establish alternative routes, to join with me in this collaborative venture.

According to Reason, the UK developments 'in co-operative inquiry have been closely linked with experiential learning and humanistic psychology' (1988: 2). Both these are parts of the foundation of youth work and youth work training. Certainly in Merton Youth Service, the majority of training for youth workers is experiential in nature. Our membership of the Centre for Youth Work Studies at Brunel University and the use of the Brunel Basic Training Scheme, with its emphasis on developmental group work, is an example of this. It was therefore a congruent choice to elect for a method of research which in itself provided opportunities for experiential learning.

Just as the emphases on the whole person and experience are common ground shared by new paradigm research and youth work, so too is the emphasis on participation. Indeed, the last major report on the Youth Service was titled *Experience and Participation* (HMSO, 1981).

Similarly just as youth workers must be wary of allowing their views, perceptions, judgements, about a young person to take precedence over that young person's perception of themselves, so too does Heron argue that the empirical basis for experiential inquiry:

> is the experiential knowledge of persons in relation to their situation, their world. And for researching the human condition and human capacity for self-direction from the standpoint of the agent; and that no other standpoint can have research precedence over the agent's standpoint. (Heron, 1981b: 159)

The methodology of the approach includes reflection and action cycles. It is because the approach is concerned with 'formed in and for action rather than in and for reflection' (Reason, 1988: 12) that it is a paradigmatic shift from orthodox science. This emphasis on action also concurred with the expectations of Brunel University and my employer – that is, that the research I was involved in should lead to the development of a real piece of work, and not simply the production of a lofty tome to sit and gather dust on a shelf.

While still intent upon researching ARQ, I could not define the research area more specifically – this would need to be done by the inquiry group if the method was to be as collaborative as possible. Instead my planning at this stage had to concentrate on setting up the inquiry group and developing a general notion of time-scale. Although the time-scale could not yet be worked out in detail, it was predictable that our work would be constrained by the deadlines placed on me by the University.

My first task then, was to invite a group of people to join me who would be:

1 Genuinely interested in the area of research – to the point of having something to gain by the development of alternative routes to qualification.
2 Experienced in growth processes of some kind (group work, counselling, etc.).
3 Keen to try out a new methodology.
4 Serious about their own growth and development.
5 Able to give and receive feedback (that is, challenge) as a natural part of their roles in groups.

Like Cunningham, I was therefore 'deliberately highly selective about the people I chose as a "core" group for the research' (Cunningham, 1988: 171).

I decided to hold a day to explain what I was interested in doing, explore the method and enable people to decide whether they wished to be involved. I made a list of all the part-time qualified youth workers in Merton whom I knew to have completed the Brunel Basic Training Scheme (BBTS) who were interested in becoming qualified as full-time youth and community workers, but who were unable to take up current options. I then wrote a letter of invitation to all those who in my perception also met the other four criteria in the list. This numbered twelve people. I also invited five people who were already full-time qualified and I perceived would be interested by virtue of their job role. This included the Principal Youth Officer for Merton; the Regional Officers responsible for training and staff development for the Catholic and Anglican Youth Services; my non-managerial supervisor (a freelance trainer who had introduced me to the methodology); and a full-time colleague who was undertaking a two-year in-service training course in experiential learning.

In the event, some people did not take up the initial invitation, and we were left as a group of eleven – eight part-time qualified workers and three full-time qualified workers (including myself) who were to be the collaborative inquiry group.

The group comes together

The first phase of the project, as I saw it, was to enable the group to get to a point of valid decision-making as quickly as possible. This simply means that all parties have access to the relevant information for their decision-making purposes; that they understand the questions; that they have time and space to formulate an opinion and that they are able to trust the group enough to express their own views, hear others' views and give and receive feedback.

While everyone knew at least three other people in the group, and most people knew the majority very well (having previously worked together through intensive learning processes), it was important to facilitate the development of this new group.

The day started with a feature which became one of the norms of our large-group meetings. As the facilitator I shared the agenda with the group and we negotiated it. Quite predictably, the first day's programme was unaltered at this stage. The key features of the 'programme' of Day 1 were:

1 Getting to know each other.
2 Exploring the method; comparing it with traditional research methods; understanding Rowan's research cycle (Reason and Rowan, 1981: 98).
3 Exploring the roles that could be played.
4 Exploring commitment (time, etc.).
5 Exploring own feelings, thoughts and ideas about the project.
6 Making a decision whether to participate or not.
7 Deciding 'where to from here?'

The aim for this first day was to enable people to appreciate fully the equality they were being offered in this process. This was achieved in two major ways. First, it was important that everyone had as much knowledge about the method as possible, to facilitate their decision about whether to participate and prevent me, the initiator, being 'an expert' to the group. The second was through identifying what roles would be needed in our process and creating the opportunity for these to be distributed throughout the group, and the flexibility for roles to be changed over time.

The roles initially identified were both formal and informal. The formal roles included group facilitators (for planning and running our days together); organizers/administrators (for written communications between meetings); group recorders (to take notes of the whole group process); personal recorders (every member agreed to keep a recording of their own experience in the project and make this available to me for my dissertation); distress managers (we agreed that every co-researcher was available to play this role for any other co-researcher in the group); and two co-researchers agreed to take on the role of meeting with members who were absent from a day meeting in order to help them 'catch up' on what they had missed.

The informal roles can be summarized by saying that every co-researcher was supported and encouraged to be themselves and offer this as freely as possible to the whole group. In particular, the skills of giving and receiving feedback, asking questions, supporting colleagues and commitment to the project in whatever it may demand.

By the end of the day, all those who had participated had committed themselves to the project with a degree of excitement. Six people had been unable to attend this first day and arrangements were made by seven of those who had attended, to contact them and facilitate their joining us on Day 2, a month later.

The group agreed what the next day should include, and two of them volunteered to facilitate it, involving me in their planning only if they needed this. At this stage I had very mixed feelings. On the one hand I was very excited that the group had so quickly picked up the reins of equal responsibility. On the other hand I was worried that this was occurring too soon. Did the two who were to plan and facilitate our next day understand the methodology sufficiently to carry out their task? I then asked myself whether this worry was really a reluctance to let go of my power as 'the expert' and 'the initiator'? I realized that this was an example of the risk-taking necessary for me to empower the co-researchers, and reasoned that the sooner I took some of these risks, the sooner we would achieve a fully collaborative research group. In the event, the two facilitators, at their request, met with me to talk through their understanding of what needed to be done, before planning the details of the day for themselves.

The design of our project

Day 2 included a recap on the methodology which served to include a co-researcher who had been unable to attend the first day, and also as a 'rooting' for the rest of the group. We spent most of the day deciding what we would research. I gave the group some ideas to 'start the ball rolling', then we split into two small groups to add our own suggestions which were collated into one list when we came back together. Some examples from this were:

- Research on experiential learning.
- Research on validating learning from experience.
- Research on our own processes of learning.
- Research on competence – what this is and how it is acquired.
- Are full-time youth workers born or made? Can people change?
- How people think and how it affects their learning.
- How to use a portfolio for our learning.
- What skills, and level of skills, do you need to start as a full-time youth worker, and what can be left to acquire on-the-job?
- Generalist youth work skills versus specialist youth work skills.
- Management of learning.

The large group again divided into smaller groups to select two favoured research topics which produced a short list in the whole group. From this the group selected the research area to be 'How People Learn' – researching our own processes of learning. We reasoned that routes to qualification were learning processes and that whatever form they took, they should be informed by knowledge of how people learn. We, therefore, decided to research this for ourselves, in order that our ARQ could be designed on what we knew to be true about how people learn.

Day 3 saw the introduction of our final 'new' co-researcher and was the start of the research 'proper'. I distributed copies of John Heron's chapter 'Validity in co-operative inquiry' (1988: 44–59) and had prepared a summary list of the validity procedures on a flip chart (see Table 8.1). The group spent time exploring these fully in order that there was a consensus of understanding. At the outset we saw them as a list of independent procedures. Our experience showed us that many interconnect or overlap and act as mechanisms of, or reinforcements for, each other, as indicated below.

Table 8.1 *Heron's validity procedures*

Research cycling
Balance of divergence and convergence
Balance between experience and reflection
Aspects of reflection
Falsification
Balance between chaos and order
Management of unaware projections
Sustaining authentic collaboration
Open and closed boundaries
Coherence in action
Variegated replication

Source: Heron (1988)

Research cycling we agreed to mean the interaction of experience and reflection for both the individual and the whole group, ensuring that individual experience and reflection was open to influence by collective experience and reflection, and vice versa. Our method was to use small groups and the whole group for experience and reflection phases, with individuals having solitary reflection phases for recording which was then shared in both the small and large groups. This interactive research cycling process sought to keep the whole group maximally informed of what was happening for individuals.

The use of small groups and the whole group as well as constant interaction with individuals was a method by which we created a *balance between experience and reflection*. We spent a day together as a whole group, once a month; small research groups met weekly for two and a half hours; individuals spent time recording their experiences. Collective experiences were both experiential and reflective, the balance initially planned by facilitators but constantly open to change in response to evaluations of what was happening and perceived to be now needed. Such amendments were always collectively agreed.

The *open and closed boundaries* procedure served to reinforce our interactive research cycling in that we aimed for a closed boundary system – using co-researchers only, to work through anything the research experiences brought up for us. From the beginning, we were aware of the difficulties of this. For example, if the project raised 'old agendas' for an individual, there was a likelihood these would be discussed with non-researchers (for example, family, friends). Both despite and because of this, we challenged ourselves to see how far we could maintain a closed boundary system. One of the other validity procedures helped us in this – the *management of unaware projections*. This we took to be identifying and dealing with unresolved emotional or psychological historical episodes, what we refer to earlier as 'old agendas'. We were all aware of how easily our current experience and perceptions are 'contaminated' and influenced by our subconscious. It was important that these were prevented from distorting or contaminating our research. We did this in two main ways. First, we agreed that each would be available individually to support and help work through any issue which the research had raised and we felt unable to deal with in a grouping. This would be shared with the group, if deemed relevant, whenever the individual felt ready to do so.

The second method was our use of a 'Devil's Advocacy' procedure. Its intended use was as a *falsification* mechanism, but it acted simultaneously as a powerful tool in the management of unaware projections. The process was simple. When an individual or small group was sharing their learning, another small group acted as Devil's Advocate, asking probing questions which assumed the contribution(s) to be 'wrong', 'illusory', 'colluding', 'confused', 'dishonest', 'inaccurate', or 'contradictory'. Another individual or small group acted as supporter(s) to the contributor(s), ensuring all parties heard each other, sharing an understanding of both questions and answers. They also ensured the contributors were not overwhelmed by the pressure of the process and that the Devil's Advocacy procedure's purpose as a method of falsification was to ensure that what was being researched and learned, was real and relevant for individuals, the group and our work together. It aimed to prevent us from stating something to be true simply because we wanted to believe it to be so. As a result of this, our findings are only those things we *all* came to know to be true and could provide evidence for.

The Devil's Advocacy process was also helpful in enabling us to differentiate between the various *aspects of reflection*. It helped us describe our experience more clearly – what had happened for me, for you, for us; and also to evaluate our experience – what it meant for me, for you, for us. Furthermore, it increased our efficiency and effectiveness in practical reflection – deciding how the next phase of our work could, would, or should be influenced by these reflections.

Another unintended outcome of the use of the Devil's Advocacy procedure was the role it played in the *balance between convergence and divergence*. At its simplest, we understood this to be the balance between similarities and differences in what we were researching, how we researched it and how we recorded it. We originally built this procedure in as follows:

1   We agreed the purpose of the research to be that it would inform the designing of an ARQ (convergence).

2 We generated a list of possible research areas (divergence).
3 We agreed to research 'How People Learn' (convergence).
4 We generated a list of learning methods (divergence).
5 Individuals chose a skill of a full-time youth worker they wanted to learn (divergence).
6 Small research groups were formed based on similarity of learning need (convergence).
7 Small research groups designed a learning and research process (to include validity procedures), which met all their learning needs. (This produced convergence within the small groups and divergence between them.)

The unexpected benefit of the Devil's Advocacy procedure was that it became the key mechanism by which convergence was created for our findings, in both the small research groups and the whole group. It was the method by which individual 'truths' were tested out collectively and collective 'truths' were tested out with individuals.

The various roles which needed to be played within the Devil's Advocacy process were constantly swapped around. This prevented any individual becoming labelled or stuck in a particular role. It also ensured a distribution of power and therefore equality within the group. This was one of our ways of *sustaining authentic collaboration*. All other roles were also rotated and undertaken by all members of the group – from facilitator of collective experiences, to being individuals' supporters for the management of unaware projections. All decisions were taken collectively. Individuals' decisions and experiences were constantly shared with the collective for confirmation and/or validation.

A further major mechanism in sustaining authentic collaboration was the *balance between chaos and order*. The purpose of this validity procedure was to ensure a balance between maximum creativity and an orderliness that enabled the research process to be worked through for the whole group. Chaos usually occurred when we were generating ideas, or questioning what needed to be done next. The phases of order emerged from this when we decided that decisions and plans would now have to be made.

The chaos was often initiated in the early stages by my refusal to decide or inform the group on what needed to happen. The process of creating authentic collaboration therefore contributed much of our chaos. As the research project progressed, our need for chaos helped us sustain authentic collaboration by keeping us wary of allowing any one individual or subgroup to determine and impose their 'order' on the rest of us.

The remaining two validity procedures – *coherence in action* and *variegated replication* – we perceived as checking devices. Coherence in action meant more for us than what use we could make of our learning in designing an ARQ. It was also about what learning we were using in our actions as researchers and in other aspects of our individual lives. We believed that our learning was real when it had changed our behaviour.

The challenge of variegated replication was to communicate our experience in a way that would enable others to replicate it. This chapter is one of our attempts. It was therefore aided by the editorial skills of Peter Reason, and will be judged by yourselves, the readers.

The next stage in the process was for each of us to identify a skill that a full-time youth worker had to have, that we felt we did not have. These were listed on a flip chart and individuals with similar learning needs formed small groups which came to be known as the small research groups. These groups were given space to work out a four week action plan by which they could start learning the skill. Everyone in the same group used the same method which had to include the validity procedures. This created some convergence, while the fact that each group was using different methods provided some divergence. We each agreed to record individual progress to bring to our next day meeting.

This became the pattern of our research – small research groups meeting once a week for eight months, and large group meetings one day a month. The whole group days consisted of the small research groups feeding back on the developmental progress of individuals' learning; the effectiveness of the validity procedures used; any 'results' – things we were learning about how people learn; and any amendments to the learning methods as a result of these types of feedback. The day meetings also included space for individuals to further develop interpersonal skills; space to explore group issues; space to identify changes of formal roles and re-deciding that our structure for the research project was still relevant.

Creating and maintaining collaborative relationships – the co-researchers' perspective

The initial issue for us in the establishment of collaborative relationships was how we came to be included in the research project. Annette used some selection criteria to invite people she knew to have a vested interest in an ARQ. While this was obviously excluding (for those who did not receive an invitation), it was necessary unless the project was to work with up to 800 people!

In detailing her selection criteria in the invitation letter, Annette indicated that she valued some of the skills we had and therefore valued us. This was in itself both empowering and including for those of us who received an invitation to participate.

The design of Day 1 was intended to enable us to decide for ourselves whether we wished to be included or not. This was achieved through an explanation of the methodology and how it differed from traditional research. We also learned about the level of collaboration Annette was seeking – that we would all be equally involved in deciding what we would research and how we would research it on ourselves. Despite the fact that this freedom was daunting (and for those expecting a more directive method, confusing), everyone was excited about it. As a result, everyone present on the first day committed themselves eagerly to the project.

Another feature of the first day was that everyone shared their reasons for being interested enough to attend. In addition to the fact that we all wanted an ARQ (some in order to participate in one, others because they wanted to be associated with providing one) we all had additional motives. Some people were intrigued to explore the new research method; some were curious to discover how their developmental groupwork skills were to be used and developed; two people (including Annette) were involved in academic courses for which the research was necessary; someone else had used new paradigm methodology previously and now wanted the opportunity to try a 'full- blown' collaborative experiential inquiry for the first time. The discovery that our personal motives were as valued by Annette as our common motives was a highly motivating factor.

Through later reflection, we realized that this acceptance of the individual's right to be either 'in common with' others or 'different from' others was a feature which maintained the inclusiveness and collaboration of the co-researchers. It may be important to explain here how this came about.

On our fourth day, the small research groups shared their learning to date with the whole group. This was done using a Devil's Advocacy procedure as previously described by Annette. It was on our joint days, when these small groups came together to share and further reflect on our learning that the convergent and divergent balance was sought.

Having completed this process during Day 4, we then collectively sought to summarize any further learning which had occurred as a result of this reflective process. The most significant item emerged in discussing what we had learned as a result of the balance of convergence and divergence. Two individuals had in fact not stuck to the 'convergent' plan of learning agreed within their small research groups. Despite some initial concern that this would 'mess up' the process, it became evident that it did not matter as there were enough individuals who had used the same methodology for convergence still to exist in the total group. The increase in divergence this created added weight or validity to the further learning that had occurred, namely – all learners need opportunities to reflect on their own, to reflect with others, to be committed to their own learning by owning the need for the learning.

Furthermore, the discussion about 'ownership' brought about our discovery that learners need to own the process by which the learning takes place, to have the power to choose that learning process. This power to choose we came to call the right to be 'in common' with others or 'different from' others. As stated earlier, it was a significant mechanism in maintaining the inclusiveness and collaboration of co-researchers.

We have been able to identify ten norms which indicate how this acceptance of this right worked in our reality.

1 The whole process was designed by the whole research group.
2 Whole group meetings, while planned by the facilitators, were always negotiated with the whole group and were open to amendment as a result.
3 Any individual could stop the process at any time and negotiate a change of direction or emphasis.
4 Anyone was free to play any of the formal roles we felt necessary.
5 Individuals identified their own learning needs to work on.
6 Everyone kept a personal portfolio of their experience on the research

project. This enabled everyone to feel that their experience and contribution was as valuable as anyone else's.

7   From the beginning, the sharing of feelings was as valued as the sharing of thoughts or ideas. This prevented an intellectual hierarchy from emerging.

8   The falsification procedure we used was that of Devil's Advocacy. It enabled everyone to feel equally able to give and receive feedback to anyone else.

9   Our processes for the management of unaware projections included 'provision for every co-researcher to be available for all other co-researchers. Everyone was used and equally valued in this role. Our Devil's Advocacy procedure allowed for a group method for the management of unaware projections, resulting in everyone feeling equally included in the process of empowering another.

10   Co-researchers who experienced crises in other areas of their lives did not leave the research project unless it became inevitable (two members eventually left due to serious health problems of their own, or of a dependant). The norm was to seek help and support from co-researchers which would keep the individual included for as long as possible.

The other major factor which served to keep people included was that co-researchers used their interpersonal and groupwork skills for the benefit of others. Some examples of this were one individual's ability to rephrase what had been said to facilitate understanding; someone else's ability to formulate and articulate questions; another person's skill in keeping the group to the point; another co-researcher was able to share their vulnerabilities early, enabling the rest of us to follow suit quickly; and everyone proved to be skilled in balancing challenge with sensitivity.

Issues and difficulties in maintaining collaborative relationships

As a result of all we have just said it is true to say that the project became 'ours' quickly and remains so to this day. However, there were two elements of our research experience which served to have an excluding effect on co-researchers – albeit with differing final outcomes.

One of these elements was John Rowan's questionnaire entitled 'A dialectical paradigm for research' (1981: 107). This was sent out by Annette following Day 2, to be completed for Day 3. The purpose of the questionnaire was to provide a common framework for some of the personal recordings throughout the period of the project, by taking 'snapshot' pictures of ourselves at each phase of the inquiry cycle – Being, Thinking, Project, Encounter, Making Sense, Communication (see Rowan, 1981: 98). The questionnaires provide an opportunity for inquirers to explore their efficiency, authenticity, relationship abilities, political awareness, views of power and oppression, personal philosophy and world-views, and how each of these was affecting or might affect the research.

There was a variety of reactions from the co-researchers, including feelings of intimidation, annoyance, anger, frustration and confusion. It made people feel excluded because they did not understand all of the language or the concepts (for example, 'the paradox of rhythm and the rhythm of paradox'); this made some wonder whether they had made a mistake in including themselves in the research project. Despite this, most people attempted the questionnaire.

On Day 3, we had the space to talk about the questionnaire and the feelings and reactions it evoked from us. Annette explained her dilemma in discovering the questionnaire after Day 2: should she send it out with the questions rephrased and who was to say her interpretation was correct? Should she not send it out and miss the opportunity of our 'being' stage being recorded at the appropriate time; was she being arrogant in assuming people would not understand it?

The result of this discussion was that the group moved forward. Despite the initial excluding effect, co-researchers felt more included, more equal in their collaboration with the initiator than they had done previously. There were five reasons for this. First, those who had attempted to answer the questions had emerged with a sense of achievement. Second, the discussion on Day 3 about the questionnaire provided an opportunity for everyone's vulnerabilities about the research to be brought into the open and begun to be dealt with. Third, we finally accepted that Annette was not necessarily more fluent in the methodology than we were (there were questions she too could not understand); and also that she was capable of making mistakes. Fourth, we gained a greater knowledge and understanding of each other as people and co-researchers. Lastly, but not least, we came to a shared understanding about the meaning of some of the language and a deeper understanding about the methodology. While the exclusivity of the language had initially had an alienating effect, we worked through the issues together and increased our level of collaboration as a result.

The other element which had an excluding effect on some people was the behaviour of two of the co-researchers. These issues were addressed as they arose and also formed part of our reflections in the 'making sense' weekend. In analysing these situations we identified that the individuals concerned were perceived by other co-researchers to be 'looking out for themselves', without regard for the other co-researchers. One was perceived as trying to grab power, the other as demanding group time and attention for themselves. In the former case, the group felt that we had been offered an equal share of power in all aspects of the research project and therefore perceived the individual's attempt to take power from the initiator as a threat to our own power, and also as disruptive. It was disruptive because any power the individual wanted, was there for the asking – but it was never articulated as a request or something to be negotiated with the group. It emerged as a refusal to use their own skills, withhold knowledge or a hijacking of agendas. The fact that this co-researcher focused on Annette for the power battle was also excluding, as it was the group which held the power – not the initiator. We saw this as an attempt to make the structure hierarchical and therefore non-collaborative.

In the second case, the co-researcher's commitment waxed and waned, resulting in non-attendance at both some small research group meetings and meetings of the whole group. When attending, this person made demands for large amounts of the group's time and attention. While this was willingly given, it became apparent the individual was unwilling to give similar time and attention to other individuals, the group's issues or its work. The effect of this individual's imbalance in 'giving and taking' was to make several co-researchers feel excluded.

Issues of dependency

At the start of the research project, there was obviously a high level of dependency upon Annette, primarily regarding the research methodology. This diminished as we learned through our own experience of the project that the initiator meant what she said, that is, that *our* experiences, ideas and feelings were as important as hers.

It also diminished as we perceived the initiator less as an expert and more as an equal co-researcher. A major turning point in this was 'The Issue of The Questionnaire' as it became known. This led to co-researchers using each other for support and to answer queries, rather than addressing these solely to Annette as had occurred in the first four to six weeks of the project.

Similarly, the six co-researchers who had taken on the role of facilitator or co-facilitator of the whole group days experienced a dependency on Annette for the planning of the earlier ones. However, as we gained more confidence in this role, and our understanding and knowledge of the process deepened, this dependency diminished to the extent that Annette was not involved in helping to plan or facilitate any part of our Days 5, 6 or 7.

Another early but major dependency was the group's need to have a 100 per cent consensus on every decision – majorities, however overwhelming, were not sufficient. It was only on Day 3 when this was articulated by some co-researchers to be a block to progress, creating frustration and eating up valuable group time. Once the dependency was identified we could talk it through and came to the conclusion that unanimity in decision-making would be sought, but where it proved to be unobtainable in the time available, a majority decision would be taken. With the additional mechanism that individuals could renegotiate the decision on the following whole group day, this proved to be a constructive way forward.

This mechanism was a typical example of our reluctance to allow any issue to remain unresolved. The benefits of this were that they provided many opportunities for growth and development resulting in being a rich source of information for our research on 'How People Learn'. These situations also allowed everyone to feel valued, in the knowledge that no one researcher's issues were less worthy than another's.

The structure of the research project was one of interdependency, without which it could not have worked. Our collaboration as a whole group depended on the small research groups being reliable in carrying out what they had decided and agreed to do. Our dependency on having access to the small research groups' learning was such that on the occasions a small group had not done its work, space was provided on the whole group day for this to occur. This ensured that all researchers were able to contribute their own experiences to the project, and that all researchers had equal access to learn from each other's learning.

Where issues of dependency were short-term, they proved to be supportive and empowering mechanisms which kept other co-researchers included and helped them become more assertive collaborators. The willingness to learn and act for oneself meant that rather than remain dependent on a co-researcher's skill, individuals began to use each other as role models and worked to develop these skills for themselves.

A major outcome of our research was that we realized that when we accepted responsibility for our own learning, dependence grew into an interdependence which allowed for greater critical reflection and further growth. Without accepting this responsibility for our own learning we remained dependent, resulting not only in the lack of development of new skills, but also in a gradual abdication of use of our current skills. In other words we either moved forward through interdependence, or backward through dependence.

Our discoveries

Our project was to explore 'How People Learn', through discovering how we, ourselves, learned. Our purpose was not to add to the body of academic knowledge per se, but to discover *for ourselves*. The utility of our findings lay not only in how they might inform the design of a qualification route: much of the learning was put to use as it was learned, through the continuing opportunities which the inquiry provided. In this way, the project remained true to new paradigm research methodology itself (see Torbert, 1981: 443).

One of the complicating and dilemma-creating factors of any form of action research is the contaminating effect of the method itself. Tandon succinctly summarizes this:

> If the situation under study undergoes changes by the process of study, then what is finally studied is something different from what was originally intended. . . . To that extent, it contaminates the situation it purports to study. (1981: 301).

This did not prove to be a dilemma for us. Because we were looking at 'How People Learn', the changes – the learning – that took place, far from contaminating our research, provided us with the very material we needed. Furthermore, it was this 'contaminating' effect which brought us to refine our topic to that of looking at the role of reflection in how people learn. This evolution, or refinement, occurred as a result of our 'Devil's Advocacy' procedures on Day 4. After each small research group had undergone the Devil's Advocacy process (that is, had critically shared their learning), it became evident that despite the divergence of learning methods chosen by individuals, 'reflection' was a convergent factor; that is, all members of the group had spoken about reflection having played some part in their learning. We decided to focus on this during our next experience and reflection cycles.

Our 'making sense' weekend was facilitated by three co-researchers. We spent the majority of this time in two newly-created small groups. The intention was to share what we had each learned and the role that reflection had played in this learning. This work was supposed to have been done in pairs from the small research groups prior to the weekend. Unfortunately, not everyone had accomplished this so the process was undergone during the weekend in the 'new' small groups.

Each small group recorded those items of information that were true for all members of the group. Towards the end of the second day, we came together as the whole project group in order to identify anything which was common to all members of the entire project. The information delineated here is *only that which proved to be true for all of us*; that is, the information which was a result of: 'convergent thinking reflecting on divergent aspects and perspectives, refining each and bringing out the common ground they illuminate' (Heron, 1985: 137).

As in earlier stages of the project, members were not permitted simply to feedback. One member of the group recorded the experience and all others were involved in active, critical discussion with the 'learner'. The process throughout was one of supportive confronting (see Cunningham, 1988: 178–9). As a result, further learning occurred through the 'making sense' phase itself – this is detailed below:

1   I learn most effectively with others:
    (a) My learning stems from a choice I make – whether to learn or not!
    (b) I have to have a common language and/or common experience with the others which allows me to test out whether I trust their judgement. If I do, they become significant and powerful enablers of my learning processes.
    (c) The common experience may be nothing more than a shared learning process.
    (d) Learning is a balance of convergence and divergence. It is a cocktail of meanings, perceptions, values, thinking styles and items to be learned, some of which I need to have 'in common with' others (convergence) and in some I need to be 'different from' others (divergence).
    (e) I need others to watch/experience me perform and give me honest feedback on that performance. This feedback, to be most effective, needs to be given by interrupting my performance, or immediately on completion of it.
    (f) I have to trust the integrity of the others; that is, that they will not consciously deceive me, but share their truth with me, willingly and openly.
    (g) I learn most effectively when the others offer perceptions and perspectives which are different from my own, creating some divergence.
    (h) I need others to be critical of me and confront me with my contradictions, collusions and illusions.
    (i) When others are confronting me, I need to trust that their motives are to aid my learning. When I am sure of this, the learning is powerful. When I doubt this, the pain outweighs and impedes the learning.

(j) I need interdependent relationships as these facilitate my learning. I need to avoid dependent relationships as these lead to my regression.

2   I learn most effectively when I take responsibility for it:
(a) I need to value that which I am seeking to learn.
(b) I need to value the learning method for my learning to be most effective. However, I can alter my perception of a method I do not value, long enough to enable me to learn something I value learning. I can therefore impede my own learning by choosing not to make this effort.
(c) I need to be in a receptive frame of mind to receive critical confrontation.
(d) I need to be open as well as honest – articulating what I think and feel at the time these occur. Articulation after the event is less powerful for my learning.
(e) I need to deal with negative experience and/or feelings, as unresolved issues impede my learning and/or 'contaminate' my 'truths'.
(f) Despite the importance of others in aiding my learning, I need time to reflect on my own.

3   Some general discoveries:
(a) Unlearning is much more difficult than learning and generates more powerful emotions.
(b) Unresolved issues will continue to manifest themselves in all aspects of our lives until they are resolved.
(c) Learning increases with each interplay of shared and solitary opportunities for experience and reflection.
(d) Learning has occurred when new action/behaviour follows.

Applications for ARQ

The group is currently involved in a project with Brunel University to design an ARQ (now called an Accessible Route to Qualification). Some of the principles which arose from our research and that we are seeking to apply are detailed here:

1   The structure of an ARQ needs to be based upon small groups of people committed to their own and each other's learning.
2   The participants need a shared understanding of the principles and practices of 'How People Learn'.
3   The participants' first phase of learning needs to be the development of skills which facilitate learning: the skills of reflection, critical confronting, group dynamics, critical awareness – to name a few.
4   Opportunities for prior learning to be accredited are necessary. This validates and values the participant and her or his experience. Additionally, it leaves her or him free to devote energy to those things yet to be learned.
5   The motivation and commitment of participants will be vastly increased if they have the power to choose what to learn and how to learn it. This is possible to achieve (as we did in our research project) because we found it

to be unnecessary for all participants to be learning the same things simultaneously.
6 The ARQ needs to build in ample opportunities for collective experience and reflection as well as individual experience and reflection.
7 The ARQ needs to provide opportunities for experiences to be witnessed/experienced by others who will give open and honest feedback to them on their performance. This feedback needs to interrupt the performance or occur immediately after the performance.

A final reflection – a collaborative perspective

We must actually own some amazement at what we have managed to achieve to date as, perhaps predictably, the process was not without difficulties. The first problem has been one of time. The project has been affected by the difficulty some members had in participating in all that they had committed themselves to. While this is in part an indication of being part-time in youth work, there were many members who lived up to their agreed commitment and gave more besides. It is certainly an issue that will need addressing within an alternative route to qualification. The second aspect of the time dilemma was the decision for the whole project group to meet once a month. This was decided in order to meet the needs of one of the participants. However, most participants articulated that the group would have gelled more quickly, and participants would have achieved more challenging relationships with each other more quickly, had the group met fortnightly – at least for the first four to six months.

The second major problem area was that of familiarity with the method. The initiator of the project was concerned that we reach a stage of shared understanding as quickly as possible, but not before the method was understood. In the event, she risked handing over power too early for some – and too late for others. As a result some members in the first category still disbelieve that this was her first experience with the method, and the power battles that have occurred reflect members in the second category!

We now believe that much of this could have been avoided had we spent time at the start of our inquiry further developing our skills for critical awareness and confronting. The initiator personally knew all members to have these skills (obviously to varying degrees); indeed it was one of the criteria she applied in selecting whom she should invite to participate. However, she expected group members to use their skills earlier than they chose to do so. It is our belief that spending time together focusing on developing them further would have created the trust necessary for people to use them earlier. This is, therefore, the third major critique we have of our process.

New paradigm research methodology

The choice of research method was based on the level of congruence Annette perceived between new paradigm research methodology, her experiences as a youth worker, a trainer, her values as an anti-discriminatory practitioner and as an individual human being. Our experience in using the methodology has not only confirmed that earlier perception, but increased our conviction. Boud and his colleagues (1985) would say that we have 'appropriated' this learning, that is, that we have taken it into our value system.

We recognize the danger we are in of becoming one of Reinharz's 'converts, embracing the new 'truth' . . . in other words, mystified anew' (Reinharz, 1981: 425). However, we do not believe we would remain alone with this conviction if more youth and community workers were aware of the methodology. The process of youth work is experiential learning. The process of training 'in the field' is experiential learning. It would seem that it is only the college-based training programmes leading to full-time qualification which are less experientially based than they could be. As Heron himself says: 'Seen in another light, co-operative inquiry is a way of systematically elaborating and refining an experiential learning cycle' (Heron, 1985: 128). It follows from this (and from earlier discussions) that the skills for this research methodology are already held by youth workers. Ironically, Torbert (1981) argues that if social scientists develop these skills they can enable others to develop them:

> As social scientists master the behavioural, emotional, disciplines necessary to research their own lives with others, they can for the first time help others in this regard as well. (Of course, there is no guarantee at present that social scientists will be among the first to choose to master these disciplines). (Torbert, 1981: 443)

Some of us may say they are already behind others in the human development field in 'mastering these disciplines'. Certainly, our collaborative group consisted mainly of people who would not consider themselves to be academic – most have not had the experience or opportunities of Further or Higher Education. The initiator was a novice in the methodology. Yet between us, and without the supervision of an expert in the field, we have made an honourable effort and we firmly believe that *any* group of people committed to a particular area of research can employ a full blown collaborative inquiry method.

We are aware that much is being done within the Youth Service to promote and encourage more research to be undertaken. While there are many ways in which people learn, we believe the new paradigm methodology to be *the* research method for youth workers. At the very least, it should be given a higher profile and offered alongside the traditional paradigm. For in 'people work' we are never very far from the 'thorny' issues of emotions, values and beliefs.

> Integrity requires that we learn to speak unselfconsciously about value in matters of fact. We need to develop, in the arena of values, inquiry methods that are as sophisticated and powerful as the methods of science have been in matters of fact. (Kolb, 1984: 227)

9

Making a Space: a Collaborative Inquiry with Women as Staff Development

Lesley Treleaven

Source of the inquiry in familiar echoes

Some time ago I asked a woman I work with 'How are you?' 'Terrible', she replied, breathing out with some relief. 'Fragile', another had replied earlier in the day. 'OK . . .' another had answered on the telephone, obviously holding her breath hoping, 'but just as well you didn't ask me yesterday. I'm coming to the conclusion that I'm going to have to look for another job. I just can't work here any longer.'

There were emerging questions as I listened to the stories of women working in the University. What is it about our workplace and its culture that creates this sense of alienation? What accounts for the difference between times of despair and times when women experience their work as satisfying? How do women move between these times? What sense of agency – of capacity to determine our own lives – can and do we have in this workplace? What would need to change in the organization so that more women could feel that what they did here was not so deeply in conflict with the organization's cultural norms, explicitly in policies and structures, implicitly in everyday practices and procedures? How could we work creatively and have that full expression of our selves included as a contribution to the cultural diversity of University life?

I was interested in exploring these complex, practical challenges in the everyday life of women working in the University. They were questions which I frequently encountered in my own practice as a feminist working in a large organization, and they seemed perhaps to be questions underlying many of the stories I kept hearing.

'If you want something to happen, make a space for it'
(Movement for the Ordination of Women, Australia)

This chapter focuses on the ways a group of women in one organization made a space to explore these issues so that something could happen. In the account that follows I outline my assumptions in initiating a collaborative inquiry group and how I shaped the inquiry framework to generate participation. I describe the space we created as participants told and retold stories of their experiences of critical incidents in their working lives. I discuss the development of collaborative processes and how they changed during the life of the group. I illustrate how through this process of collaborative inquiry we developed new understandings that informed our actions towards changing some of our situations as women in an organization. Finally, I sketch some of what is happening in our workplace by making an innovative space for such a collaborative inquiry.

In offering this account of the inquiry, I am aware of constructing a 'fiction' as I systematically select and represent events and interpretations that are unavoidably partial (Clifford and Marcus, 1986: 6). Such ambiguities are heightened by the use of story itself as a valid form of researching people's lives, for the story-teller's narrative is a version that cannot be claimed as the only truth; yet the issue of subjectivity (Hollway, 1984) – how we each construct and give meanings to our experiences as we dynamically position ourselves in relation to others – is present within any human inquiry and its representation. Thus Hollway (1989: 42) argues for a shift of focus 'from methodological conditions that will enable the discovery of truth to one of understanding the conditions which produce accounts' that are themselves located within discourses, history and relations.

This account has developed over the 18 months of our collaborative inquiry. I have drawn on multiple sources of data: a description of the preparatory stage which I wrote at the time and submitted to the group; tape recordings that were made of all meetings, discussions and interviews; notes that I have taken at these sessions; written reflections and evaluations by group members, and extensive journal entries. Given the group's inquiry into its own processes, there was little disagreement as participants read my developing text. We engaged to clarify meanings until in recognizing 'Yes, that fits with my understanding', we can claim validity for the participants of this current account.

However, some 12 months after first putting this chapter together, I now find aspects of this narrative problematic, for it presents our work through a framework that for me is constantly changing as I continue with the research, especially as I examine the discourses within which our meanings were shaped. This situation serves to highlight that the account's validity is both partial and temporary; not peculiar to this piece of research, except perhaps that it is acknowledged.

Locating the inquiry as staff development: beyond the deficit model for women

As a Staff Development manager, responsible for providing a range of training and development opportunities for all staff in the organization, I was in a position to initiate an inquiry process that derived from questions in the working lives of women. Participation in such a programme is intimately related to the development of individual women on staff as well as to the organization's development. Furthermore, Staff Development is required to make specific provisions for women: under Australian legislation the University is required to submit Equal Employment Opportunity (EEO) and Affirmative Action (AA) Plans for monitoring by Government. However, in Australian Higher Education where most forms of staff development are either short courses delivered within the institution or professional development activities such as conference attendance, upgrading formal qualifications or sabbatical leave, a collaborative inquiry approach is significantly different.

Many affirmative action training programmes rest on an assumption that women have a skill deficit. Thus it is argued that training women in management skills which have traditionally been exercised by men and learning assertive communication, meeting procedures, and financial skills will help address the imbalance between the sexes in the middle and senior levels of an organization.

The major difficulty of this deficit approach to training lies not only in its failure over the last ten years to produce significant change by increasing the presence of women in management (Still, 1993), but also in the ways it has continued to perpetuate the masculine as a norm against which women are judged negatively (Marshall, 1984; Burton, 1991).

A further difficulty with such an approach is that it individualizes and often psychologizes women's absences and silences in management. Training is therefore directed towards developing the competencies of the individual woman and often assumes she needs to overcome psychological traits which are undesirable in positions of responsibility and decision-making. This happens because psychological characteristics attributed in Western society to the masculine (competitive, aggressive, rational) are privileged over those attributed to the feminine (co-operative, nurturing, emotional). In turn, these gendered polarizations produce a web of systemic practices and normative values which permeate an organization (Burton, 1991; Blackmore, 1992). For example, a female manager concerned with the working conditions of her staff and who was herself under-resourced for the workload, was seen as 'not coping' when she made repeated requests for change. Her angry outburst at being stalled by managers recursively fed the gendered beliefs that she was irrational and emotional: 'When you've put a rational argument on paper, I'll look at it', she was told. However, it was only after a health crisis and her worker's compensation claim, that several new positions were allocated to the section.

The systemic effects of gendered practices show up individually in women's alienation from the organizational culture, and organizationally in the absence of women in leadership positions. How could an innovative form of staff development begin to address these challenges?

By initiating a collaborative action research group as a leadership development programme for women it was possible to move away from both the deficit training model and traditional approaches to management training. Furthermore, by focusing on leadership rather than management, it was possible to move beyond hierarchical position and status as the only source of organizational power and influence, to action research the diverse ways women's leadership is expressed (or can be reconstructed) in the workplace.

Theoretical roots

A collaborative action research group provided a suitable framework for this staff development programme. In contrast to an instructional or skills-orientated course, participation in action research informed by critical theory (Lather, 1986) can be empowering as participants engage directly in understanding and acting on issues of concern in their own lives.

The collaborative inquiry rested on assumptions that women managing complex lives already brought evidence of considerable management skills. A further assumption was that women's socialization in awareness of others and their listening skills (Tannen, 1990) could be affirmed and revalued in a collaborative inquiry process. So in lieu of structured training, my interest lay in facilitating the development of a listening space in which the women participants themselves would shape the inquiry, so that appropriate structures and processes would unfold over time: 'I don't have a plan which I carry out, step by step. I move step by step and the design takes shape, with no image of the final form' (Stevens, 1970: 118).

Barry Stevens' statement could have been written to describe my way of action researching. It is also a way of proceeding which I have observed in the everyday lives of many women whose activities are often highly divergent, and where a linear way of being is neither desirable nor feasible. Such a familiar way of inquiring is only recently being accorded the status of a research methodology and the knowledge gained being accepted as valid. The variously named academic approaches of emancipatory collaborative action research, participatory research, co-operative inquiry and now human inquiry (Lewin, 1946; Torbert, 1976; Heron, 1981b; Reason and Rowan, 1981; Carr and Kemmis, 1986) is a field strangely populated by men. Women's development of these research approaches (Mies, 1983; Stanley and Wise, 1983; Lather, 1986; Fine, 1992, to name only a few) have come principally out of feminism. Their contributions, often in Women's Studies and on the margins of professions or disciplines dominated by traditional (positivist) scientific research, have been less visible (Ward and Grant, 1991: 262; Fine and Gordon, 1992: 2). The work of such writers has, however, strongly informed the theoretical framework of this inquiry.

Furthermore, women have brought to this inquiry skills in producing knowledge for action (praxis) that has come out of practical participation in the community, health and welfare sectors, in environmental groups and in education's equity and disadvantage programmes. Here their commitment to service provision and political change has come ahead of documenting processes which they have not necessarily conceptualized as research, though their community consultations, submission processes and needs analyses rest solidly on research activity, frequently as collaborative inquiry. Perhaps too, women activists have mistrusted academic theorizing as Grimshaw (1986) claims, for theory has so often failed to reflect women's experiences.

Such an absence is apparent for me in action research theory. For example, I have found the circular model of sequenced steps – plan, act, observe and reflect, then re-plan (Kemmis and McTaggart, 1988) to be an incomplete approximation of action research, taking no account of implicit structure embedded within a situation, nor allowing for other forms of knowing beyond that of the conscious, rational mind. This is to ignore knowledge constructed in many forms: from emotions and the body, in creative expression (story-telling, poetry, drawing, music and dance), from synchronicity (coincidence to which meaning is given), and from dreams: 'Aware is not just knowing, it's getting in touch, letting my knowing be felt all through me, before moving on' (Stevens, 1970: 117). Such a gestalt approach differs markedly from that of Western rational enlightenment man.

In approaching the inquiry, I brought with me commitments to feminist praxis – knowledge produced about the world for action to change it equitably – and a concern with how we find out what we know – the domain of methodology and epistemology (Harding, 1986). I did not expect to find some universal truths that could be uncovered by 'objectivity', but instead accepted that knowledge is itself a social construction. I valued lived experience as a source of constructed knowledge and drew, in part, on the significant contribution to the women's movement of feminist consciousness raising (Weedon, 1987; Fonow and Cook, 1991). As women told their stories and were heard, they developed understandings of the political issues embedded in personal experiences and ways to change

> our subjectivity through positioning ourselves in alternative discourses which we produce together: the feminist practice of consciousness-raising takes as its object women's experience of our lives . . . [The] very process of sharing experience with other women leads to a recognition that the terms in which we understand things are not fixed. Experience is not something that language reflects. In so far as it is meaningful, experience is constituted in language. Language offers a range of ways of interpreting our lives which imply different versions of experience. . . . It is possible to transform the meaning of experience by bringing a different set of assumptions to bear on it. (Weedon, 1987: 85).

Later in the inquiry I drew on other postmodern contributions to feminist theory (Hollway, 1984; Walkerdine, 1984; Riley, 1988; Grosz, 1990; Fine, 1992) and its critique (Luke, 1992) as I tried to find a useful place to stand in relation to the politics of feminist theory and practice.

Shaping the inquiry framework

In my experience of collaborative inquiry, it is in the initiatory phase that participation is generated and shaped by attention to two formative dimensions. One is the creation of a space where the inquiry can happen by establishing a framework of enabling structures. The second is the development of a context within this space that is itself productive of collaborative processes. Hence the preparatory phase of the inquiry needs to be congruent with collaborative processes and grounded in responses to exploratory dialogue. Furthermore, language is used with awareness of its capacity to shape participation and collaboration.

Within one organization and its culture

An obvious design factor was locating the inquiry within one organization. It enabled the group to research collaboratively the network of discursive practices as they operate within a single organization and in the process to reduce some of the isolation of women in their workplace. However, the masculinist culture and politics of the organization within which the inquiry was sited was itself a subject of inquiry and this produced complex challenges in establishing a suitable inquiry framework.

With a history as an Agricultural College, and later as a College of Advanced Education, the fields of study in this institution have been traditionally staffed by men. All senior appointments, with the exception of the Dean of Nursing appointed 12 years ago, are still held by men. The student culture is still dominated by conservative rural male values that have successfully resisted change towards including a diversity of values despite the appointment of the first female academic staff in 1968, the arrival of female students in 1969, and the College becoming a University in 1989. A new School of Humanities may well attract further diversity in 1995.

With a background of strongly held traditional attitudes towards women among those staff who have little experience of accepting women as peers or those administrative staff recruited from the Defence Forces located nearby, there was hostility to Affirmative Action; one story may suffice.

A year before this collaborative inquiry, leaflets advertising staff development activities were widely distributed across the campus. The full programme included the first courses specifically provided for women under the EEO/AA plan. In one tearoom there was an angry reaction. One of the academic men concerned 'shot the whole bundle of programmes in the bin', with a comment designed to threaten women who stepped out of their prescribed roles by acquiring the assertiveness skills advertised in one of the courses. None of the women present in that tearoom registered for the programmes.

To reduce the backlash that negatively labels women's participation in specifically targeted programmes, we found it effective to adopt several strategies. First, a memo to all senior and middle managers informed them in advance of the programmes, drew their attention to the EEO/AA framework within which they were provided, and requested their managerial support by encouraging their female staff to nominate (under NSW legislation EEO responsibilities are written into all supervisory and managerial position descriptions). This worked as a defensive strategy but did not produce affirmative action on the part of managers encouraging staff to participate. Second, a written invitation to participate in staff development programmes was sent to each female member of staff on the payroll, in preference to the practice of advertising in the organization's information newsletter.

Additionally, women's participation was encouraged by personal contact.

Ironically, the decision not to advertise the inquiry publicly, together with my status as an insider rather than as a consultant invited by an inquiring management, constructed the collaborative inquiry initially without organizational visibility. The political benefit, cost and strategic implications of that choice however, places the responsibility on the inquiry group itself for making our action research public knowledge.

Within an unstructured space

The inquiry framework needed to provide a space within which there was freedom from the tyranny of structured training as increasingly demanded in the Australian education and training environment determined by government policies based on foundations of economic rationalism. Since the collaborative inquiry was located within a staff development programme, it was necessary to develop a framework that supported open exploration rather than instruction or structured training.

Paradoxically, in making space for the spontaneity and creativity of inquiry, I have observed that implicitly structuring processes emerge. They are not the explicit structures that a facilitator may lay down in order to direct, focus or control the direction of the inquiry (though at times we have indeed negotiated such facilitation). They are implicit ordering processes that are responsive to felt need, enable expression and lead to subsequent action. They will be highlighted in the following account of our inquiry.

With interested participants

In representing the nature of a collaborative inquiry to possible participants, I was aware that it could evoke anxiety with its lack of structure, excitement with its open-endedness, and uncertainty with its unpredictability regarding specifically desired outcomes. I wanted to include those who were new to such a research process while representing it adequately so that self-nomination would lead to a workable group. I therefore spent a lot of time making initial contact with women personally or by telephone, talking with them about their experiences as women working in the organization, sharing the patterns that I was making from these conversations, and exploring what a collaborative inquiry could offer them. This 'getting in register', actively listening and using language that expressed their own concerns and interests, enabled me to establish the inquiry framework in response to participants.

The invitation phase is not a task that can be delegated, but one integral to the formation of the collaborative group. My hunch is that this is because language itself shapes the inquiry, just as attention to recursivity (every part of the inquiry process informing the next) informs the development of an appropriate framework. This process is well illustrated by how I moved in the initiation phase from sending a written invitation for self-nomination, to a verbal invitation which women could accept or reject, to an exploratory dialogue which created participation in a space of inquiry. As I engaged in numerous conversations with women individually, I was able to develop my understanding of what I heard in this phase as:

- Women had their heads down and tails up – they were isolated and busy.
- Women wanted to know how they could manage themselves and others in an environment where thriving/surviving in a gendered culture were the greatest challenges.
- Women wanted to find ways to bring leadership in an effective and powerful way to diversify the organizational culture currently based on dominant masculine norms.

The group was therefore formed on a self-nomination basis from the open written invitation, telephone contact and the informal networking of the snowball technique (where those interested are asked to suggest others who may be interested). Yet one participant later interpreted my personal approach as 'an acknowledgement that I had something to offer . . . knowledge is power'. The snowball method has obvious limitations as she indicated: I know [now] of people who would desperately like to be included for support and for other information. Because you've been part of it, you can now identify people who could be interested.'

From dialogue to collaborative group: an introductory session

Scheduling the initial meeting was well worth considerable consultation to find the optimum time for those who had indicated interest. By placing it around both sides of lunchtime, staff could readily opt to participate in different parts of the introductory programme. The three parts were developed in response to the dialogues of the initial stage and further illustrate the recursivity of collaborative inquiry. The first purpose was to bring together women who were scattered across the campus as many had indicated their isolation. The second was to provide time over lunch for informal networking. The third, and primary purpose, was to clarify the staff development opportunity and for women to make an informed choice about participating in the collaborative inquiry of the Leadership Development Programme. In this third phase, women addressed the following questions:

- What is the inquiry that we each bring to this group?
- What is collaborative action research and what might it mean in terms of this inquiry?
- What do we need of each other to work together? (group commitments and ethics)
- How shall we arrange our inquiry process? (logistics)

Within the introductory group, most women were not only comfortable but welcomed an opportunity where they did not have to fight to be heard and could have uninterrupted time to gather their thoughts on issues that they wanted to explore collaboratively. Some women chose only to take up the chance to network briefly with women from other faculties, while a few others considered that issues applied equally to men and women in their department.

Participants

Who then formed the first collaborative inquiry group? Eleven academic women from four of the five faculties: the sciences (agriculture, horticulture, food technology and science) have a long tradition of male appointments; nursing has traditionally been staffed by females. Thus the group was well placed to explore workplace issues of sex and gender in a university.

Some aspects of the group are particularly homogeneous: all are white with English speaking backgrounds reflecting the lack of diversity in female staff appointments at the University. Heterogeneity in the group has come from our differing families of origin and current personal circumstances, enabling us to consider more widely the issues of race and class and age that braid with gender. The group includes tenured, contract and part-time staff; some on staff for 25 years, some only recently; thus there are senior lecturers, lecturers and tutors. Some have held management positions within their faculty or on University committees, others have no experience of these aspects of University life. The variations of employment provide opportunity to examine differences within the University, across faculties, and over the period of the inquiry while the University underwent restructuring at national and internal levels.

Awareness of the organizational culture from which participants came into the collaborative inquiry group was vital. While an academic culture often promotes tolerance for ambiguity in the pursuit of knowledge and supports individual freedom to engage in that pursuit with considerable autonomy, the administrative culture of the institution as a whole and that of some faculties demands accountability and demonstrable productivity on a task basis that is often very closely supervised. This has placed pressure on women who have internalized this supervisory gaze or experience it through peers. For these reasons, a transition period within the life of the collaborative inquiry enabled some participants to revalue other ways of being that were unfamiliar in the context of this organizational culture but not unfamiliar to them in their everyday lives:

> 'As you all know I was very loath to join this group. I resisted like hell [laughter]. I was a scientist, and issues were cut and dried. There was an acceptance that we ran meetings with an agenda. What we've been doing here, I was doing with mothers and women friends. That wasn't of any value. It's interesting how set groups [those with a set agenda] come to the same place as we have without structure.'

Story-telling as inquiry

Stories as a rich expression of human experience have been approached by researchers in several ways: by Peter Reason and Peter Hawkins (1988) as a source of explanation and expression in human inquiry; by Frigga Haug (1983) as a way of examining collective memories; by Jean Houston (1987) in connecting people with myth as inspiration; by qualitative researchers like Bronwyn Davies (1989) using story to reveal how children construct their gendered worlds; by Maria Mies (1991) in consciousness raising as a way to tap collective stories; and by Carolyn Steedman (1986) who examines biography (her own and her mother's) to unsettle theories of working class and gender that fail to be useful in explaining these two lives.

In making a space where we could tell our stories, we moved slowly through an organically structured process which enabled stories to emerge. How did we do this? Quite simply, we began in the introductory session by introducing ourselves by name, faculty, how long we had been here and the gender patterns in the faculty. I took on the role of facilitator by phrasing some core questions like these which were written up on a whiteboard (to the side of the room so it did not dominate the more informal space). Thus a space was systematically made by each woman giving specific data about her workplace. We then moved to a reflective and more interactive process of sharing a little of what it had been like working here drawing on our experiences, by asking: 'What draws each of us here this morning?' With this sequencing, we drew on our own and others' stories quite readily.

One night, preoccupied with the research methodology, I had the following dream:

> I am looking for the big myth. . . . I am on my hands and knees in the desert. Coming up out of the ground is a mat of very tiny, newly emerging wildflowers. It is like a cut carpet, and I take great care in examining the new shoots. It is hardly one big myth. More like many, many stories that make the mat.

I felt confident that through the gathering of these incipient blooms, it would be possible to discern a larger pattern, though it might stop short of the mythic and reveal something more everyday!

So we began our inquiry by telling our stories, using our experiences of the everyday situation to hand as a rich source of data for critically examining different working lives in the one organization. We did this in several ways: initially in a spontaneous, unstructured space that I find useful to refer to as the emergent phase. Later, in a residential space we used a highly structured process (Southgate, 1985), which I have called Listening Circles (Treleaven, 1991), as a way of bringing our daily life stories into the group, as a basis for reflection, understanding and action. More recently, we have been revisiting old stories in new forms as we have moved in a spiral outward from the experiences of individual women into action at the organizational level.

Stories emerging in the space

When we met to begin our inquiry, Edith arrived in a rush straight from a meeting carrying a bundle of papers.

> 'Can I tell you where I've just come from and why I'm late, it's relevant I'm sure to the group . . . I've just been to see the editor of the centenary history because I was

asked to write a history of women for it. I'm feeling very tentative because I don't know whether it'll be accepted as I've written it because the people I've interviewed have not always . . . but I've tried to be quite fair in putting in what they've said rather than my own judgements . . . thought I've been quite objective and scientific and I'm aware that people will say you've been very emotive . . . I'd like to read some of it to you if you want to hear it.

It's very much a commentary on motting . . . Motting is basically to do with initiation: "The 1971 intake was motted. . . . The activities included: being run through the sheep yards like sheep with human dogs barking and biting, being sold to 'Sirs' (third years) by auction to be their slaves, being taught the College war cry and traditions, general mental torture and physical unpleasantness, eating cornflakes like sheep, scrubbing the front drive with a toothbrush, swimming through pig effluent, all spitting into a bowl and then being fed it back again (it turned out to be egg white)" [Parker, 1991, p. 372].

I didn't put in bum running . . . some of it's almost unprintable . . . based on the barstardisation in public schools . . . The staff were always amazed that the Home Economics girls participated really willingly and fully in motting because they chose to. I don't think they really did choose to. Some of them really remember it as wonderful but some of them remember it being absolutely terrifying. There was one girl who reported that she got blood poisoning from swimming through the pig stuff and she was too scared to go to the local doctor because the press were around, so she went to the Penrith Hospital where they wouldn't know she was from the College . . . It's been modified because all this brought on a government inquiry in 1983 . . . but what happens when you bring rules in to change things is that a whole lot of things go underground and a lot of this is still happening.'

The point is not whether both girls and boys were motted, nor whether such bullying behaviour was 'just boys being boys', but rather the nature of the masculinist culture and its domination. Working in an institution that tolerates such practices serves to illustrate the underlying values from which many women feel alienated.

In constructing the story of women's places, changing roles and unchanging status in the institution's 100 years, Edith had conducted research based on 330 questionnaires and interviews with male and female members of the Old Boys' Union (a telling title itself). From Edith's herstory and a well known refrain, 'Hawkesbury and women are like oil and water, they just don't mix', we began to see how the roots of our group's inquiry were deeply bound up in the institution's history.

Such synchronicity at the beginning of our inquiry affirmed the unstructured process of making space for a way of inquiring that was not the function of planning or controlling content. One story evoked another, creatively releasing the memory of others. We told our stories as a way of building relationship, and the meaning of the stories was not hurried by applying analytic processes in the early stage. Thus a crucial aspect of participation was to allow the process of collaborative inquiry to unfold. It is a way of engaging in 'a process, which is seen as simply happening and is not to be forced or achieved by an effort of the will . . . [it] is a mixture of attentiveness and contemplation' (Ulanov, 1983: 41).

Stories facilitated by the Listening Circles

In a residential soon after the inquiry group began, there was sufficient time for an activity which invited participants to share one trauma, trivia and joy (Southgate, 1985) from their experiences of working in the organization. This developed into sustained story-telling that broke many of the silences between women in the one workplace:

> 'I was supporting a workshop where a group of senior staff used, with much glee, the particularly sexist metaphor of pack rape to describe the lack of collaboration in a recent decision taken to introduce condom vending machines. I found their behaviour both inappropriate and offensive. I decided later to speak to the initiator about my own response as a means of engaging responsibly with change. His initial reaction was "It's none of your business what men say in the privacy of their own company." He had forgotten that there had been three women present, and that it was a University activity, even if it did include dinner. Three months later, it was still on his mind; he called me over at a staff function: "I've thought about what you said. I can see your point." Since then I haven't been in the position to work with those staff . . . and I hadn't made that connection till now . . . I do feel vulnerable breaking my silence . . . but if we don't tell these stories, and they aren't part of our research to point to how men construct women and relate to women's issues, then how can we demonstrate that things need to change?'

We debriefed, analysing the individual stories we told in the Listening Circles in a structured group process (for a detailed example see Treleaven, 1991). This format enabled us to move our collaboration into identifying themes embedded in groups of stories and advocating ways of acting/responding that we elicited from our 'reading' of the stories themselves. For instance, Donna heard in one group of stories women's tendency to go and talk with a colleague when a difficulty arose. When a man responded instrumentally to this interpersonal approach by dealing with the situation impersonally through bureaucratic or formal procedures, she noted that the women felt frustrated at not being heard. These stories illustrated how the dominant culture operated to produce taken-for-granted communication patterns that worked against these women's preferred style in given work situations. In advocating possibilities, Jill recognized that the women seemed cautious of on the spot responses, and noted that some of the best resolutions had occurred when the story-teller was aware of her feelings, bodily reactions and had taken time to consider a way of approaching the situation, occasionally using an advocate. There was concern in the group that adopting the norms of organizational communication was to negate our diversity, and thus further questions for inquiry were posed. These engagements with the data by the group also highlight intersubjectivity in collaborative inquiry quite explicitly.

Stories of spiralling action research

Stories have interwoven. As emergent processes within different individual stories have unfolded, changes have been produced in the everyday lives of some of the women, in the way the group conducts itself, and more widely in the horizontal diffusion into parts of the organization. This centrifugal process of diffusion has brought stories of action research cycles which could be described as spiralling outward, connecting women within and beyond the group.

Mary arrived one time waving our local University Information Newsletter: 'Has anyone seen this? There wasn't a single female staff rep elected for next year on any of these committees.'

We asked some obvious questions about how many women had stood, and then why there had been none standing. Some of the group recognized their need to find out how the nomination process worked, what the politics were of standing as a female staff member across faculty interests or as the faculty rep who was female. We discussed what membership of such committees required in terms of workload and prior experience, women's expectations of themselves as committee members and by contrast, the reported behaviour of men in terms of what they required of themselves in performing such membership roles in terms of time commitment and preparation for meetings. Participants told stories of the ineffectiveness and frustration of being token committee members, and also of the need to have (at worst even) a woman's presence that circumscribed some limits around the men's behaviour from equity perspectives. One spoke about how offering the different viewpoint sometimes meant that another woman more likely to agree with the men would be invited to join a committee or working party on subsequent occasions. Few of the inquiry group had experienced being a useful or valued committee member at University level within this masculinist organization. Yet committees were acknowledged as the major decision-making forums, so the debate continued about how women were going to change what we could not take part in effectively.

Some of us acknowledged resistance to take up committee membership because of our sex; we did not want to be positioned as the token woman/women; we did not believe that it was an effective location in which to use our energy in wanting to change practices; nor that we would have much influence to do so in this institution. If requested to join a committee, we wanted to join on the basis of what we had to offer. Naïve perhaps until that value is established. In summary, women examined their silences and found that we wanted to find other effective ways of being heard that did not position us as targets of sex discreditation (Spender, 1992). We wanted to explore how we could create space on our own terms, rather than respond to others' needs (for a token woman). What were these reconstructed forms of participation?

Some months later Linda brought a story continuing these themes.

'The Dean walked into my office last week and said, "I'd like you to join the faculty management committee. We need a woman and I value what you have to offer." I told him firstly that I didn't want to be invited on as a woman, and secondly that I had no evidence of him valuing me. I shut the door and confronted him about what I'd been upset about last year: why I'd sometimes chosen silence; how it was difficult not only to represent a whole different agenda, but also a whole different way of doing things . . . the story that I'd told in the Listening Circles. He listened but he didn't engage with the personal, only the safe intellectual stuff about representation and token women . . . I told him I'd have to think about his request and get back to him. That was ten days ago and it feels really powerful to have been able to take that time to work it through rather than give him an answer straight away.'

In previous meetings of the inquiry group we had explored how we said, 'yes', on the spot, to the constant stream of requests from staff, students, family and friends. We recognized that this was part of our socialization as girls and the expectations of us as women: 'It was also extraordinarily difficult to hold that space open. I could hardly . . . bear to pass him in the corridor I felt so guilty.'

We understood that such ways of responding continually placed us in a reactive position. We found it useful to explore ways of 'putting a foot in the door before it slams shut' so that we were not locked in to others' demands of us and later regretting it. Some members of the group decided to take time to consider requests before giving an answer, and others told stories of using administrative procedural knowledge to refuse requests that were not our responsibility. What we wanted was a sense of control over our own lives, enabling us to make choices about what we did want to put our energy into, rather than finding ourselves doing things without any apparent choice.

Linda continued with her story in another meeting of our collaborative group:

> 'I got the other women in the faculty together and we discussed it [the Dean's request] . . . we agreed that the position should be rotated . . . and that it was important that we find other creative areas we could be involved in.'

It was at another lunchtime gathering that Linda spoke about a research application that this newly formed group of women had put in for seed funding by the University.

> 'We decided in the faculty that we didn't want to necessarily respond to the requests about committees, and we can't respond to all the requests made of us anyhow. So we started to ask as a group, what's the best way to use our own energy, to set our own agenda? We made a clear decision to do things in the faculty that came out of a feminist consciousness. And that's a direct result of this inquiry group, I wouldn't have approached the other women without this structure of collaboration . . . They were like the spot fires we talked about at the beginning.'

We recalled many times an image of spot fires that I brought to the group after bushfires had threatened our house. The process of horizontal diffusion seemed to be well described by the metaphor of sparks being ignited in joint collaboration, starting another fire at some distance separate from but connected to the same source of energy; of the fires clearing heavy loads of undergrowth, forcing seeds open in the heat, and encouraging the cycle of bush regeneration.

This particular cycle seemed to have gone full circle and spiralled outwards: not only were the women successful in their submission for research funding, but later Linda joined the new faculty management committee. After a major restructuring of faculties and a promotion, this time it was Linda's own choice to stand as a woman. She said she felt able to represent different points of view in that forum, due to recent leadership experiences in the absence of the Department's director, and that she would be one of few staff able to bring a sense of the department's history to impending decisions. Rather than a response to a hierarchical request from the Dean, this was now a test of putting herself forward.

The ways in which Linda reconstructed the nomination process and her options for decision-making as a committee member negotiating back with the staff group, were part of the rich tapestry of spiralling action research for herself and the other inquiry participants. It was not surprising, given the multiple and conflicting discourses within which women are located in their working lives that, for all this resolution, there was a hint of ambivalence and an escape clause in Linda's account. Her throwaway line 'I can always leave' was soon forgotten.

Developing collaborative processes

Developing collaborative processes is a deliberate and dynamic activity. As initiator, facilitator, convenor, researcher, housekeeper and participant, I have been differently positioned during the life of the group, and as the group reshaped itself during the course of the inquiry. For example, as a staff development professional with group skills, I positioned myself as facilitator of the transition process into a collaborative inquiry. The women unfamiliar with collaborative action research and those anticipating a more instructive mode also positioned me as facilitator first of their learning, and then of the group process.

Trust as a basis for collaboration

In the transition phase there was a need to build trust between the women in the group and trust in the process of inquiry. We did this initially by sharing our hopes and concerns related to the inquiry and its process, examining what commitments we were each willing to offer, and what we would each require of ourselves and other participants in working towards fulfilling our stated interests. We explored our varying understandings of confidentiality and its relationship to trust as it ranged from personal trust to the political complexities of trust in the workplace. Within the inquiry group, we were committed to sharing power (though of course we had people or topics that tended to dominate), and to individually being responsible for creating value from our participation in the collaborative processes (though there were times when we forgot and just felt impatient!).

Our approach was typical of feminist practice with explicit agreements that enabled each woman to have space in which to be heard without interruption (though in practice we had enthusiastic interrupters from time to time), to speak only for herself, and to respect each participant's contributions to the inquiry as confidential. These ways of working together were significantly different from the workplace culture, reflected in a passionate poem that I wrote in a burst of energy after sitting reflectively in a meeting with some very vocal men:

No longer am I willing
to fight in the cut and thrust of conversation
to make space to hear my voice
assuming my contribution is most worthy.

No longer am I willing
to state my piece
when the ebb and flow means it no longer connects
to what is now present.

No longer am I willing
to allow invasive thrusts to consume my energy,
to divert the flow of creative revelation
that stillness can allow.

> I will speak where I can be heard.
> In here is a resounding cave.

(Treleaven, journal 1990)

The development of trust and group bonding are conditions which fundamentally influence participation and the extent to which people are willing to explore issues through situations grounded in their experience. Initially, it was relatively easy to assume and hence draw upon trust based on our shared identity and structural subordination as women (Finch, 1984). However, the boundaries of trust have been mobile; expanding and contracting as each woman has implicitly or explicitly assessed her position given varying contexts; sometimes women have spoken in the absence of another member from her faculty, others have chosen occasions not to trust colleagues in situations where there is professional competition, and women have made varying choices about trusting the group when their personal situations have changed, seeking either support or time out. Trust is particularly highlighted in this inquiry group because it is located within the one dispersed yet common workplace. Unlike a group formed beyond the boundary of the workplace, perhaps on assumptions of past and continuing friendships, what is at stake differs for members of an inquiry group formed within an organization. The only commitments to each other as colleagues are those that we choose to construct from our membership of the inquiry group and shared commitment to the project(s) of the group: these are richly diverse, often contradictory and always changing. Thus, a collaborative workplace group has the advantage of placing the research within the many complex and ambiguous social situations that impact significantly on women, as we think and act, feel and respond – sometimes choosing silence, other times to tell our stories.

Creating a listening space

Establishing conditions that would generate a listening space in the workplace was a significant aspect of developing collaboration. The venue chosen was relaxing, away from the classrooms and staffrooms where there were interrupting demands and no confidentiality. In contrast to a training room with audiovisual hardware and chairs at desks, the room was furnished with low comfortable chairs, an attractive mat under the large coffee table where there was a collection of books, articles, flyers and fresh flowers. The meeting place did not change and thus the taken-for-granted security of re-entering that space over time became conducive to engagement in a different way of being. 'One of the reasons it could stay relaxed and different' Susan thought 'was that the space wouldn't be invaded. Quite often you might sit round at work in this way, and then a man or someone else, it didn't have to be a man, would walk in and it would be different. Whereas you knew here that wouldn't happen . . . it was part of the calm.' Women would tune in as they entered, very often bringing a similar topic.

A simple but varying lunch was provided, and in the sharing of food and drink some of the implicit time-honoured associations of the ritual were evoked. (As for the housekeeping role, I sometimes wished I knew exactly how many to prepare for!)

We agreed to work with the ambiguity of women's busy and complex lives, by meeting monthly at first, and later fortnightly, for two hours over the lunch period. We agreed that as there was no common lunch time across the campus, women would come when they could, and stay as long as they could, as often as they were able, given the multiple demands made of them.

In one sense the space was like a family lounge room with people coming and going throughout the two hours, grabbing a bite to eat, sharing something of their current story, hearing some others, and departing to go on with their everyday activities. Thus my intention at the outset of the research project was that it should be:

> Action researching as a way of being – in our lives, at work, at home, such that the inquiry is a form of consciousness that we bring to our daily interactions, rather than a research topic we undertake. I imagine most of the action researching taking place outside the group itself, as praxis. (Treleaven, journal 1990)

Yet, there was an expressed commitment by the women to the inquiry group and their ongoing participation over 18 months. Unlike other programmes that necessitate confirmations of attendance, the women took responsibility for their own attendance, placing it high in their competing priorities. At the beginning of a new year when teaching and study timetables changed, two women discontinued after approximately six months and another joined on her return from leave. Usually there were six of the nine women able to make our on-campus meetings. It proved easier to attend a dedicated period off campus for sustained inquiry but I found trying to plan these as a full group extraordinarily trying.

Keeping the space open

At each meeting there has been a productive gathering, unrelated to the size of the group. Rather it would seem, that the significance lay in keeping the space of inquiry open and active, using the opportunity of differently constituted groups to make more spaces for different aspects of the inquiry, 'with each day having its own ecology' as Edith put it. One time we talked of daughters and of their expectations, assumptions and anticipated choices in the interaction between work and family; but we did that only when we were a group of mothers with daughters. It allowed us to reflect on our own patterns and to reconstruct some of the meanings that we had attributed to our own lives, by placing them in a historical context.

Including body and emotion

As participants with emotions and bodies which are themselves often ignored sources of our knowing (Crawford et al., 1992), we made space in our workplace inquiry to speak about our bodies, and to allow ourselves and each other to express emotions that accompanied our stories – anger, despair and grief as well as joy and its accompanying laughter or well-being, have been catalysts to new understanding and acting. Helen noticed the frequent use of apology, theorized its impact, then devised a forfeit that had us laughing each time one of us fell into using 'I'm sorry' and had to take up an appropriately repentant position on her knees. When we considered our inquiry process, Helen drew our attention to her impression that 'we spend as much time laughing as we do crying', and my listening to the tapes confirmed this view. Menopause and breast cancer wove through some of our lives and so were present in our inquiry as people and structures demonstrated varying capacities to respond.

Extending the spaces

In addition to our basic meeting pattern, the group took up the opportunity for off campus residential workshops which are a structural feature of our Staff Development approach to in-depth learning (for a literature review see Brown and Atkins, 1988). Each year, a residential of two days with an overnight stay was designed collaboratively within the group, including its location to take account of family responsibilities. The first was highly successful in enabling the development of trust and the focus of the inquiry. The second clearly reflected how the inquiry had developed to challenge individual women's career decisions and had moved towards collective action on projects of shared interest. Another supportive space was made off campus in the informality of a participant's home one day during a particularly difficult period.

Widening the collaborative network

As part of resourcing the Leadership Development programme, women beyond the group have been invited to share their stories with us. At the second residential, a senior academic from an established university narrated her career story, weaving together aspects of study, employment, mentoring, personal decisions and strategies. Engaging with her story from a less masculinist culture provoked new questions and challenged the extent of possibilities for some of the women. Invitations like these provide a new staff development alternative to the 'expert' role of the external consultant; offer resourcing congruent with the form of collaborative inquiry and an orientation towards inquiry rather than didactic or solution-orientated approaches. They also enable networking that is professionally based, in contrast to the consultancy situation.

With external participation, it is possible to avoid several of the implicit dangers of collaborative inquiry. Participants are not assumed to fully resource their own inquiry but are able to draw on knowledges beyond the group (Reason, 1988: 104). External voices can also present a challenge to the paradigms within which the inquiry/co-researchers are located. For example Susan, who struggled against drawing on procedural knowledge as a valid way to create change between people, came to accept for herself the value of such knowledge in this wider context of the senior woman's story, and her later stories reflected changes in action.

Initially I was reluctant to 'impose', from outside the group, others' theory or even my own interpretations when the research project was basically conceptualized as a grounded theory approach (Glaser and Strauss, 1967) where theory is constructed principally from data. However, as I explored these issues with the group, with my supervisor and in the literature (Adler and Adler, 1987), I came to see the obvious – that there is no *tabula rasa* (blank slate) to which data are gathered anyhow. Rather, validity rested on participants engaging in collaborative inquiry, constructing new understandings that informed their subsequent and thus different actions which were themselves examined in the spiralling research process through later stories. My tension of holding back as a fully participating co-researcher began to disperse; only to resurface when I found that I was the principal person bringing theory to the group. Again, I adopted the self-reflexive approach of bringing this to the group; they saw our inquiry as testing out whether such theory was useful for them.

Shifts in collaborative processes

There have been several transitions in the collaborative processes within the group. Many of the early stories that participants brought into the inquiry group allowed 'a slow sorting through' that was reflective for the story-teller, a source of 'data' for collaborative inquiry by participants, and increased our knowledge of the organization and its power regimes. The listening space was characterized by the spontaneity of content in the form of story, critical incident or diffuse conversation.

What distinguished the early stories was 'the high emotional energy, almost as though a lid had been taken off the stories that we had been living over the top of'. Mary expressed the oppositional bonding process well: 'I've made the connection with others and it's pain, the way they've been treated', and carried it beyond the group in a project she later initiated, demonstrating what Lather (1986) refers to as catalytic validity – the capacity of the research process to impact participants' knowing of their reality and energize them towards self-determined action. Our stories included images and laughter in unexpectedly creative ways that shifted our ways of being with our everyday experiences of working in the institution; the endorphins released in our laughter often helped us lighten up.

Our collaborative processes have also been characterized by responsiveness to what has been brought to the group in ways that are affirming and sometimes challenging. When Edith was preparing a talk for a Women's Network event, she ran it past the group. When Jill dismissed her life as really quite trivial, some of the group challenged her, and she recognized the sense of loss she felt now, having been 'a clever child destined for great things'. We have collaborated around specific situations in our working life, theorizing, exploring options and tracking their development in later stories. Stories often provided material for examining power relations as we experienced their effects on our employment and promotion. As a sense of identity politics developed, our collaboration broadened and action research projects were established with women beyond the group, as, for example, in seeking a permanent women's room on campus.

Our engagement in the group has been with respect and an ethic of care for the well-being of those present (Gilligan, 1982). Problematically for the research, this has sometimes meant avoiding conflict (Brown and Gilligan, 1992) and not examining our differences. It is a complex situation: some women want to protect the supportive context of the group given our particular workplace; some have chosen to respect the different styles of handling conflict and not confront those who have indicated their unwillingness; some have discussed differences beyond the group.

However, some women have a strong desire to reconstruct new identities as women aspiring to or holding positions of leadership in such a way that would, of themselves, challenge the masculinist norms of the University. In recognizing that this is no easy task, some of the group were impatient to move to a reconstructive phase. Such a phase required a change in the collaborative relations to include the exploration of difference without avoiding productive conflict or confrontation.

We came up to this place many times as a group. At our last meeting for the year we had a powerful exchange of difference between two women. We explored through dialogue the choices they made about strategies and whether these compromised their (feminist) principles, such as lobbying senior staff to sponsor an invitation to a female to apply for a recently advertised position. This challenging exploration of feminist politics energized significant change in my own understanding of the assumptions and difficulties in 'shared identity' and how to proceed with a feminist project; in particular, I concluded that action now needs to be directed towards gender inclusive behaviour by men if we are to further women's participation. The group also learned that we could dialogue through differences in ways that were productive even while they challenged our values profoundly.

Analysing and documenting collaboratively

It would be inaccurate to describe the analysis and writing processes of this project as a separate linear phase. Indeed, much of our work in the inquiry has relied upon collaborating to name issues as part of the spiralling movement into action both in the workplace and in our own ways of framing our situations. Some of our analytical work has been informed by theory that we have brought into the group. Some of our theorizing has emerged like the wildflowers in my dream, coming up out of the ground of our inquiry within the group as a second order analysis (Guba and Lincoln, 1989). My own systematic third order analysis of our data for discourses and subjectivities within which the stories are located, is a further source of material for collaborative inquiry and is thereby producing a fourth order analysis.

Yet as a researcher, the interests in theorizing and documenting our inquiry are my own. One is as a co-researcher with my colleagues examining the experiences of women surviving/thriving in a masculinist organization, especially as we take action towards inclusive forms of participation and leadership; a second is as a staff development practitioner in action researching my professional practice with our client groups; and the third is as a postgraduate student undertaking a doctoral research project with a collaborative inquiry methodology. In practice, this nesting of activity one within the other somewhat like Russian dolls, has been an effective way to bring together parts of my life that would otherwise have been fragmented. It has not proved problematic as much as it has required the reflexivity (Stanley, 1991b; Steier, 1991) of observing the interaction between positions, and reflecting on and engaging in the ambiguities and contradictions, as a part of the research process itself. I have often used my journal for reflection and explored with group members their expectations and perceptions. It has been a fortunate reminder that research is not a tidy, clear-cut activity but that at some level, the subjectivity of the researchers is always present.

There is demonstrably a new level of collaboration required for the documentation of our inquiry. Here each of us is positioned differently: in part, because of individual research and study commitments in disciplines outside our inquiry. The energy in the group is most strongly constellated around participation in the process of the inquiry and its integral action outcomes. As a researcher wanting to see an account of our praxis made more available, there are new challenges to develop congruent forms of collaboration in this phase. It will also be necessary to negotiate in practice the ethics discussed in principle when the group was forming. These include confidentiality, visibility in the text, rights of the co-researchers to varying interpretations, intellectual property, publication, and the production of a thesis for an academic award.

Outcomes and ownership

Participants' ownership of the outcomes of our collaborative action research are embedded in our ways of inquiring and in the collaborative processes that unfold towards action. As one woman reflected: 'I don't take on a project because I have to but because I want to.' Outcomes and ownership are integral to the recursive nature of our work together.

While some outcomes were expected and formed the basis of the proposal, others could not have been predicted given the generative nature of the inquiry. This has made the work most exciting.

Broadly speaking, participation in the collaborative inquiry is producing changes that can be clustered in three domains. First, there are the anticipated staff development outcomes in individual personal and professional development. Second, there is the potential for long-term organizational change: by drawing attention to the gendered culture and reconstructing forms of leadership and participation that are inclusive of women. Such 'outcomes' are quite diffuse; they also meet resistance and elicit backlash (Faludi, 1991) since they fundamentally challenge existing regimes of power. Third, there are research outcomes: in the substantive issues of the research, in the research methodology, and for participants as researchers (for a full discussion see Treleaven, in preparation).

Individual outcomes

In recognizing our own stories that we share with other women in the organization and in listening to stories which are different, women's isolation has been reduced and collaborative networks that live well beyond the inquiry group itself have developed. The politics of this is a significant issue given the organizational culture.

Since much of the research method relies on viewing stories of critical incidents as 'data', by gathering such data over time it has been possible to evaluate outcomes through actions located in later stories. These stories are understood in the context of being produced within women's subjectivities rather than being viewed at 'face value' as fact. Changes in the stories themselves and changes in how women later retell their stories indicate shifts in women's construction of their subjectivities. Linda's stories of joining the Faculty Management Committee, for example, are illustrative of the process whereby the story-teller herself takes up a new position (Walkerdine, 1984) as agent in relation to an earlier situation concerning women's participation and leadership.

While information as new knowledge is certainly one outcome for participants, an outcome for some has been a transformed position with respect to their identities and possible futures as women in academia. It is reflected in women asking new questions and making space in their working lives to engage with them. As a nurse, Rosemary gained from her inquiry colleagues and our residential visitor a sense of 'Now I know what it means to be an academic', and the decisions that she makes have begun to come from this perspective rather than from trying to advance her career by gaining approval from her seniors.

Bani Shorter suggests 'initiatory seeing comes in the performance of ceremonies that draw on myth, metaphor and ritual; it is not the mere acquisition of knowledge, nor the subsequent interpretation, but a change of being' (1987: 41). Such a transitional space has been evoked and available in our listening to the stories in our meetings over lunch and in the Listening Circles, where we have explored ways of positioning ourselves differently and collectively sought to produce alternative discourses within our workplace. This kind of integrated learning can enable an ontological shift – a change in the way of being of a person – and is one of the fundamental claims to the validity of this inquiry process as a form of Staff Development.

Another significant individual outcome is related not to women changing but rather to women in the group affirming the various ways in which their values and approaches are brought to their work in a culture that they feel devalues their differences and strengths: 'I just didn't know how much strength there was in coming together like this; I've come to see the value of putting in my twopenneth worth when I try to get people to work together in our department: it really is a worthwhile contribution.'

Diffuse outcomes

The most intriguing outcomes are in the ways that women are acting together to challenge the basic assumptions of the dominant masculine values in the organization. While such actions often spring from women's grievances and disadvantage, women are also finding forums in which to take their own initiatives and influence practices which have kept reproducing the established norms of leadership. Their active participation in bringing new ways of acting in decision making forums will help diversify notions of leadership. Elizabeth's story is illustrative.

Elizabeth was invited to take part in the consultative process to review the organization's structure. At the wrapping up of one meeting, she challenged the Chair's concluding summary as being representative of all who had attended. She noted that very little had been heard from the three women and the one non-English speaking background man, and that in such silence the consensus of 'Well, we're all agreed that . . .' could hardly be presumed. Her challenge was followed by a long silence. She then continued that the meeting's recommendation for cross-faculty communication and co-operation was already happening with a group of academic women who met regularly in the Academic Women's Leadership Development group. One of the most vocal men cut across her, 'Who's your leader?' Contained within his demand to know who headed up the group were numerous assumptions about his own construction of leadership. 'The women are', was the thoughtful response from another woman in our inquiry group also at the meeting. Stunned, he tried again. 'You mean you haven't got a leader?' 'Yes, the women.' From the exchange that followed, a space was opened up for a member of the Review Committee to consult with our inquiry group. In turn, we sought to broaden women's input into the Review by inviting many interested women to this meeting. The inquiry group then took responsibility for preparing a submission to the Review Committee that both identified issues affecting women staff and gave different perspectives on the University's future shape from those already canvassed. In this way, Elizabeth's challenge demonstrates both the recursivity and horizontal diffusion of collaborative inquiry.

In this brief discussion of outcomes, I am suggesting that this particular collaborative inquiry as a form of staff development points to its potential for being both individually and organizationally productive of change towards a more equitable and diverse culture in the workplace, by unsettling acceptance of the dominant modes of decision-making, leadership and women's participation. However, in the interim, in terms of staff development for women, outcomes suggest that learning is supported and integrated through such a process as collaborative inquiry.

A collaborative inquiry with women

What is distinctive about this collaborative inquiry? Foremost it is collaboration with women from one organization; with women in a masculinist organization, across traditionally gendered areas. It lies ambiguously between a workplace group of colleagues and the many groups constituted by women outside an institution. In the space created by women in this collaborative inquiry, it became possible using the situations to hand in our everyday working lives, to allow emergent processes in shared stories to unfold, producing knowledge for action. The inquiry developed out of feminist values of sharing power, responsibility and knowledge among participants, with attention to our processes of inquiry.

The collaborative inquiry began round women-centred ways of working. We began with assumptions that perhaps women had a different voice (Gilligan, 1982) and different ways of knowing (Belenky et al., 1986). In the course of our inquiry, we unsettled some of our fundamental understandings of what we each meant by the category 'women', while recognizing that there were ways of working characterized as feminine that were devalued and excluded in an organizational culture based on the dominance of values ascribed to the masculine. Some of the approaches attributed to the feminine were accessible to us in contexts beyond our workplace, and their persistent and systemic exclusion from the diversity of expression within the workplace produced an alienation many women felt.

The inquiry enabled us to examine ways in which such a gendered culture is produced and reproduced in our workplace. Our explorations provide rich data for analysis of both the discourses operating within the organization, and for analysis of female subjectivity – the ways in which women are positioned by others and by themselves within these discourses. We heard in the stories how positions taken up by men and women are not equally available to each sex, since both discourses and subjectivity are themselves gendered. We looked at how we found ourselves positioned within competing and contradictory discourses, and could identify how individuals take up one rather than another position according to the relative power available in a particular position at a particular time. From our collaborative action research, it became clear that the dominance of masculinist discourses produced female subjectivity as a site for the reproduction of gender within the organization (Treleaven, in preparation). The telling of our stories in an open space enabled participants not only to contribute rich empirical data, but also to engage in the emergent processes of the research from which new understandings were generated collaboratively through reflection on action.

There is abundant evidence of the need to reconstruct (particularly in our workplace) those traditionally gendered expectations of women to support in quiet, invisible ways the 'real work' being done by men in patriarchal organizations which, like the church and the medical profession, universities exemplify (Poiner, 1991).

For some of us, our choice to continue working in the organization is dependent on finding new ways to express ourselves creatively beyond the absence and silence bestowed by gendered politics: to draw on notions of our agency in producing and reproducing the conditions of our lives, and to work collectively with others beyond the inquiry group in a politics of shared action. Change directed towards revaluing 'the feminine' which is split off, devalued and then projected on to women to carry is, I suggest, at the heart of making a workplace genuinely gender inclusive. For the exertion of personal power over others is driven by the fear of difference and is accompanied by the need to exclude difference which cannot even be acknowledged as threat. A politics of change that pays attention to the dynamics of subjectivity and investments in power is indicative of a way forward.

How we can make such shifts in an organization so that there are diverse and integral spaces where women can work creatively and participate fully continues to be the subject of inquiry. For the present, it seems that when we are able to make listening spaces, we allow a form of knowing from which spontaneous action flows. It is like a shower of rain in the desert that produces a profusion of wildflowers.

Acknowledgements

I warmly acknowledge my colleagues at the University of Western Sydney, Hawkesbury, with whom I shared this collaborative inquiry over two years, and whose feedback on drafts until this account represented our shared truths was an integral part of our collaboration. They continue in many different ways to make new spaces in which something can happen in the working lives of women. I am delighted by the widening network of women researchers across the University and have appreciated the encouragement given by many. Rosemary Leonard, Penny Rossiter and Caroline Williams offered valuable feedback on the initial draft. Jenny Onyx has kindly kept me in touch with the fire kindling this project. Lesley Johnson has played a significant role in my grappling with feminist theory, as I relate it to my practice. Peter Reason engaged with me in editorial email communications that were stimulating. Fiona Plesman offered friendship that kept me going over the rough ground. To you all, my heartfelt thanks.

Lesley T

10

Developing a Culture of Learning through Research Partnerships

Lesley Archer and Dorothy Whitaker

The partnership arrangements described here are between university-based researchers and a service-providing organization. By a 'service-providing organization' we mean one that provides some form of social or health or therapeutic care and support, usually to vulnerable populations such as children at risk, elderly infirm people, adults with learning disabilities, or people with mental health problems. A research partnership is created for the purpose of planning and conducting a piece of research of interest to the organization. It goes on for whatever length of time a given project requires: typically two to three years. In addition to producing research findings relevant to the operation of the organization, a partnership arrangement can also contribute to team-building and be a form of training. If all goes well, it can create a culture or climate of learning in service-providing teams which persists beyond the life of the project.

After providing background information which shows how it is that it seemed necessary to us to devise partnership arrangements, the structures and procedures involved in a research partnership are described, first in a brief summary, and then by naming and discussing successive steps involved. As part of the step-by-step description we will point to factors which our experience to date tells us facilitate or hinder the partnership process, and give thought to whether and how hindering factors be dealt with. Some examples will be provided. A concluding section compares this partnership structure with other, perhaps more familiar, ways of mounting research, considers the issue of fit (or non-fit) with characteristic organizational structures and procedures, and points to some learnings and benefits beyond those generated by the research itself.

Background: experiences which led to devising research partnerships

The two authors of this report have had an abiding interest in making research an integral part of practice. In 1981 we offered a short course for practising social workers, designed to assist them to plan and carry out a piece of research on an issue arising from their own practice experience. Two further courses were carried out in 1982 and 1983 (see Whitaker and Archer, 1985;

Archer and Whitaker, 1989; Whitaker et al., 1990).

These courses worked well in that all of those who participated in them devised viable research plans and learned about research methods through working within a small cohort of course members. Some then carried out their research, but some did not. It became clear that when research was not carried out, it was mainly because of the worker's position in his or her employing organization. Sometimes the worker changed jobs and the research topic was no longer seen as relevant to the new position. Sometimes staff shortages meant that to allow a worker to go on pursuing research was seen by his or her manager as an unaffordable luxury. Both course members and their managers tended to see research efforts as extra to a social worker's regular duties, and somehow a personal self-indulgence. Course members had a commitment to and a sense of ownership of their own research but their managers did not and could not, since their role was restricted to allowing a modest amount of time off (a few hours a week) for attendance at our early-evening, once a week, sessions.

This led us to see that if we wanted research efforts to count in the workplace we needed a structure which avoided placing the worker in a position in which he or she was isolated from own organization and management. We also wanted to avoid a situation where the research became a burden on already stretched workloads for on-the-ground practitioners. If not, research became an empty exercise, often aborted.

Thus, any focus for systematic investigation, and any framework for carrying it out, had to make sense to the organization and its management as well as to the practitioners. It needed to contain ways of sharing tasks. Some tasks were already within the compass of those doing them; others, such as those done by agency-based practitioners (who became research associates with the authors in a Project Workers Team) could be acquired by a form of working alongside training.

We hoped that what we would achieve would be a way of conducting research that mattered to the agency, to the on-the-ground practitioners (and increasingly to their clients) in ways that included all levels of the organization in the research. We planned that all participants would be kept in touch with both the processes and the findings from the work as it went along. We expected that the different perspectives of the staffs and the managers on the issue would become visible not just to the researchers but to each group and that this would have an impact on service provision as well as the research. We hoped for a sense of ownership to be developed. At the end of the work, we also expected that those closely involved, especially the seconded practitioner-researchers and the on-the-ground staff teams, would have integrated a research way of thinking into their day-to-day work.

It will be seen that in order for the model to function as intended and for it to achieve its potential benefits, it is necessary to work regularly and closely with a service-providing organization: with managers at several levels, with 'coal face' staff, sometimes with clients or residents, and with different combinations of these or of their representatives.

Brief description of the research partnership structure and procedure

The research structure and procedure, as evolved, supports the interests just described. A research partnership moves through three successive phases and is supported by two groups of people, differently composed and with different functions, which exist throughout the life of a project and serve its needs.

Preliminary to any work taking place, an agreement is reached between the university-based researchers and upper management in the service-providing organization that a piece of research will be carried out within a general topic or issue. The university-based researchers ask these managers what issues are currently pressing. From among these, one or more general issues will be selected by the key people in the organization as important to understand better or evaluate. Any general topic also has to be perceived as potentially researchable by the university members of the partnership.

As we will show, the *legitimization for the work* has to come from the top of the organization if it is to be successfully accomplished, but the *process of partnership research* is controlled by staff from all levels of the agency working collaboratively with the university-based staff. Often, the issue as it is identified by managers is expressed as a general concern, for example 'the quality of life of elderly people in homes run by the authority' or managers point to a new activity and responsibility, such as that they are now responsible for learning disabled people being rehoused from hospital into group homes run by housing associations. The focus of the research comes from agency managers. The university-based staff make clear that within this general focus they will need a range of units – some which are functioning well and some which are experiencing difficulties – with whom to work. The idea of partnership research and what it comprises is also fully discussed and agreed in initial meetings. A three-phase structure is agreed, and the agency or department accepts that some of the time of the staff will need to be released in order for the partnership to work.

Two groups are then set up which will exist throughout the life of the project. These are the Project Workers Team and a Project Coordination Group.

The Project Workers Team is responsible for the day-to-day conduct of the work through all its three phases. They will have the authority for carrying out the research. The team includes the university-based researchers and from one to four or five employees of the organization – either practitioners or line managers, depending on the issue being researched. The staff to be seconded to the Project Workers Team are selected by agency managers after a full discussion with the university-based researchers about what kind of person we are seeking. Agency seconded members of the team need to be people who fully understand the focus of the research – for example social work with older people. They do not have to be 'researchers' and usually are not. Together, the members of this team plan the details of the work. They keep in close touch, through frequent meetings and telephone contact.

The Project Coordination Group oversees the project, keeps in touch with events as it moves along, and advises on key aspects of the work (such as the form of the final report and dissemination procedures). This group includes all the members of the Project Workers Team plus managers and workers up and across the organization, and sometimes people from outside concerned with the issue or with that aspect of the organization's work. Core members of the group are selected in initial discussions with managers when the focus for the work is identified. Sometimes, others join the group as the work proceeds. The group meets every four months or so through the life of the project.

The membership of these two groups is established as soon as possible after a general agreement to pursue the work is agreed. All members of these two groups contribute to the partnership character of the work in different ways. The members of the Project Workers Team are most closely and consistently involved, and take joint responsibility for moving through all three phases of the work and for communicating to the Project Coordination Group. The members of the Project Coordination Group receive information and reports from the Project Workers Team and use this as a basis for commenting and advising.

The project moves through the following three phases. Phase 1 has to do with planning: it 'maps' the organization, identifies that which is already known and understood about the topic or issue by organization members, and spells out what needs to be understood better or evaluated. Workshop methods are used with members of the organization with direct experience of the issue. Often, these are on-the-ground workers – those who provide direct service or care in their day-to-day work. The outcome of this phase is the identification of specific detailed purposes within the general topic or issue already agreed.

Phase 2 has to do with such detailed planning of research design as is then necessary, and with carrying out a piece of research which meets the purposes which have been defined. This is the longest phase of the three. Its outcome is a full written report of the completed research.

Phase 3 is a dissemination and research utilization phase. Once the findings are available, ways of making them known throughout the organization are worked out, and one or more 'research utilization' activities is planned and carried out. This phase seeks to make the research 'count' in the workplace and to make a difference to practice.

This structure – that is the two groups set up for the life of the project and the three phases – is firm enough to contain a piece of partnership research and at the same time flexible enough to accommodate different topics and organizational structures. For example, while there will always be a 'Phase 1' which uses workshop methods, the number of sessions, those invited to attend, and the tasks to be worked on can all be varied to suit circumstances. While there will always be a 'Phase 2' in which the research is carried out, design details will differ from project to project, and best data sources will also be different, depending on the focus of the work and the ways in which work units are organized and responsibility for work allocated. A partnership research structure can contain research which is essentially exploratory, evaluation research, process outcome research, or action research (see Whitaker and Archer, 1989). It tends to be small-scale and intensive in character – perhaps because this is the preference of the university-based researchers, but also because the issues which the organization wishes to pursue are usually close to practice, which means close to the interactions between staff and clients/residents. In all pieces of partnership research, there always is a final report and a 'Phase 3'. It will, however, be up to the Project Coordination Group to think out how the report can best be 'mined' for points to put before different target groups within its own organization and beyond.

Successive key tasks in a partnership research project

1   It is useful first of all to speak informally with someone in a management position in the agency, in order to establish an initial point of contact and get some idea of what issue might be of interest and what operational group(s) it might make sense to work with.

It has proved very helpful if we already have contact with someone in an agency who has a potential interest in research and can clue us in to the character and structure of the organization. With such a contact person we can get some idea of what issue or issues might be of interest to the agency and identify which managers within the organization should be contacted to take the next steps forward. Sometimes these contacts are made in the course of other tasks which we are engaged in, sometimes someone from the agency will approach us and sometimes we make contact with someone we know to ask if their agency might be interested in being involved in such a piece of work.

2   The next task is to meet with those managers within the organization who can confirm or agree an overall purpose or focus for the work and release resources.

Sometimes, our original contact person will form part of this small group. Sometimes he or she negotiates directly for overall permission on our behalf and then becomes the key operational manager within the Project Coordination Group. Sometimes he or she provides names and is not further involved.

The negotiation with key managers includes agreeing the overall focus for the work, the operational groups it might make sense to work with and setting up the partnership arrangements, for example how cover will be provided in a residential home while the whole team meets.

We have found that at this stage it is possible to be blocked in our hopes for a partnership arrangement to go forward. We think this is because the term 'research' carries meanings for some managers which puts them off the idea. They may assume that research is something which researchers come in and do *to* people rather than *with* them and expect our work to be like this. They may have ideas that research has to be quantitative and 'objective' to be 'respectable' and if so, this much restricts what can be done. They may, when they have been told something of the framework which we propose to use, assume that they 'do that already', in their training section or in the normal course of the work. This phenomenon of saying 'we do that already' has been noted by other researchers (see Marsh and Fisher, 1992). It is an argument hard to counter, even when it is evident (to us) that this is not the case.

When we say that what we are doing is research but also training and team-building, managers sometimes do not know what to do with this. They do not know which pocket to reach into in order to support a partnership effort. If money is to come out of a training budget, it looks and is very expensive, considering how training budgets are ordinarily used. However, we have also found that our explanation of partnership research provides enthusiastic managers, who catch on to what we are doing, with degrees of flexibility in both presenting the package to Committee and in finding the money. For example one manager, who wished to extend the dissemination phase, found spare money in a mental health budget and argued successfully that the planned workshop was likely to improve the mental health of both his staff and the client group.

3   Decisions now need to be made as to who from within the organization will function as project worker(s), which people or units will be the primary foci for the work and/or providers of data, and who will become members of the Project Workers Group.

Once a topic is agreed and the partnership structure thoroughly discussed, these decisions usually follow without difficulty.

Managers know their staffs well enough to judge who might be interested in and capable of working along with us as project workers. Any nominated person can of course decline to participate, but on the whole we have found enthusiastic responses to the opportunity to look closely at some aspect of the work. All project workers with whom we have worked have had a commitment to the practice issue and a wealth of experience on which to draw.

At this stage it becomes evident to both the managers and the university-based researchers which individuals or units are appropriate as sources of data or foci for investigation. For example, if the overall purpose already agreed is to understand better what constitutes and contributes to a satisfactory quality of life for elderly people in residential care, then it will follow that X number of residential facilities with Y number of elderly residents and Z number of staff might become the focus for the work.

The managers and the university-based researchers also agree as to who should become members of the Project Coordination Group. This is done by role within the organization. For example when the foci for a project were homes for elderly people, the heads of each home and the neighbourhood team managers, who were their line managers, were invited to join the Project Coordination Group. Sometimes people outside the organization become members of the group, for example, foster parents, when the issue has to do with decision-making for children in care.

4   An initial series of meetings of the Project Workers Team takes place to do the necessary planning for Phase 1 and to induct the agency-based workers into partnership research.

The research-related tasks undertaken in this set of meetings include:

● Planning the Phase 1 workshops.
● Gaining entry to those functioning units which are to participate in the workshops.
● Identifying and carrying out related administrative tasks
● Making brief preliminary visits to units in which workshops are to take place.

At the same time, attention is necessarily paid to getting established as a group which is to work together for a considerable period of time. This involves sharing background and interests and includes, in particular:

● The university-based members sharing something about their own practice backgrounds and their stance towards research.
● The agency-based members sharing something about their practice or supervisory experience, especially when it bears focus for the research.
● Dealing with any assumptions or fears on the part of agency-based members about what research is and what working with university-based staff is likely to be like.

We are making a distinction here, familiar to social psychologists, between task and group maintenance functions of this operating group. The first set of tasks has to do with the work itself; the second set has to do with establishing and maintaining the group as a group. Since this group is to take on so much responsibility for the work, it is essential that it become a well-functioning team. Our experience to date is that, providing we have got this far in a partnership research project, creating a well-functioning team is no problem. When such a group works together over a long period of time, relationships between members of the group become very close. Time is necessarily spent in learning about each other as people as well as researchers.

These initial Phase 1 tasks and activities can take a longer or shorter time, depending on the nature of the work and the degree of sophistication and knowledge of the agency-based members. Any concerns on the part of agency staff about working with university staff are soon dispelled, once we have met and acknowledged our different roles, and it has become clear that agency-based staff have something important to bring to the research task and will be taking on tasks not dissimilar from familiar work. The way in which the project workers work together evolves: as experience accumulates and confidence builds, agency-based members take on more of the research tasks.

It is almost always the case that a certain amount of time is spent in talking about the agency-based members' positions in their own organization, especially if the agency is undergoing significant changes. We note what is said as we go, since what they say often provides valuable contextual information.

5   From two to five Phase 1 workshops are carried out with one or more staff
    groups who actually provide the service or care in their day-to-day work.

The staff groups who participate in the Phase 1 workshops may be jointly
responsible for a home for elderly people, for work with children at risk, etc.
The key point is that they will have had direct experience of whatever is the
focus for the research.

Usually, one or two of the university-based members of the Project Workers
Team work with one of the agency-based members in each of the units. This
proves to be a good combination, since the agency-based members know the
language and ethos of the staff team or group participating in the workshop(s)
and the university-based members know the research requirements and are
experienced in workshop methods.

The details of these workshops will vary from project to project, but they
always involve opportunities for workshop participants to share their experi-
ence-based understandings of the task (their 'practice wisdom'), to give
thought to issues which puzzle or concern them, and from this formulate
views as to what it would be useful to understand better or evaluate. In order
to assist in achieving this, the Project Workers Team works out a framework
for the workshop series, framing questions to stimulate discussion in either the
group as a whole if it is small enough, or in subgroups. For example, a group
of staff in a home for elderly people might be asked to explore: 'If your mother
or father or uncle or aunt had to come to live in a home for elderly people what
would you look out for in selecting the home?' or a group of specialist child
protection staff might be asked to tell one another about recent referrals to the
caseload, how they felt about these and what they did as a consequence of the
referral.

Any Project Workers Team has to develop considerable skills in order to
manage Phase 1 of the work: the framework has to match the interests and
ability level of the staff with whom we are to work; there has to be a willingness to accept all opinion as legitimate; there needs to develop an
understanding of group dynamics such that the facilitators are aware of group
defences, affect and subgrouping. The skill lies in becoming aware of group
dynamics and noting these. We would intervene if and when we judged that
certain of the group dynamics were interfering with the task. For example, if
a staff group got into an argument over whose opinion was the correct one, we
would intervene to legitimize contradictory views. We have always been fortunate in working with agency-based workers who have training in such
understandings or who are open to learning such skills.

Workshops are lively and exciting experiences – especially with groups of
staff who may never have been brought together as a group and may have little
experience of group discussions. Alongside the tasks discussed below, members
of the research team sometimes have to help inexperienced participants not to
talk all at once.

Key tasks for the project workers include:

● Facilitating the discussion.

- Hearing what is being said without judging in any way.
- Asking for clarification but not otherwise interrupting the flow.
- Recording what has been said.

Members of the Project Workers Team take full notes of the discussions. Everything is recorded, even when it may be contradictory. The point of these workshop meetings is not to arrive at consensus (though there is often substantial consensus) but to gain as full a picture as possible of the experiences and views of those participating. What has been said is written up by the Project Workers Team: points may be reordered and regrouped but nothing substantive is changed or omitted. These 'minutes' are brought to the next meeting for discussion and amplification. If the minutes reveal that any misunderstandings occurred within the staff group, or between that group and the researchers, these are corrected. When workshop members hear this feedback, their practice wisdom, their views and their concerns are immediately evident to them. It is at this point that contradictions can be addressed – sometimes resolved but often simply held as offering differences which characterize the team.

Once Phase 1 workshops are completed, a draft report is drawn up which includes a summary of all the themes discussed in all the units worked with, and a preliminary list of detailed purposes for the research proper. This report is used as the basis for the next steps.

In our experience problems do not arise with such workshops (although we do not always negotiate our way into setting them up). We believe that the reasons are that the workshops provide opportunities for those participating to reflect on their experience, to have their views heard and respected (and never misrepresented), and to receive a message from management-sanctioned researchers that what they have said is important and will be attended to. We have often noted that the typescript record of discussions surprises the participants. They see that their comments are 'taken seriously'. A less sophisticated group of staff are often amazed by how much they know and there is often a good deal of humour when they recognize what they said, recorded exactly as they said it. With more sophisticated or cynical groups we believe that the fact that their views are presented fully and uncritically does much to counter any doubts they may have about the idea that we mean what we say: that this is a partnership between us and them.

6 A meeting of the Project Coordination Group is arranged at this point.

The summary report of the Phase 1 workshops is distributed to the members of the Project Coordination Group in advance of the meeting. At this meeting there is the opportunity for those members of the group who have not participated in Phase 1 to add their perspective on the work, and their views as to what purposes should be addressed in Phase 2, which is the actual carrying out of the piece of research. On the basis of this meeting, the report is amended to include a full list of detailed research purposes and the report made available to all the people who have participated so far.

At this meeting agreements are usually made as to the intervals at which the

Project Coordination Group will meet in the course of Phase 2. Usually a four-month interval seems about right to those concerned, and is agreed.

By this stage we have a sense of full commitment from participants at all levels of the organization. The detailed purposes represent the views of all levels of staff, the two groups are established as groups with a common aim, and the communication channels from the 'top' to the 'bottom' and 'sideways' in a large organization are established.

7 Phase 2 is carried out: the research plan is finalized, the research is conducted and a report is written.

Phase 2 is the research activity conducted on the basis of plans agreed in Phase 1. It extends over a period of one to two and a half years. Depending on the purposes identified in Phase 1, it may take the form of a piece of exploratory research or a series of action-research cycles[1] or be a piece of evaluative research. (For a full description of the kinds of research likely to interest social agencies see Whitaker and Archer, 1989).

Phase 2 requires:

- Members of the Project Workers Team to carry out the actual work in the setting of one or more service-providing units.
- Monitoring how this goes and trouble-shooting if indicated.
- Maintaining the team as a functioning research team through frequent meetings and dealing with any problems which might arise as the work proceeds.
- At the same time meeting, at less frequent intervals, with the Project Coordination Group, in order to maintain communication up, down and across the organization.

Over the agreed period of time, depending on the design and character of Phase 2, the agency-based project workers (and sometimes the university-based staff alongside) will either be collecting data in Phase 2 or assisting one or more teams of staff to do their own action research. They will also be collecting information about the processes of their interactions with the agency teams and clients as they go. Regular monthly meetings of the whole Project Workers Team are held in which the progress and the processes of the work are discussed.

We have found that however carefully the research is designed, it is not possible to anticipate all the opportunities and problems which may arise.

The members of the Project Workers Team engaged in the field have to be alert to problems as they arise and to take action within the spirit of the overall research to deal with them. For example, in a piece of exploratory research into the quality of life of staff and residents in homes for elderly people we devised a structured sample of staff and residents across three homes (Whitaker and Archer, 1987). This meant that only some staff in each home were to be interviewed. Staff, who had become intrigued about and interested in the research in Phase 1, felt left out when they were not to be part of the sample. Our explanations for interviewing a sample rather than everyone satisfied some staff, but there were others who still wanted closer involvement. Together, we were able to devise a secondary piece of work for them to do alongside what we were doing.

Another piece of research was planned as action research with whole teams. In one of these teams, we found that the team was without a team leader and very stretched (Archer and Whitaker, 1991). They did not feel able to meet as a whole staff group, which was required by the research plan. They were preoccupied with their future viability, with problems of taking decisions, and with a poor relationship with their neighbourhood team. The agency-based researcher happened to come from their neighbourhood team. Staff in the unit spent a lot of time in blaming him for the failings of all the social workers in his team and beyond. We therefore decided that the action research cycle would have as its goal helping this team to better their relationships with the team by taking some control over the way clients were admitted to the unit. Strictly, making this decision did not conform to the research design, since the plan was for teams to identify their own goals and carry out action towards them. However, it was in the spirit of the research and, as the team felt to be more in control of its admission policy through work carried out by the project worker, it became more interested in identifying other goals and carrying out action towards them.

In yet another project, two foci for research were envisaged initially: one having to do with the interface between care workers and residents – in this case, learning disabled adults – and one having to do with the character of consortia which were managing the small group homes. As data began to be gathered and analysed, it became clear that quality of care was highly dependent on quality of work life for staff and became an additional focus for the research.

In carrying out partnership research, problems can also arise within the Project Workers Team itself. For example, one member of a Project Workers Team, who was for the rest of her week a social worker in a generic team, found that she could not always get to monthly meetings. On one occasion we heard that her team was in a state of crisis, with two members of staff off sick, the team manager on leave and that she was the only social worker left on duty who was qualified to deal with allegations of child abuse which needed immediate action.

An interesting issue sometimes arises which has to do with the appropriate balance between research and consultation *vis-à-vis* the units from which research data are being collected. Sometimes, we have felt it necessary to move into brief periods of consultation or advocacy when the research effort has been threatened by events in the workplace. It becomes necessary to give proper attention to the boundary between research and consultation and to avoid turning into practitioners with the working staff as clients.

The Project Coordination Group is an important forum for airing problems arising from staff shortages and stress. Group members also sanction any modifications in Phase 2 activity arising from what we are finding. They might take action within their organization to ease the path of the research. For example, a senior manager might communicate to colleagues who were not part of the research that staff shortages are causing particular problems to a team. Action could then be taken on the team's behalf. When a team manager and his or her line manager are members of the group, it is easier to sanction difficulties being shared more widely in the organization.

From the point of view of the university-based researchers all of the above has to be held together. We have the task of seeing that the research as research is differentiated from other tasks, such as responding in sympathetic ways to snags which occur in carrying it out. With the other members of the Project Workers Team, we need counselling skills as well as research skills. We have to make time and energy to respond to crises and troubles in facilitating ways and in ways which will serve the research task.

8   At the conclusion of Phase 2, a full written report is prepared of the research.

The university-based researchers take the main responsibility for writing a report, since we have had substantial previous experience of such a task, but the partnership emphasis is retained. We draw up an outline of proposed contents which is discussed and agreed within the Project Coordination Group. This usually includes a full and extended section on data collection methods, so that the work can be replicated elsewhere in the organization.

A problem we sometimes encounter is that it takes a considerable time to write a full report which does justice to both the content and the processes of the work. This can mean that there is a time gap between the end of Phase 2 and the start of the dissemination phase of the work.

9   A plan for disseminating learnings is worked out.

A draft plan is drawn up in the Project Workers Team and this forms the basis for an agenda for the Project Coordination Group. In large agencies, such as Social Services Departments, dissemination plans are likely to include a report to the relevant committee of the Local Authority, a full workshop day with staff who do the same job as those involved in the research and summary reports for various levels of the organization. In smaller agencies, meetings and summary reports may be planned for managers, and for committees or trustees who may not have been much involved beyond sanctioning the work. Other forms of dissemination for use with client groups, such as posters and the like, may be drawn up from the full report by agency staff.

10   Dissemination and research utilization are carried out.

Staffs from all levels of the organization who have been part of the research in some capacity or other are part of this process. Sometimes the university-based researchers are involved, sometimes they are not. For example, the university-based researchers are likely to be involved in large-scale workshop events, reports to committee and in writing papers for the field, usually with agency staff. However, a team of staff in a unit may devise its own dissemination exercise with a group of other staff from a nearby unit or elect one or two of its staff to try out some exercise from the research process or conclusions. For example in a project on 'Improving and maintaining quality of life in homes for elderly people' there was a workplan for assessing difficult residents and thinking out how best to respond to them (Archer and Whitaker, 1991). One of the homes in the study used this plan by asking a student on placement with them to carry out a survey of residents, a year after the research was completed.

11   The project is closed.

A final meeting with the Project Coordination Group is held with the purpose of marking what we have achieved together and acknowledging that the project has now come to an end. This often turns into or is accompanied by a social event, so that others with whom we have become closely involved can say their 'goodbyes' to us and to one another. While this marks the end of the partnership project it does not, we hope, mark the end of learnings and application.

Some examples of partnership research: difficulties and what can be expected when it is successful

We have chosen the stories below to illustrate points where the process of partnership research can become difficult and to show what can happen when it is going well.

Example A: A project which could not be taken beyond Phase 1

We had been given money by an outside funding body to do some work on a particular issue. At the same time we had approached an agency with a view to making a partnership arrangement. We made the mistake of trying to combine the two activities. The money we had would pay for a Phase 1, and we assumed that being given permission to spend it in the agency meant they were likely to feel committed to providing financial support for Phases 2 and 3. We also assumed that they had really understood that the Phase 1 was not of and by itself a piece of research. A Project Coordination Group was set up. However, events showed that the managers in it were not committed to the idea of partnership research. The idea for the overall focus of the research had not come from them.

It was agreed, however, that a Phase 1 would be conducted with a team of experienced practitioners, who had comparable responsibility within the organization but did not ordinarily work together. We did not set up a project workers team, judging that one could be drawn up from among the workshop members at the end of Phase 1.

When Phase 1 was completed, we produced a report which included a list of issues generated by these experienced workers which they wished to pursue further. The report also included an idea that the people whom we had brought together for Phase 1 should continue to meet on a regular basis, since they had found the whole experience to be a very supportive one. The managers received the report as if it were a full research report. They decided they could not find the money for further work. They disliked the idea of the workers meeting as a group informally without a manager being present. They thanked us for our efforts.

What had gone wrong? First, the agency had made no real commitment to the work in prospect beyond giving permission for six or seven workshop meetings with a number of their staff. The idea for the focus of the work did not come from them and they had made no financial commitment to its completion. The management group had ideas about the nature of what we were offering, which were at odds with our own, but we did not properly understand this at the time, or confront this. The agency itself had long before dissolved its own research group as being a costly extravagance. We later speculated that the managers with whom we worked viewed what we were doing as 'training' rather than research. When we produced a full report of Phase 1, its apparent completeness was sufficient to satisfy their expectations of what we were to do. They had no commitment to finding additional money, especially for research. We also learned from this experience something about management structures and styles. The organization was strictly hierarchical in character. The idea that workers might provide mutual support for one another, outside formal support structures, was incompatible with the organization's assumptions about control and training. The experienced staff group was working on issues which might bring the organization to the attention of the media. In the United Kingdom at the time we were doing this work, newspapers, radio and television were filled with reports of social workers failing in their duty to young people who were at risk. Managers consequently felt a need to be aware of everything social workers were doing, in case something happened which brought the agency to media attention. These particular staff were already supported by a supervision system within the agency and, because they were experienced, were assumed not to require anything more, especially as they were already hard pressed to cover their case loads.

From the point of view of taking a piece of partnership research through to completion, it would have been better not to start, though we could see that Phase 1 activity was useful to the participants, and we ourselves learned much about the dilemmas facing the workers.

Example B: A staff group which could not find the time or energy to co-operate with the research

The staff of a home for elderly people had agreed to participate in a series of action research cycles as part of a larger partnership research project. They had chosen a goal for the home and then took no action towards achieving it. We wondered why this was happening. Discussion with the agency-based project worker who was going into the home regularly revealed that the staff group were suffering considerable stress. The neighbourhood team manager had moved elsewhere in the department and temporary cover was provided by a manager who was already in charge of another team. The home's unit manager had gone off sick with a bad back. They had lost their cook and were finding it difficult to replace her.

We decided to take steps to try to understand the stress, rather than to pursue the direct research plan. We met with two of the deputies. They began to talk about all the things which had happened in the last six months. We found that the home was having a wing converted for the use of elderly learning disabled people at the same time as the rest of the home was being decorated. The loss of the cook had meant that care staff were having to prepare meals. Residents were having to be moved round the home and, as many of them were confused, this was adding to their confusion. One old lady was regularly eating the workmen's sandwiches. Other residents were becoming very ill. The support which members of staff were getting from the agency was beset with problems: a committee member of the Local Authority Committee, responsible ultimately to the electorate for the conduct of the home, arrived with a bunch of daffodils on the day a washing machine broke down and flooded the boiler house – the staff were embarrassed to have no water to put the flowers into.

As the deputies talked about all these events, some important, some merely irritating or even funny, we began to realize that the research effort was just another burden. We decided that we would keep a log of all their stressors and make what the staff was enduring visible to the members of the Project Coordination Group. It took a further nine months for this home to get into a position to pursue the research.

What had gone wrong? Despite the best efforts of the staff, the external problems continued. Decorators, who came for a few weeks, stayed for months. During their stay, the kitchen was out of commission for several weeks and the cook was still not replaced. Food had to be supplied during the week by a voluntary agency 'meals on wheels' which normally supplies food to elderly people in their own homes. At weekends, staff had to go out and buy in fish and chips or other kinds of take-aways for residents while the kitchen was out of commission. The head of home continued to have a bad back which meant that from time to time, she had to stay off work. Several residents died. The neighbourhood team manager changed twice and support to this home from the neighbourhood team was patchy until the post was filled more permanently.

As a research team we learned a lot from this experience about what needs to be in place for a staff group to be effective. We especially learned that staff have to have time and available energy if they are to do more than do the practical care tasks. There is little room for more difficult emotional tasks and no room at all for forward planning since all energy is diverted to the twin tasks of dealing with day-to-day chaos and personal stress. We also learned how crucial it is for first-line managers to be in place and to be interested in what staff are doing. We learned that there may be less sympathy on the part of higher management for a staff group suffering from a build-up of small stressors than when faced with a major crisis.

*Example C: A team of workers whose understanding of the people in
their care expanded through certain of the research findings*

In a partnership research project which focused on the quality of care for residents in a home for the elderly, interviews were carried out with a sample of
old people which invited them to complete sentences, of which the first few
words only were provided. The stems of sentences included, for example, 'For
me a good day is . . .'; 'The hardest thing to get used to about this home is . . .';
'When I see a new person coming here to live, I . . .'; and so on, to a total of
about 20 such items. The results showed that residents vary considerably in
what, for each, constituted and contributed to a good quality of life. A number of different and preferred life-styles could be identified. When these
findings were fed back to the care staff they could see that certain of their residents preferred a quiet life and creature comforts; others wanted days out and
treats of a particular sort and liked being waited on; and still others wanted to
do things which helped them to feel that they were competent and able to
make useful contributions to others. The findings were of general interest and
also helped staff to be sensitive to individual difference among those in their
care.

   This example illustrates the kind of research finding which might equally
well have emerged from research conducted without an emphasis on partnership arrangements. Phase 2 of this research had been quite orthodox
exploratory research except that data were collected by an 'ordinary' social
worker rather than a researcher, who regularly met with other members of the
research team. But the subjects of the research did not challenge the findings
or regard them as any kind of external threat. The difference, we believe, is that
staff paid serious attention to the results because their own ideas had been
solicited early in the planning stage of the research, they knew that the
research design had taken their interests into account and, during Phase 2,
they had been given a lot of support by the project worker who listened to their
troubles and concerns every time she came into the home. They regarded the
research as being done with them, rather than on them.

*Example D: Teams of care workers who participated in an action
research project and internalized the idea of monitoring and
evaluating their own work*

A research partnership was set up with a Social Services Department in which
one focus was on work carried out in small group homes for learning disabled
adults. An action research approach was adopted in Phase 2, in which staffs
were encouraged by the research worker to identify goals towards which they
would like to work, devise a plan, carry it out and evaluate the outcomes. This
was done in successive action research cycles. Goals might have to do with
individual residents, the resident group as a whole, own organization, the
neighbourhood, and so on. The hope was that staffs would not only be
assisted to achieve good results, but that they would produce their own
research data as they went.

In action research a potential for learning from own experience is present, such that habits of goal-setting, making plans which look to fit goals, close attention and observation, self-evaluation, and so on, can become a habitual part of the work effort. We have seen this come about. At first a staff moves through action research cycles in a step-by-step fashion under the guidance of the researchers. However, especially as experience accumulates, they may move outside the 'letter' of the action research cycle while retaining its spirit. Some staffs have become quite ingenious about what they undertake: for example, keeping diaries of holidays or of successive accomplishments of individual residents, writing up 'A day in the life of (the home)' in which activities and interactions of residents and staff were tracked over a 24-hour period and written up. Staff have been prepared to revise goals when they have proved to be over-ambitious, and have learned to learn from apparent 'failure'.

These we consider are *process* learnings which can emerge from a certain form of partnership research.

Facilitating and hindering factors in partnership research projects

It will be seen from what has already been said that some stages and aspects of the partnership research process seem to present few or no problems, while others can prove difficult to manage or surmount.

Factors which facilitate the process include:

- Locating a contact person or 'transactor' who can facilitate entry into a service-providing agency at an appropriate management level (see also Smale, 1992).
- Managing to communicate the essence of the partnership idea even when it is unfamiliar to agency-based personnel and seems to them not to fit into existing organizational structures and procedures (see also Chisholm and Elden, 1993).
- Establishing agreements with managers at a sufficiently high level in the service-providing organization for decisions not only to be taken but to be held to (so that agreements cannot be easily countermanded by those higher up in the organization).
- All concerned being willing to tolerate a degree of open-endedness and uncertainty at certain stages of the work, especially in the beginning before Phase 1 has been completed.
- Relative freedom from pressure and stress in units providing direct care, such that members of staff and teams have sufficient time and energy to involve themselves in partnership work.
- Sympathetic line managers who are prepared to listen to the on-the-ground staff, and share in goal-setting, planning and action.
- A management system and ethos which leads individual managers and management as a group to be open to ideas from on-the-ground staff and to respect their experience and their understanding of the task and of the people in their care. Related to this is the readiness to appreciate that not

all instruction, control and assurance of good practice has to come from the top of the organization and be imposed downwards.

- University-based researchers who hold to the rigours of systematic research, but who are also able to fulfil a counselling role and to be sympathetic to events in the real world which inhibit the research. They also require the capacity to turn set-backs into opportunities for further understanding.

Factors which hinder the partnership process are for the most part the converse of the above:

- Failing to find at least one manager in the service-providing agency who is sympathetic and intrigued by the possibilities of partnership research, and sufficiently highly placed in the organization such that his or her views are listened to. Without such a person there is a danger of the university-based researchers who are presenting the ideas getting into an unproductive adversarial relationship with managers, which can then prove fatal to collaborative work.
- Misunderstandings and failures to communicate well, especially during the early, pre-Phase 1 stage of the research.
- Bad luck: especially when factors outside anyone's control put pressure on agency resources and lead key managers to feel that they cannot honour earlier agreements.
- Lack or loss of energy and available time on the part of on-the-ground staff whose participation and co-operation are essential to the viability of the project.
- An entrenched severely hierarchical management system which involves a great deal of top-down control, and a distant, blaming attitude on the part of management and a complementary defensive attitude on the part of staff further down the hierarchy are bound to interfere with the partnership research process.
- Distractions, of whatever kind and from whatever source which sap energy and generate preoccupations which are extraneous to the task and to the partnership research effort, will interfere with the process. Many of these can be dealt with if facilitating factors are largely in place and if the Project Workers Team is prepared to be patient and to interrupt the work for a period of time, but some such preoccupations are intractable and virtually impossible to deal with.
- The university-based researchers have to cope with colleagues and the research establishment seeing this kind of research as 'applied' and therefore less scholarly, and somehow diluted by bringing non-researchers into the research enterprise.

When a unit or team is unable to work to a partnership research structure because of hindering factors within the unit itself, we have employed two strategies to counter the effects of this. The first is to monitor what is happening and to make this a part of the research process and a source of learning.

The second is to make use of the Project Coordination Group to discuss how problems might be alleviated.

Problems located in the larger organization may prove to be intractable: there is no leverage available to us as outsiders. In consequence, efforts may need to be abandoned, or if serious blockages become evident early on, it seems to us to make sense not to continue with efforts likely to be futile.

The lists of facilitating and hindering factors just presented have been influenced by our experience of the most likely loci of problems. There are a number of potentially hindering factors which we have not mentioned here because they have not, in our experience, occurred. There are a number of facilitating factors which we have not mentioned because they are likely to be present and so go unnoticed as an expected part of the process. We have not said, for example, that it facilitates matters if on-the-ground staff who participate in Phase 1 workshops are responsive: we have never known them not to be so. We have not said that lack of skill and sensitivity on the part of agency-based members of the Project Workers Team is a hindering factor because we have never encountered this. We have said that increases in work pressure on the members of the Project Workers Team can get in the way of the work, because this does occur from time to time.

Finally

In this final section we consider the similarities and differences between this partnership arrangement and other, perhaps more familiar, ways of mounting research, raise the issue of fit (or non-fit) with characteristic organizational structures and procedures, and point to some learnings and benefits which go beyond producing research findings.

Similarities and differences between partnership research and more
usual ways of planning and carrying out research

We take the more usual ways of planning and carrying out research to involve one or more experienced researchers working out research aims and a research design, then seeking support for it and then seeking co-operation from those organizations or individuals who are to be data sources. The co-operation of any service-providing organization may be restricted to permitting access to data sources, though feedback of research results to co-operating organizations is often built into a research plan. Research partnerships, as has been shown, involve collaboration throughout all stages of the work, from agreeing purposes, in many cases finding the funding for the university-based researchers' work, through to carrying out the work and providing for dissemination and research-utilization within the agency.

In some ways a partnership structure does not affect the character of the research. As in any piece of research, purposes need careful and specific spelling out, research design and data collection and analysis methods need to fit purposes, and conclusions need to be carefully drawn on the basis of findings. However, there are also important differences.

In partnership research, planning takes longer because of the need to tap into the experience of so many people before firming up the agreed set of purposes, let alone a plan. Although the overall focus for a study is agreed very near to the beginning, a set of detailed purposes waits upon the conclusion to Phase 1. All concerned need to accept this and live with a certain amount of uncertainty during this early phase. Prior to Phase 1, a prospective plan needs to be thought out in broad outline, so that reasonable estimates can be made of the time and money likely to be required. These estimates need to include not only the costs of the university-based researchers, but also the additional resource costs of seconding staff to the Project Workers Team for part of their time, their travel expenses and those additional resource costs incurred by bringing staff together for Phase 1 meetings and to the Project Coordination Group. However, any such plan has to be held *provisionally* so that it can be adjusted in the light of outcomes of Phase 1.

Phase 2 – detailed planning and the actual conduct of the research – is undertaken by the university-based researchers together with one or a few people seconded from the agency. The agency-based members of the Project Workers Team are almost always experienced practitioners or first-line managers: they are unlikely to be experienced in research. This means that frequent meetings are required to help agency-based staff develop the considerable skills they will need and to keep the work moving along. Time needs to be invested in, for example, thinking out any differences (and similarities) between practice as an activity and research as an activity (Archer, 1990). Because the Project Workers Team works closely with operating teams or staffs, real life events affecting groups of workers while the research is going on need to be acknowledged and taken into account. Sometimes such events suggest new possibilities for investigation in Phase 2. While maintaining the integrity of the plan which was agreed in Phase 1, the project workers and other members of the coordination group need to decide whether such possibilities are too good to miss, and whether further purposes should be added in. In other words, the issue of the proper boundaries for the work is not necessarily settled once and for all at the beginning. Yet the research must not be allowed to expand willy nilly, in response to any and every intriguing development on the ground. It is also the case that now and then some aspect of the research has come to a standstill because of some crisis or accumulation of stressors among those providing data. The project workers then have to wait until the situation changes and the on-the-ground staff are again in a position to have the energy for the data-providing task.

This means that the progress from *purposes* to *plan* to *execution of plan* to *assembling findings* is not as smooth or uninterrupted as might otherwise be the case. On the other hand, by retaining flexibility in the ways described, the research effort often achieves understandings not always possible to anticipate at the start. One tends to trade certainty for richness.

One further difference between research partnerships and more conventional ways of planning and conducting research has to do with dissemination and research utilization. While publishing accounts of the research in the usual ways for the field as a whole, there is inserted a dissemination phase (Phase 3) for the participating service-providing agency. This is one of the pay-offs for the agency and is also a rich source of learning for all concerned, as it provides opportunities for learning how findings are received, and whether or not obstacles are seen to application and implementation.

The fit between the ethos of partnership research and the culture of a service-providing organization

The way in which partnership research is structured and the procedures it follows involve collaborative work among a number of differently situated and differently skilled people, most of whom are employees of the participating agency(s). Partnership research at its best creates a spirit of collaboration and a prevailing sense of mutual respect among those participating. Different people bring different perspectives to the work whether they be part-time care workers or members of higher management. These perspectives are shared, especially within the Project Coordination Group. It becomes evident that on-the-ground workers have accumulated much practice wisdom which it is useful for management to know about, and that, in the other direction, managers are aware of requirements, pressures and constraints which are unknown to or ill-understood by the on-the-ground workers, even though their work lives are influenced by these through guidelines and inspection procedures.

Within a partnership project, people within the organization who are not ordinarily in face-to-face contact are brought together, and for purposes of getting research done, views are sought from all and heard by all. Although the organizational hierarchy remains in place, within the Project Workers Team and the Project Coordination Group, there is a flattening of hierarchical relationships and an open acknowledgement of which strengths are brought to the work by whom.

Sometimes this works as intended, and the research effort is the richer for such open communication. Sometimes it works less well. We have encountered at least one situation (see Example A) in which the assumptions of management, and the associated management structures and procedures were such that the project could not go ahead. We have encountered another in which management structures and procedures appeared to harden when managers were confronted with more open communication with an on-the-ground staff group.

In other words, partnership research seems to work best when there is a degree of compatibility between the culture (expectations, assumptions, norms, etc.) which is integral to partnership research, and the culture of the participating organization. This does not mean they must be exactly alike, which is impossible given the differences in scope and task, but it does mean that they must be near enough so that the partnership effort does not threaten the integrity of the organization as perceived by upper management, and that the organization does not stifle the research process.

This is something we are learning more about as project follows project. We hope to have more to say about it as experience accumulates.

Some learnings and benefits that go beyond the production of research findings

One ordinarily expects a piece of research to yield findings, well supported by evidence, from which conclusions can be drawn. This is the case for partnership research as well as for any other structure for getting research done. However, we find that through the process of living through a research partnership project, understandings are acquired which cannot be said to be *findings*, but nevertheless emerge from the work as *learnings*.

What appears to happen is that this form of research immerses the researcher in events: those which occur in the settings in which data are collected, and those which occur in the temporary groups set up to support the work – the Project Workers Team and the Project Coordination Group.

For example, in one piece of work in residential homes for the elderly, by soaking up the atmospheres of a number of homes, members of the team learned much about readily tolerable and hard to tolerate stresses on staffs; about how it is that common-sense assumptions about people's motivations can sometimes support the work but sometimes lead staff to misunderstand residents' feelings or needs; how quality of work life for staff appears to be essential to the provision for good quality care; and the like.

From noting what goes on in the project coordination group meetings, we may become aware of what about management surprises on-the-ground workers, and what about everyday events in service-providing units surprises managers.

Insights so gained cannot be called 'findings' in the traditional sense of the term, since we cannot name an 'N' on which such understandings are based. We have also called these *learnings* rather than *findings* because they were not listed in the original detailed purposes of the research or added to the list of purposes as the research progressed. We did not set out to *find* them but having *learned* them within a rigorously recorded structure we were often able to make them part of our conclusions. Sometimes an important insight is based on a single or rare incidence such as several resident deaths over a period of months, or the reaction in a project coordination meeting to the absence of a high level manager.

Because they do not fit into the notion of 'research findings' we do not consider that these learnings are unimportant or should be ignored. Such learnings and the processes by which they are acquired are a matter for further thought and enquiry. When and on what basis can one have confidence in an insight which takes the form of a 'learning' rather than a 'finding'? We are curious about how such learnings fit into the spectrum of that which can be understood through research.

We have already alluded to benefits which can accrue to a service-providing organization through participation in a partnership research project. To summarize them, team-building is supported by Phase 1 activities, where all members of an operating team or staff are assisted to make explicit what they have already learned from experience, what they still need to learn, and what they would like to direct attention to. A convention is adopted where all that is said is important and worthy of noting, including views which are on the face of it incompatible but are nevertheless a part of the team's experience. If the research is such as to involve staff further in the actual conduct of the research, for example by instituting successive action-research cycles, then this too supports team-building.

Partnership research can be a form of learning on the job: through paying attention to own experience; through noting the consequences of one's efforts with clients/residents; through critically examining assumptions made about events and interpretations put upon them and comparing these with assumptions and interpretations made by others. This is especially the case for agency seconded staff who join the project workers team and also if action research is involved, when members of the staff team gain experience in setting goals proactively, making plans which can then be expected to move towards goals, noting the outcomes of efforts, registering what went right and what went wrong, and why. If this becomes established as a stance towards work, a habit of mind, such ways of thinking become internalized and outlive the project.

Partnership structures tend to increase the body of shared information available to those occupying different positions in the organization. They can make the expertise acquired and held by different members/levels of staff visible and available to others.

In the experience of the university-based researchers such partnership structures require additional work and effort, far beyond that which is required in more conventional research. Only some of the time required for this can be costed into any proposal. However, the benefits for us are considerable. We are beginning to achieve our aim of making research and research findings an integral part of practice. We have made research count in the workplace – the work we have done is taken seriously and has made a difference to the quality of life of many of those who have participated. We have been able to use our social work and groupwork skills as well as our research skills and learned more about what discriminates them. We have made learnings that would not have been routinely available to us if we had been doing more conventional research and still been able to hold to the demands of orthodoxy. We have not been limited by our own knowledge and expertise of the substantive issue. Our knowledge has been expanded through a partnership with the expertise of those doing the work in many fields. The research partnerships provide a variety which has kept us in touch with most recent developments in many areas of social welfare. We have, on the whole, made friends rather than enemies at all levels of complex organizations and we have had a great deal of pleasure from working close to the tasks of those who care for disadvantaged people.

These benefits are over and above what is learned from the research itself.

Note

1. The term 'action research' is sometimes used very loosely to refer to any work which involves ongoing contact with the field. We are using the term more precisely. The action research model we use closely follows that developed by the social psychologist Kurt Lewin – who first used the

term – in the immediate post-Second World War years in the United States (Lewin, 1947, 1951). This model involves a particular sequence of steps, repeated in successive action research cycles, and distinct roles for the researcher/facilitator and those from the field. The sequence of steps within each action research cycle involves (1) identifying a goal (concrete and relatively short-term); (2) devising a plan to work towards achieving it; (3) carrying out the plan; (4) assessing the outcomes and consequences; and (5) on the basis of this, either revising the plan, changing the goal or choosing a new goal. Step (5) initiates a new action cycle. We do not use 'action research' to refer to Phase 1 of the work because the goals of Phase 1 are to identify research goals and Phase 1 is only one part of partnership research. Nor do we use action research to refer to the research partnership as a whole. When action research is used in Phase 2, it is a research method chosen because it fits the purposes of the research. The goals for any action research cycle conducted in Phase 2 are chosen by the staffs in the unit, they do the work on them and the research team assist them in that task. Partnership research seeks to understand the process of any kind of research which is undertaken in Phase 2 by teams and units, whether the method chosen is action research, survey research, evaluation research or exploratory in character.

11

Reflections on Participation in Human Inquiry

Peter Reason

In this chapter I attempt to look at the examples presented in the previous six chapters, to highlight what seem to me to be interesting issues, and to make some comparisons between different approaches. I will also use the framework of forms of participation developed in Chapters 1–4 as a means of further illuminating the process of participation in human inquiry. Essentially the present chapter contains my own musing and reflections, my own sense of the interesting comparisons, my own comments on the different methods. I circulated a draft of the chapter to all contributors and received a number of comments in return, many of which I have incorporated. Sometimes I have added to or changed my original comment, sometimes I have noted a difference in my perspective as reader/editor from that of the writer/co-researcher. My purpose is not to be 'right', but to stimulate further reflection.

Hilary Traylen: Research with health visitors

Hilary is almost forced in to participative research. In her earlier interviews and observations she comes to recognize that the issues she is concerned with in health visiting practice are complex, difficult to express, sensitive and of vital importance to the potential participants in the inquiry. They require reflective action in a co-operative inquiry group if they are to be properly addressed and honoured. Indeed, almost as soon as the participative group is established a new and important issue – that of hidden agendas – is identified that was not articulated in the earlier interviews, and proves to be the focus of the inquiry.

Hilary carefully prepares for the early stages of the inquiry. Some of her concern about her competence to run an inquiry may have been unnecessary agonizing, but this was also a time when she thought carefully and deeply about what was needed and prepared herself internally. She builds on the contacts she has made already in the earlier phases of her research (indeed, the interview and workshop phases can be seen as critical preparations for the establishment of the inquiry group). She carefully plans an introductory session, talks personally to those who cannot attend and demonstrates in her behaviour her genuine interest in developing collaborative relationships.

Once the group is established it moves quickly to co-define the topic for the inquiry, both at the overall level of exploring hidden agendas, and at the more concrete level of choosing the specific issue each participant wishes to explore. It is through this co-definition of the topic that the group develops its autonomy.

The foundation for the inquiry then lies in a concrete engagement with important issues of practice for the participants. At an early point of difficulty, after the group is established, when they are 'circling around these problems' and 'feeling at a loss' Hilary makes a critical intervention, inviting each member to describe a particular hidden agenda in their practice. This enables them to drop from the abstract to the practical, and to move into several cycles of highly profitable exploration of specific issues in a period of deep detailed engagement with the topic of the inquiry. In this way the group members learn about the process of co-operative inquiry by doing it.

In her facilitation of the group Hilary can best be described as naïve and genuine. She claims to have minimal group facilitation skills, but she works from her heart and joins with them. She shows deep identification with the experience of the participants (in her dreams and in her concerns for them) and through the inquiry worked very hard to be of service to the work.

One of the most interesting features of this inquiry is the repeated mirroring of the personal and the professional, the ways in which the personal concerns of the group reflect the topic of the inquiry. First, Hilary comes to realize that her choice of topic is based not just on rational considerations but on personal needs and concerns about her own competence. Second, she realizes that the co-researchers' concern about confronting and raising issues with their clients mirrors her concern about how much to confront the group process. Third, the group members realize that there was an important link between their need to feel good in their work and the clients' need to feel strong and confident: the notion of well-being lies at the root of a healthy life for everyone.

Throughout the inquiry the experience of anxiety and stress of all those engaged is close to the surface Indeed it is central to the inquiry – it would not be possible to engage in depth with these sensitive issues using an inquiry approach that did not acknowledge and work with the anxiety. By engaging with these underlying feelings, and by providing support for experimental behaviour in confronting them, the group becomes an empowering agent for them all.

There are two crisis points in the inquiry. The first, when the group moves from circling round the issues to deep engagement, I have already mentioned. The second comes later, when they try to reflect on the role of the health visitor. One thing to notice is how they stick with it, engage together with the chaos of not making progress. As Heron wrote, 'new order is created by perturbation' (1988: 52); it is important for an inquiry group to recognize and accept emergent chaos, not try to tidy it up prematurely. The chaos arises as the group shifts from deep engagement with their actual practice to more generalized sense-making. In particular they get stuck with a very abstract 'professional' statement about health visiting practice.

The organizational context of Hilary's inquiry is not discussed in her chapter but is of some importance. Her work was supported by her Health Authority as part of the programme in collaboration with the School of Management at the University of Bath. Despite this formal overall approval, she ran into difficulties with the more local organization when she set up the co-operative inquiry group: managers of the health visitors could not understand why such a group was needed and viewed it as a threat to their authority. Hilary, deeply concerned with the experience of the health visitors and their clients, was taken by surprise by this response and was obliged to retrace her steps, explaining and getting local support (albeit not always enthusiastic) for the inquiry.

Bessa Whitmore's participative evaluation

Bessa Whitmore's chapter shows participation employed to reach across a cultural divide between the privileged providers and the disadvantaged recipients of a service. The initiative for the inquiry, its primary purpose, and the methodology are defined by the funding agency and by Bessa as the initiating researcher rather than by the programme participants. The participation is with a group of representative women employed as co-researchers.

It is worth noting the very different role of the co-evaluators from the greater number of women who are interviewed. The former are closely involved in the research programme and they influence its development; they are educated into their role as co-researchers; they contribute essential insights into the culture of the interviewees; and they are clearly empowered by the programme, albeit in the limited sense that Bessa herself notes. On the other hand, the women who are interviewed, while they are approached and interviewed in a manner sensitive to their situation which respects and honours them and their experience, are treated in the same way as orthodox research treats its informants: data are gathered, taken away and made sense of elsewhere.

Another feature of this approach is that the information gathered is not directly linked with action: neither the co-researchers nor the other women involved can engage with their experience in a way that leads to constructive action, either on their own or in collaboration with the providers of the antenatal service. It would seem that in this instance it was simply not possible: holding the group together and completing the evaluation was a remarkable achievement itself.

On the other hand, the strategy taken does mean that information can be gathered from a much wider (and presumably more representative group) of people. In contrast to Hilary Traylen's research, in which the co-operative inquiry is limited to a very small group of professionals, in this project information is collected from as many of those involved in the programme as is practicable. Thus the research does lead to an evaluation of the programme which may provide the basis to develop the programme, or a similar programme elsewhere.

This strategy is clearly appropriate given the intention to evaluate the ante-natal programme in a way that bridges between two cultures. The incidental learning from the project (which is probably the most important piece of learning for our exploration of participation in human inquiry) is how very hard it is for this bridging to be successful, and how hard it is for well-mean-ing professional researchers who intend to work with a collaborative approach to get it anywhere near 'right'. As Bessa points out, it is easier to teach disad-vantaged women the skills of social research than to teach middle class people to enter another culture.

Other learnings from this project emphasize what we already know about participatory inquiry. Time spent on building the group is essential; in partic-ular time spent nurturing a sense of belonging and building open communication channels is time very well spent. We also see how important it is for this group building to take place in a manner which is appropriate to the culture: if group building games and exercises do not fit the culture and are thus inappropriate, it may be better to pay attention to and try to amplify the natural developmental processes of the group. And we also see how important it is to capture the moments naturally offered for building more open rela-tionships, often at unexpected times like driving downtown.

We do not learn from Bessa's chapter anything about her own supervision or support for this work as facilitator of this group. I would speculate that reflecting on her relationship with the co-researchers, talking it through with a supportive friend, might have been helpful. It might also be helpful in such supervision sessions to use role play or psychodrama to explore what was going on experientially (Hawkins, 1988; Krim, 1988). In response to my queries, Bessa wrote to me,

> I did have one friend, who was familiar with the programme (and knew the women involved) as we talked a great deal about the ups and downs as we went along. That was most helpful and I would deliberately build in some form of support next time. I also wrote quite an extensive reflexive log – writing to myself is one way I process experiences and try to make sense out of them. It helped me to get a handle on my own feelings, on what happened (or didn't), on the process, the women's reactions (expressed and non-verbal) insights into the evaluation (content) plus analyzing it all as we went along. (Whitmore, personal communication, 1993)

Another important feature of this project is its organizational setting. We are told that the antenatal programme is set up to be informal and to match the culture to which it is offered. The evaluation programme continues this ethos, and is fully and quite actively supported by the Community Advisory Committee; the sympathetic and supportive manner in which it played its part is most significant. There is of course a more distant organizational con-text in the government funding agency which may be more judgemental and less sympathetic, and which has to be placated by carefully written reports!

Bessa comments at the end of her chapter that we need to understand bet-ter the dynamics of oppression. It would seem that one way to do this is through some form of participatory inquiry which helps people reach deeply into their experience and to learn to reflect on it from within. One question which remains is the impact on the women co-evaluators and whether they are empowered by the experience? As best we can judge, they did gain in self-esteem and confidence through having been exposed to new ideas and a different cultural setting. I find myself wondering whether they were given a tantalizing glimpse of a different world before being dropped back into their disadvantaged culture with only a greater sense of dissatisfaction. In response to this comment, Bessa took me to task, writing

> it sounds as if I had the power to 'lift' them out of (or drop them back into) their world into mine. What would make me think I had such power? In addition, I'm not sure they necessarily would or should want 'my world' or that it is necessarily all that much better. Materially and economically it is, of course, But there are other aspects, which are so much part of 'who we are' as persons, that cannot necessarily be evaluated in this way. Who defines disadvantage and what that means? Maybe I'm being reactive, but I find your comment is full of assumptions about the superiority of 'my' way of life. I object to the implication that their world is inherently inferior in *every* way and that they want to join what they see as a bunch of pretty tight assed folks who don't have much fun.

The great pity is that we have no comments directly from the women co-researchers on these issues.

Sara and John's multidisciplinary inquiry

Sara and John portray themselves as strong initiators in search of a group with whom to collaborate! The characteristic quality of this research endeavour is the enthusiastic and proactive conduct of the two facilitators in originating the project, working to make it happen within its organizational context and actively facilitating the group inquiry process; while at the same time being intensely concerned that the project is owned by the organization and the group members. It is as if they create a paradox which demands that they work hard in the service of a creative outcome.

They tell the story of their nurturing the project through the organization so well that it does not need elaboration here. But it is worth emphasizing the detailed attention they pay to these questions of context; in this way their work parallels that of Lesley and Dorothy in establishing frameworks for participative research in organizations.

The process of the inquiry itself raises all kinds of interesting issues. The difficulty of pulling together a disparate group of people without proper preparation; the contrasting demands of group process and research task when time is short; the continued tension between facilitator initiative and group ownership; keeping the inquiry alive over holiday breaks in the context of very busy work lives. These issues arise time and again in inquiry projects.

Sara and John present us with a model of strong and active facilitators in the service of the group and inquiry process: they design activities to help the group get together; they listen to the tapes, feed back summaries and prepare agendas; they listen for and support group member initiatives; they support and then get out of the way when the group responds with its own creativity.

The great advantage of this approach is that it can accelerate the group's development and its ability to undertake co-operative inquiry. Activities such as summarizing, feeding back, identifying inquiry agendas can be crucial in teaching the group the process of co-operative inquiry through doing it.

The danger of this style is twofold: the facilitators may take over the inquiry process; or their competent activity may deskill group members, inhibiting the development of independent competence in the group (it contrasts with Annette's abdication of authority early in the inquiry process which, she argues, creates space for the development of peer authority). However, if the activity is coupled with careful attention to group development and ownership, and willingness to step aside at the moment the group takes the initiative (or perhaps just that critical instant beforehand), this can be a fruitful path of facilitation.

Bessa's account or her project would tell us to be careful about taking such a high profile if the cultural divide between group members and facilitators is too wide – what are intended as helpful interventions will misfire. But while Sara and John are in some ways dealing with a complex multidisciplinary group, it is in its way quite homogeneous: all group members are educated middle class professionals who can comfortably meet round a table in a conference centre. Sara and John, as experienced group facilitators, can trust their ability to make appropriate interventions at least most of the time.

They also provide an interesting model of co-facilitation. They chose to collaborate by focusing on different arenas of group behaviour so that their behaviour is complementary and they do not get in each other's way. And they spend a lot of time in self-conscious reflection on the process of the inquiry. Their chapter reminds me of a maxim I learned early in my training as a facilitator, 'Never do alone what two can do'.

While their facilitation is highly planned and active they acknowledge the place of serendipity in this work – things fall into place at the right time – which we also saw in Bessa's story. Like chaos, serendipity cannot be planned, but if you are clear with your intent and work as well as you are able towards it, the universe does seem to bring opportunities that can be seized. The attitude needed is one of control and surrender, bringing discipline to the work while always watching for the unplanned opportunities that arise and being willing to go with them, riding the wave. 'Capture the moment', as Shepard had it (Shepard, 1975).

The process of group development, which they characterize as ascent, flight and descent, echoes that of other accounts of inquiry groups. I find the difficulties they have with closure particularly interesting. In characteristic form, they reflect critically on their own behaviour as facilitators, musing as to whether they could have done better. My own interpretation of the process of the group ending is that the awkwardness was at least in part brought about because the group was really only just beginning. Having worked very hard and against all odds over six short sessions to get a disparate group working together creatively, the project is cut short in its prime. As it ends, the group members are just about ready to go out into their worlds to do the real work of a co-operative inquiry in improving the approach to child protection in Northamptonshire: 'The group has stopped meeting: there are no more dead-lines but it does not *feel* finished'. Writing reports is all very well, but does it address in practice the crucial issues, which 'matter enormously'?

For as a co-operative inquiry this group attends primarily to the reflective stage, the stage of making sense of experience so far. That this is important is not doubted, particularly given the multidisciplinary nature of the work. But reflecting on the past draws attention to the needs of the future; a well formed group almost naturally attends to the important task at hand (as we see from Lesley Treleaven's women's inquiry which quite naturally moves into creative action on the basis of its reflection). So we might say that this group has been denied the opportunity to continue its work.

Moira, Annette, Lyn and Nancy: the youth work inquiry

The co-operative inquiry into youth work provides us with an example of meticulous attention to the values of equal participation throughout. Annette, as the initiator of the project, aims to exercise no more power than is needed to establish the project – allowing power to devolve to group members as quickly as she is able. The group defines the focus of the inquiry, agrees a range of member roles early on, takes a strong part in peer facilitation from the second meeting, albeit with Annette's support. Paradoxically, when she reclaims power to circulate John Rowan's questionnaire she actually provides a focus for a discussion which leads to a new emphasis on the co-operative group.

Annette's willingness to share power continues through the project. The account of the inquiry in Chapter 8 was written collaboratively; and though it was to her that I extended the invitation to contribute to this volume, and she undertook the work of coordination, her name does not appear as first author of the chapter.

The concern for power sharing is mirrored by a concern for creating and maintaining collaborative relationships among group members, exemplified by the development of norms which allow co-researchers to maintain the right to be 'in common' or 'different from' the rest of the group. And it would appear that the emphasis on an ethos of collaboration, individual freedom and responsibility is not just lip-service: they actively address issues of dependency, the disruptive behaviour of two group members and other issues of group process.

In contrast, I get the impression that the group relied quite heavily on the external written authority of John Heron, John Rowan and myself as 'experts' on co-operative inquiry, who provide a clear framework within which collaboration could take place. There are advantages and disadvantages to this: accepting an externally defined discipline does provide an arena in which co-operative learning can take place; on the other hand it may prevent the inquirers from stretching to develop their own unique approach to their work.

Taking the role of devil's advocate one might wonder whether all this attention to establishing collaborative relationships is too idealistic and impractical.

As Randall and Southgate (1980) show, it is the 'living labour cycle', integration of work on a worthwhile task with attention to individual and group needs, that leads to a creative group process. One might wonder whether the group's concern for collaboration would lead to the establishment of a profoundly egalitarian and loving group that was incapable of *doing* anything effective.

But this is shown not to be the case: the group designs a quite complex structure for its inquiry, with detailed work in small groups feeding into the large group effort; and with space for individuals to pursue their own learning needs in the context of a larger group project. They reach some conclusions about their own learning process which, while not wildly original, work for them and provide texture and experiential verification to principles of humanistic learning. And they contribute to the project of an Alternative (or Accessible) Route to Qualification by showing how co-operative inquiry can provide a learning framework for training of youth workers.

I suspect there are a number of processes which make this possible. First of all, Annette provides an excellent role model from the very beginning of co-operative working: she is well prepared for the first meeting of the group and also open to negotiation, demonstrating a balance of initiative, authority and democracy which runs through the whole project. Second, the group is relatively homogeneous in that it is composed of people interested in youth work who share values of humanistic groupwork and experiential learning; they are not people who have to defend their patch or the organization they represent; they are not hard thrusting achievers, but relatively democratic and open in their relationships; and they are quite skilled in working in this kind of group and as facilitators.

This example, along with Hilary's, shows how the co-operative inquiry method can truly democratize research, providing a means by which ordinary, non-academic people can engage in self-directed inquiry into aspects of their lives that matter to them.

Lesley Treleaven's women's staff development group

Lesley Treleaven circulated the draft of my comments to the women in her group, and provided me with copies of their comments as well as providing her own. I have endeavoured to include their comments and feedback as a counterpoint to my own reflections, rather than provide one cleaned up account.

I see Lesley as providing an account of an inquiry which is innovative in several ways. First, there is the creative use of the staff development programme as a vehicle for inquiry. By doing this she not only creates a degree of organizational legitimacy for work which confronts entrenched cultural patterns, but is able to contribute to changing the image of staff development for women from repairing 'deficits' to a creative, educational and genuinely developmental process. This provides another example of how collaborative inquiry can provide a framework for education programmes.

Second, the inquiry is firmly rooted within the organization in which it takes place, and provides a safe space for women in which they can explore their own experience and needs, and from which they can venture out to create changes in the wider organization. Thus this inquiry exemplifies the feminist maxim that the personal is political. And of course this commitment to a feminist position runs through the whole chapter: the inquiry is emphatically woman-centred, and draws on the literature of the women's movement as a theoretical underpinning, thus demonstrating how inquiry can be grounded in an explicitly chosen ideological position.

My use of the term 'feminist' to describe the inquiry provoked considerable response. Several participants wrote that they did not see themselves as feminists, or that they were not consciously building an ideology of feminism. One woman saw my use of the term as a 'put-down', as a label which pigeon-holed them in a negative way. Lesley herself thought my emphasis on feminist ideology overwhelmed other aspects of the inquiry which she sees as equally important:

> We were a group of women staff, and while my own approach is declaredly feminist in the writing, there were a range of diverse positions taken up within the group that changed over time for each of us I think . . . I do not wish to delete my own feminist perspective from the writing, however I did not assume that those participating in the inquiry were self-identified feminists, nor was that the desired 'destination'. (Treleaven, personal communication, 1993)

The third important aspect of this project is the use of the notion of inquiry as creating a space for something to happen. Lesley is critical of accounts of inquiry as a sequence of steps, which she sees as an incomplete approximation of the inquiry process, and argues for a vision of inquiry which allows more space for the implicit structure of the situation to emerge, for creative expression and synchronicity.

While arguing this, the inquiry is not without structure. There is an emphasis on equal time and space for all members (although as Lesley points out, this was not always achieved), on story-telling and on listening circles. There is also agreement about the essential ambiguity of structure, an acceptance that members may come and go as they are able. But it does appear that the structure *emerges* as required, from the early getting together, through the deep immersion in story-telling, into more active responses to the organizational situations that arise and which offer opportunities for re-visioning the position of women in the University. This inquiry points to the potentially creative paradox in the tension between structure and lack of structure.

While Lesley's inquiry has these novel features, it is also deeply familiar. She writes about the care and attention that goes into the formation of the group – the formal letter to managers, the personal contact made to potential participants; and the planning and preparation that goes into the initial meeting – choosing a time and space which will be suitable, preparation of an agenda and structure which will include people. We also learn about the continued physical as well as emotional nurturing of the group – lunch, flowers on the table – which we found in Bessa's story and in Sara and John's account.

I find it interesting that we learn little about Lesley as facilitator from the chapter. She mentions the careful work she undertook to set up the group; she does refer to herself as 'initiator, facilitator, convenor, researcher, housekeeper and participant'; and we do learn of her personal responses to the group from her dream and poem. But otherwise the account is of what 'we' – the inquiry group – chose to do. This is in marked contrast to the emphasis Sara and John place on their reflections and on their choices as facilitators. I find myself wondering whether this became a genuine 'leaderless' group, framed and contained by a shared feminist or woman-centred perspective; or whether much active leadership and facilitation is hidden behind the rhetoric of 'making space'. In particular it would be interesting to learn more about how the group managed the episodes of confrontation and conflict which arose. Lesley wrote in response:

> I am genuinely surprised by your comment about learning little about my facilitation. My facilitative role changed from the initial positioning of me by some of the group as facilitator, to times when we used a structured process like Listening circles which I facilitated, to frequent times when the group functioned without a facilitator but with participants actively responsible for all or part of a session . . . I've found your comment stimulating – obviously – but remain concerned about the polarization you have constructed between 'leaderless' or 'hidden leadership'. I wonder if there isn't a masculinist assumption that 'active leadership' must be present, identifiable or otherwise hidden and unacknowledged . . . One of the group's challenges was the re-framing of traditional notions of leadership/management. (personal communication, 1993)

I do not think my comment contained a hidden assumption, it was more a gentle wondering about how the group worked internally, wanting to know more about how it managed itself.

It is important to note that while the group continues to emphasize listening, caring and nurturing, there is a lot of action in this inquiry. The women participants are supported by the group as they confront sexist remarks, resist tokenism, raise issues of equal opportunities in University committees, and as they begin to devise a coherent strategy for raising the profile of women in the decision-making forums of the organization. So as with the youth workers' project, we can see that attention to individual and group needs can lead beyond introspection to action in the world. The maxim that co-operative inquiry is 'learning through risk taking in living' is also exemplified here, as it is in Hilary's account.

Lesley Archer and Dorothy Whitaker: research partnerships

Lesley and Dorothy's account of research partnerships is of interest for precisely the opposite reason to Lesley Treleaven's: it shows how an approach to participative research can be formally organized into a series of phases and activities. In this way the participative approach reflects the ethos of service-providing organizations, while the structured approach fits with the formal organizational setting in which they wish to operate.

Their account will read as familiar to people acquainted with the literature on planned change and organizational development. We read of the need for the work to be legitimized from the top while controlled by staff at all levels; how a Project Workers Team is established to conduct the work, while a Coordination Group provides an arena for communication with the wider organization; and how the project moves through a series of planned phases firm enough to provide clarity yet flexible enough to be tailored to different situations.

Lesley and Dorothy's approach includes the use of research workshops as structured opportunities for organizational members to share their 'practice wisdom' and to identify issues the organization needs to address. These are very important ways in which large numbers of people – members of organizations or communities – can genuinely participate, perhaps not as full co-researchers, but as significant contributors to an inquiry. Such workshop structures are common practice among action researchers working on quality of working life projects (Gustavsen, 1992) and in a different way by proponents of participatory action research (Fals-Borda and Rahman, 1991). Thus the research partnership proceeds through a series of temporary participative structures which run in parallel with the formal organization structure, jointly managed by the external researchers and organizational members (Bushe and Shani, 1991).

It is important to note the more traditional view of research activity espoused here, for example where they differentiate between formal 'findings' and experiential 'learnings'; and also in their emphasis on the research itself as a separate phase of activity conducted in a traditionally rigorous fashion, but bringing together that experience of those in the field with the methodological expertise of university-based social work researchers. In this way their work is comparable with Bessa Whitmore's research, which uses a traditional interviewing method in an innovative fashion; and stands in contrast to the work of Lesley Treleaven and Hilary Traylen which is grounded fully in the experience of the participants. Both may have their validity. What is important is to see that this more orthodox approach to inquiry can be integrated fruitfully within a participative inquiry strategy.

The other important contrast is between this approach of research partnerships and the examples of full co-operative inquiry. In research partnerships the authority structure of the organization and of the research process is the accepted framework for the research. The participation is consultative in style within this framework, and the researchers appear to work as benign authoritative leaders; in contrast, Hilary, Annette and Lesley Treleaven allow and encourage their co-researchers to take much more power in defining the range, style and content of their inquiries. Lesley and Dorothy comment

> This of course raises the extremely interesting question of power and where it lies. We do not think of ourselves as 'benign authoritarian leaders'. We do not think of ourselves as leaders at all, but as facilitators. Any authority which we have derives from a background of experience with research, just as others concerned possess authority derived from their, equally important, realms of experience. We hope that we are benign, but then so is everyone else: the ethos of partnership research is mutual respect for what each person concerned can bring to the project. We would like it noted that the power over the focus of the work, and the research purposes,

derives from people in the organization. Our role in formulating purposes consists in facilitating their articulation. (personal communication, 1994)

Research partnerships also reflect the political orientation of representative democracy in establishing groups to steer and manage the project whose members can speak for their constituents. Bessa Whitmore's chapter is similarly based on representation of a wider group in a different way – although without the formal constitutional arrangement which characterizes research partnerships. Representative democracy stands in contrast to direct or participatory democracy, in which individual members are directly involved in decision-making, rather than through representatives (Bachrach and Botwinick, 1992). The ideology of co-operative inquiry tends towards that of direct democracy, with Lesley Treleaven's inquiry being probably the most radical example.

The many faces of participation

This review of the contributors' chapters shows the many faces of participation: so simple on the one hand, so subtle and complex on the other; so easy to say, and yet so difficult to practise; and so rich in the experience for all involved. A number of themes have emerged which I shall note.

Forms of participation

I want first to reflect on the different forms of participation in the inquiries using the framework developed in Chapters 1–4. To what extent are these projects examples of original participation, unconscious participation and future participation?

While the health visitors' experience cannot be described as original participation in Barfield's sense of unconscious embeddedness in phenomena, there is a sense in which the health visitors that Hilary interviewed were originally flooded by their experience and sunk in the stress of their work; this can be seen as a degenerate form of deep participation. The first task of the inquiry was then to recover a sense of connectedness and valuing of their experience: to shift the group to a valid form of deep participation. Thus the work of exploring their practice is deeply engaging: Hilary notes that their primary modality was story-telling which is congruent with deep participation. She also points out how difficult it was to move the group to reflect on the inquiry as a whole. However, by building on their concrete experience the group moves into productive and quite risky cycles of action and reflection, which I would suggest can be seen as a move towards their own form of future reflexive participation.

In contrast to this experiential work, the formal statement of health visitor aims to which they later turn for a definition of their role exemplifies formal alienated consciousness. They struggle with the contrast between their experience and this statement, and from the dialectical tension between these two comes the more deeply based realization that health visiting practice must be based on the 'development of well-being'. As Hilary points out, for the inquiry group 'well-being' is not just another abstract statement. It is grounded in their own intuitive experiential knowing – they have developed a feel for their own well-being as professionals and for the well-being of clients through their exploration of hidden agendas. It is made manifest through the practical skills they have been developing. And it is expressed through a statement which makes sense to them and communicates to their colleagues. Thus experiential, practical and propositional knowings are congruent, build on and reinforce each other. The group can be seen as taking a further step towards future participation, developing a way of knowing which is both deeply embedded and reflective.

In Bessa's account the women who participated in the antenatal programme can be seen in terms of deep non-reflective participation: they have been supported through their pregnancy and delivery by the programme and they have been asked to tell the story of their experience to an understanding and sympathetic listener with whom they can identify. They are embedded in their culture, which is characterized as quite defensive, and have not been asked to reflect or make sense of their experience.

The four women co-researchers are taught social science methodology, they are taken into different cultural milieux which present novel experiences and through this develop a degree of critical reflectiveness. But they do not lose their capacity for deep participation – reading the stories of their encounters with committees and conferences I am struck with their continued spontaneity. Thus they appear to be making their idiosyncratic transition, albeit limited, from deep participation to a reflective future participation.

Bessa, on the other hand, seems to be making the journey towards a reflective participation in the opposite direction. Despite her value stance and epistemological position, she characterizes herself at first as quite awkward, ignorant of the culture, working from the models of her social science training rather than from a deep intuitive participation. We are treated to a very honest account of her struggles to learn from her experiences, her 'stumbling gait' towards participation, as Torbert (1991) might describe it. Again we see that good heartedness and willingness to learn may be more important than getting it right all the time.

Sara and John seem well on the way towards a reflective participation in their work as facilitators. They certainly are deeply engaged with their work and also systematically take time to stand back and reflect. It is worth noting that engagement and reflection are still separate activities to a large extent: there are clearly times when they are swamped by the experience, and their sense-making follows with some delay, but that is to be expected.

On the other hand it is not clear how much the participants in the research project have moved towards a reflective consciousness. Since the project is so thoroughly (and successfully) facilitated I find myself suspecting that for much of the time the participants were carried along by a process which they were not able to make fully conscious for themselves.

Lesley Treleaven's women's inquiry demonstrates the possibility of grounding an inquiry in deep experiential knowing: the group affirms the importance of experience, intuition, story-telling, of knowing with body and emotions as well as with intellect, of structures and processes emerging from the needs of the moment. Confident in the experiential base of women's shared pain in the organization, the group seems to include conscious reflection as part of the process throughout – although there is of course an increased emphasis on making sense towards the end of the inquiry as documenting becomes important. The sense-making continues to hold awareness of the ground on which it arose.

The members of the youth work inquiry start from their experiential embeddedness in their work and their desire for qualification. Since most of them have been involved in experiential learning for a while, it would seem reasonable to assume that they are rooted in valid deep participation with a degree of reflective consciousness. They use the tools of co-operative inquiry – research cycling and devil's advocate procedures in particular, to enhance their self-reflectiveness. There is one particularly interesting incident, a vignette of the dialectic process, when Annette, by taking her authority in distributing the Rowan questionnaire, causes a major debate about power and democracy within the group.

Lesley and Dorothy's account of partnership research is important because it provides a framework within which collaborative research can take place. This can be seen as creating a contradiction between the formal structures of the 'parallel organization' they help to create and the experiential involvement of people. Successful projects are those in which this tension pays off in new creative understandings. Unsuccessful ones are those in which energy slumps or the hierarchy dominates. Again we can see the dialectic process at play: by creating a structure a space is created within which spontaneity can arise.

It seems from this retrospective analysis that the dialectical framework of developing participative consciousness which I outlined in Chapter 3 does help to make sense of these projects. However, in more proactive use the framework would illuminate the development of future participation as it unfolded through the history of an inquiry. It would provide both facilitators and participants with a way of looking at their experience, making sense of their interactions and choosing the form of their developing relationships.

Methodology

Formal methodology is approached in very different ways in the six examples. The youth workers, health visitors and child protection groups draw quite formally on co-operative inquiry method, adapting it for their purposes yet staying within the framework. The pre-natal programme evaluation draws on the tradition of participatory research and links it with a more traditional qualitative methodology. In partnership research Lesley and Dorothy have developed their own methodological form grounded in the principles of action research and organizational intervention. In contrast, Lesley Treleaven sees all statements of method as oversimplified and argues for an emergent process of inquiry. I have much sympathy with her perspective, having found that in my own work co-operative inquiry, which started off as a radical alternative to orthodox inquiry, has developed an orthodoxy of its own, so that students sometimes feel that they have to undertake a 'proper' co-operative inquiry. On the other hand, Lesley's work *is* informed by a range of participatory ideas and by woman-centred values and practice, and it takes place at an institution where collaborative forms of inquiry do have a voice in that they are advocated and supported in at least one subculture.

I believe that method is important. I believe, as I have argued in Chapter 4, that it presents a discipline which will encourage the development of reflective participative consciousness and of a community of inquiry. This discipline offers a tension between the messiness of experiential engagement and the structure offered by cycles of action and reflection. And yet, if method becomes a new orthodoxy it will degenerate and again stifle creativity. Discipline is important in translating the intellectual ideals of participation into a form of practice.

My advice to those who want to use collaborative methods is that they should study what others have done, explore the range of methods that is available, and then invent their own form which is suitable for the project they wish to undertake:

> The methodologies we teach are best seen as sets of general principles and heuristic devices which need to be adapted creatively to different research issues. They raise questions rather than offer answers . . . . We see ourselves as working with people on the questions behind the formulae of academic research, inviting them to create and frame answers for themselves. (Marshall and Reason, 1994)

Ownership, power and collaboration

The question, 'Whose research is this?' runs centrally through many accounts. What is fascinating is the amount of work and attention the initiators have devoted to developing participatory group relationships. The group first has to be created and established with enough clarity of purpose and method that it has some chance of success, a culture of collaboration developed over time, and then space has to be provided for initiatives from participants to take over and transform the inquiry beyond the original dreams of the initiator.

This is accomplished in several ways: at one extreme Annette gives away power as soon as the group is established; at the other Lesley and Dorothy provide guidance to the participants through the steps of the research. Hilary identifies strongly with her participants, while Sara and John provide professional facilitation. There is an interesting contrast between Bessa working across cultural boundaries in the interest of a disadvantaged group and Lesley's feminist identification with the difficulties of women in her institution.

It seems also that participation in inquiry may range from the tacit to the explicit. In a way, in all inquiry participation will be tacit to begin with, from the time the initiator conceives the idea until it has been shared and agreed with co-researchers. Our students at Bath have found that they may have to work within their organization for quite a while, sowing the seeds of collaborative inquiry, inviting people to join with them, before making the explicit proposal to establish a co-operative inquiry group. In other situations, for example with people belonging to other subcultures, inquiry may need to stay tacit for quite a period, while trust and understanding are built up. As Bessa points out, it may be quite impossible to make an explicit agreement for co-operation with the disadvantaged women. Indeed, it may rarely be possible to establish a full relationship as co-researchers with some constituencies, although Sheila McClelland has shown that the limits of collaboration may be broader than we imagine by working with mental health patients as co-researchers (McClelland et al., 1993).

Facilitation

The contributions show a wide range of approaches to facilitation. On the one hand there is the intentional application of professional competence of Lesley and Dorothy in research partnerships and Sara and John with the child protection inquiry, all of whom have extensive training in group dynamics and facilitation. Bessa finds that quite often her professional competence is disabling as it takes her too far away from the culture of her co-evaluators. On the other hand there is Hilary's relatively naïve facilitation by identification, and the shared facilitation of the youth workers group.

   Hilary's facilitation worked well in the circumstances: a homogeneous group working to a clear purpose engaged in creative cycles of inquiry (Randall and Southgate, 1980). It illustrates well that co-operative inquiry can be used by 'ordinary people' and is not just the prerogative of professional researchers. At the same time, one can imagine situations with larger groups with more diverse composition and more difficult circumstances in which the group process could become difficult, turn sour, and lead a naïve facilitator beyond their skills. I strongly believe that all those involved in co-operative inquiry should have an understanding of group process (for example, through reading Srivastva et al., 1977; Randall and Southgate, 1980; Heron, 1993) and some introduction of facilitation skill (see, for example, Heron, 1989).

Organizational context

The inquiries took place in very diverse organizational contexts. The programme of research partnerships is designed as a way of taking inquiry into formal organizations as part of a programme of planned development. Lesley and Dorothy have built a solid reputation for their work and established relationships with their client systems over the years, centred in the University of York. The child protection project is formally sanctioned and paid for by the sponsoring organization, but since it is not (as yet) part of a long-term programme of co-operative inquiry, each step of legitimation has to be invented and painfully negotiated. The evaluation of the pre-natal programme is sponsored by an organization which clearly appreciates the values of participation and invites proposals which will be in keeping with the nature of the project. And the norms and expectations of the youth service that provided the context for the youth service inquiry are congruent with those of co-operative inquiry.

In contrast, Lesley Treleaven uses the opportunities presented by equal employment and opportunity legislation and the staff development programme as a kind of organizational jujitsu, reframing them so that her inquiry is both within and outside the organization in a way that provides a base for her women-centred project.

Hilary's research with health visitors takes place in an organizational context – her project is sponsored by the NHS regional organization, and takes place within the local organization. However, since her concern is primarily with the participants she fails to anticipate that her project runs counter to organizational norms and will stimulate opposition. She is obliged to spend some considerable amount of energy mending fences and restoring confidence in her work before she can proceed.

All these examples show how important it is to attend to organizational context: one may choose to go with it or to oppose it; to find the cracks in the formal organization in which the seeds of participation can be planted. But one cannot ignore it.

By way of conclusion

I write these final words the day after the first session at the University of Bath with our new postgraduate programme in action research. The group includes experienced professionals from business and public sector organizations, from health care, social work and education. Their concerns include organizational learning and development, questions of gender and race, and conflict resolution. We spent two days together, at first tentatively, and then with more confidence sharing what we hoped to get out of our association and our fears of disappointment. The desire for community is strong: many saying how deeply they feel the need for support, friendship and challenge; and at the same time there is some fear of losing individual purpose in the whole. The desire for clarity about method, and truth, and meaning is strong, yet there is suspicion that words and theories may potentially distort experience. We have begun to build a participative community of inquiry.

My image for these exhilarating and exhausting two days is rather different from Hampden-Turner's one of steering between the rock and the whirlpool (see Chapter 3); for both rock and whirlpool are to be avoided – dangers on which one can be wrecked. Rather it is the image of a sailing boat, beating down a tidal channel in a fresh wind, *working* between wind and tide: for wind and tide can both carry you along and can also turn against you. Sometimes they work together as when the wind in the sails and the tide under the hull carry you on a fast passage; sometimes they are in harsh opposition, when wind against tide gives rise to a sharp, choppy and dangerous sea, especially around a tricky headland; and sometimes wind and tide work together in creative opposition as when the tidal stream counters the wind's leeway and allows the boat to steer a more direct course. In my metaphor the tide is the water in which we all swim, the deep participation of membership, of flowing together, of empathy; and the wind in contrast brings separateness, difference and critical consciousness. It is in knowing their ways and in working their contrast and contradiction that skilful sailors – and inquirers – make a forward passage.

References

Adler, P.A. and Adler, P. (1987) 'The history and epistemology of fieldwork roles', in *Membership Roles in Field Research*, Sage University Paper Series on Qualitative Research Methods (Vol. 6): Newbury Park, CA: Sage.

Allen, P.G. (1986) 'Tribal cultures'. (Contribution to Cultural Sources of New Paradigm Thinking.) In *ReVision* Special Issue: Critical Questions about New Paradigm Thinking, 9 (1): 26–32.

Allen, P.G. (1992) *The Sacred Hoop: Recovering the Feminine in American Indian Traditions*. Boston: Beacon.

Archer, J.L. (1990) 'Research and practice as related activities', in D.S. Whitaker, J.L. Archer and S. Greve (eds), *Research, Practice and Service Delivery in Social Work*. CCETSW regional publication.

Archer, J.L. and Whitaker, D.S. (1989) 'Engaging practitioners in formulating research purposes', *Journal of Social Work*, 8 (2): 29–37.

Archer, J.L. and Whitaker, D.S. (1991) *Improving and Maintaining Quality of Life in Homes for Elderly People*. Humberside SSD Polkington Office, Flat 2, Wold Haven, Pocklington, England.

Argyris, C. and Schon, D. (1974) *Theory in Practice: Increasing Professional Effectiveness*. San Francisco: Jossey Bass.

Argyris, C. and Schon, D. (1978) *Organizational Learning*. Reading, MA: Addison Wesley.

Argyris, C., Putnam, R. and Smith, M.C. (1985) *Action Science: Concepts, Methods, and Skills for Research and Intervention*. San Francisco: Jossey Bass.

Ash, M. (1992) *The Fabric of the World: Towards a Philosophy of Environment*. Bideford, Devon: Green Books.

Avens, R. (1980) *Imagination is Reality*. Irving, TX: Spring Publications.

Bachrach, P. and Botwinick, A. (1992) *Power and Empowerment: a Radical Theory of Participatory Democracy*. Philadelphia: Temple University Press.

Bakan, D. (1966) *The Duality of Human Existence: Isolation and Communion in Western Man*. Boston: Beacon Press.

Barfield, O. (1957) *Saving the Appearances: a Study in Idolatry*. London: Faber and Faber.

Barfield, O. (1977) *The Rediscovery of Meaning and Other Essays*. Middletown: Wesleyan University Press.

Baring, A. and Cashford, J. (1991) *The Myth of the Goddess: Evolution of an Image*. London: Viking Arkana.

Bate, P. and Mangham, I.L. (1981) *Exploring Participation*. Chichester: Wiley.

Bates, B. (1983) *The Way of Wyrd: Tales of an Anglo-Saxon Sorcerer*. London: Century Publishing.

Bateson, G. (1972) *Steps to an Ecology of Mind*. San Francisco: Chandler.

Bateson, G. and Bateson, M.C. (1987) *Angels Fear: an Investigation into the Nature and Meaning of the Sacred*. London: Rider.

Bateson, G. (1979) *Mind and Nature: a Necessary Unity*. New York: E.P. Dutton.

Belenky, M., Clinchy, B., Goldberger, N. and Tarule, J. (1986) *Women's Ways of Knowing: the Development of Self, Voice, and Mind*. New York: Basic Books.

Bell, J. and Hardiman, R. J. (1989) 'The third role – the naturalistic knowledge engineer', in D. Diaper (ed.) *Knowledge Elicitation: Principles, Techniques and Applications*. London: Ellis Horwood.

Berman, M. (1981) *The Reenchantment of the World*. Ithaca: Cornell University Press.

Berman, M. (1989) *Coming to our Senses: Body and Spirit in the Hidden History of the West*. New York: Simon and Schuster.

Berry, T. (1988) *The Dream of the Earth*. San Francisco: Sierra Club.

Bion, W.R. (1959) *Experiences in Groups*. London: Tavistock Publications.

Black Elk, W.H. and Lyon, W.S. (1990) *Black Elk Speaks: the Sacred Ways of the Lakota*. San Francisco: Harper and Row.

Blackmore, J. (1992) 'Post masculinist institutional politics: hegemonic masculinities, bureaucratic culture(s) and feminist practise in educational organisations'. Paper presented to the Conference on Gendered Culture: Educational Management in the 90s, Victoria University of Technology, St Albans, Victoria, Australia.

Bookchin, M. (1991) *The Ecology of Freedom: the Emergence and Dissolution of Hierarchy*. Montreal and New York: Black Rose Books.

Bortoft, H. (1986) *Goethe's Scientific Consciousness*. Tonbridge Wells, Kent: Institute of Cultural Research, Monograph Series No. 22.

Boud, D., Keogh R. and Walker, D. (eds) (1985) *Reflection: Turning Experience into Learning*. London: Kogan Page.

Brown, G. and Atkins, M. (1988) *Effective Teaching in Higher Education*. London: Methuen.

Brown, L.M. and Gilligan, C. (1992) *Meeting at the Crossroads: Women's Psychology and Girls' Development*. Cambridge, MA: Harvard University Press.

Buber, M. (1965) *The Knowledge of Man*. London: Allen and Unwin.

Burton, C. (1991) *The Promise and the Price: the Struggle for Equal Opportunity in Women's Employment*. Sydney: Allen and Unwin.

Bushe, G.R. and Shani, A.B. (1991) *Parallel Learning Structures*. Reading, MA: Addison Wesley.

Campbell, J. (1960) *The Masks of God: Primitive Mythology*. London: Secker and Warburg.

Campbell, J. (1962) *The Masks of God: Oriental Mythology*. London: Secker and Warburg.

Campbell, J. (1965) *The Masks of God: Occidental Mythology*. London: Secker and Warburg.

Cancian, F.M. and Armstead, C. (1993) 'Bibliography on participatory research', in P. Reason (ed.) *Collaborative Inquiry*, No. 9, Centre for the Study of Organizational Change and Development, University of Bath.

Carr, W. and Kemmis, S. (1986) *Becoming Critical: Education, Knowledge and Action Research*. Geelong, Victoria, Australia: Deakin University.

CETHU (1977) *The Function of the Health Visitor*. London: Council for Education and Training of Health Visitors.

Chisholm, R. and Elden, M. (1993) 'Features of emerging action research', *Human Relations*, 46 (2): 275–98.

Clifford, J. and Marcus, G.E. (eds) (1986) *Writing Culture: The Poetics and Politics of Ethnography*. Berkeley: University of California Press.

Colgrave, S. (1979) *The Spirit of the Valley: Androgony and Chinese Thought*. London: Virago.

Colorado, P. (1988) 'Bridging native and Western science, *Convergence*, 21 (2/3): 49–68.

Comstock, D.E. and Fox, R. (1993) 'Participatory research as critical theory: the North Bonneville, USA, experience', in P. Park, M. Brydon-Miller, B. Hall and T. Jackson (eds) *Voices of Change: Participatory Research in the United States and Canada*. Toronto: OISE Press.

Cosier, J.P. (1991a) *Setting Up a Quality Organisation: a Senior Manager's Improvement Workshop*. Private publication.

Cosier, J.P. (1991b) *Achieving Improvement: a Workshop for Everyone Involved in Improvement*. Private publication.

Crawford, J., Kippax, S., Onyx, J. and Galt, U. (1992) *Gender and Emotion*. London: Sage.

Crook, J. (1993) 'Review of Ash, M. (1992) *The Fabric of the World: Towards a Philosophy of Environment*', *Resurgence*, 156: 46–7.

Crook, J.H. (1980) *The Evolution of Human Consciousness*. Oxford: Oxford University Press.

Cunningham, I. (1988) 'Interactive holistic research: researching self managed learning', in P. Reason (ed.) *Human Inquiry in Action: Developments in New Paradigm Research*. London: Sage Publications.

Davies, B. (1989) *Frogs and Snails and Feminist Tales*. Sydney: George Allen and Unwin.

Devall, B. and Sessions, G. (1985) *Deep Ecology: Living as if Nature Mattered.* Salt Lake City: Gibbs M. Smith.

Eckman, B. (1986) *Jung, Hegel, and the Subjective Universe.* Dallas: Spring Publications.

Eisler, R. (1990) *The Chalice and the Blade.* London: Unwin Hyman.

Falk, R. (1992) 'Politically engaged spirituality in an emerging global society', *ReVision*, 15 (3): 137–44.

Fals-Borda, O. and Rahman, M.A. (1991) *Action and Knowledge: Breaking the Monopoly with Participatory Action Research.* New York: Intermediate Technology Pubs/Apex Press.

Faludi, S. (1991) *Backlash: The Undeclared War Against American Women.* New York: Doubleday.

Fernandes, W. and Tandon, R. (eds) (1981) *Participatory Research and Evaluation: Experiments in Research as a Process of Liberation.* New Delhi: Indian Social Institute.

Finch, J. (1984) '"It's great to have someone to talk to": the ethics and politics of interviewing women', in C. Bell and H. Roberts (eds) *Social Researching: Politics, Problems, Practice.* London: Routledge and Kegan Paul.

Fine, M. (1992) *Disruptive Voices: the Possibilities of Feminist Research.* Ann Arbor: University of Michigan Press.

Fine, M. and Gordon, S.M. (1992) Feminist Transformations of/despite psychology', in M. Fine (ed.) *Disruptive Voices: the Possibilities of Feminist Research.* Ann Arbor: University of Michigan Press.

Fisher, D. and Torbert, W.R. (1995) *Personal and Organizational Transformations: Continual Quality Improvement and beyond.* Maidenhead: McGraw–Hill.

Fonow, M.M. and Cook, J.A. (eds) (1991) *Beyond Methodology: Feminist Scholarship as Lived Research.* Bloomington: Indiana University Press.

Fox, M. (1983) *Meditations with Meister Eckhart.* Santa Fe: Bear and Co.

Fox-Genovese, E. (1987) 'Andocrats go home!', *The New York Times Book Review*, October 4: 32.

Freire, P. (1970) *Pedagogy of the Oppressed.* New York: Herder and Herder.

Gaventa, J. (1980) *Power and Powerlessness: Rebellion and Quiescence in an Appalachian Valley.* Chicago: University of Illinois Press.

Gilligan, C. (1982) *In a Different Voice: Psychological Theory and Women's Identity.* Cambridge, MA: Harvard University Press.

Gimbutas, M. (1982) *The Gods and Goddesses of Old Europe.* Los Angeles: University of California Press.

Glaser, B.G. and Strauss, A.L. (1967) *The Discovery of Grounded Theory.* Chicago: Aldine.

Goldberger, N.R., Clinchy, B.M., Belenky, M. and Tarule, J.M. (1987) 'Women's ways of knowing: on gaining a voice', in P. Shaver and C. Hendrick (eds) *Sex and Gender.* Newbury Park, CA: Sage.

Goodwin, B.C. (1992) *A Science of Qualities.* Milton Keynes: Development Dynamics Research Group, The Open University.

Griffin, D.R. (1989) Introduction to SUNY series in Constructive Postmodern Thought, in D.R. Griffin, W.A. Beardslee and J. Holland *Varieties of Postmodern Theology.* Albany: SUNY.

Griffin, D.R., Beardslee, W.A. and Holland, J. (1989) *Varieties of Postmodern Theology.* Albany: SUNY.

Griffin, S. (1984) 'Split culture', in S. Kumar (ed.) *The Schumacher Lectures Volume II.* London: Abacus.

Grimshaw, J. (1986) *Feminist Philosophers.* Brighton: Wheatsheaf.

Grosz, E. (1990) 'Conclusion: a note on essentialism and difference', in S. Gunew (ed.) *Feminist Knowledge: Critique and Construct.* London: Routledge.

Guba, E.G. and Lincoln, Y.S. (1989) *Fourth Generation Evaluation.* Newbury Park, CA: Sage.

Gustavsen, B. (1992) *Dialogue and Development.* Assen/Maastricht: Van Gorcum.

Hall, B. (1993) 'Participatory research', *International Encyclopedia of Education.* London: Pergamon.

Hall, B., Gillette, A. and Tandon, R. (eds) (1982) *Creating Knowledge: a Monopoly? Participatory Research in Development.* New Delhi: Society for Participatory Research in Asia.

Hampden-Turner, C. (1990) *Charting the Corporate Mind: From Strategy to Dilemma.* Oxford: Basil Blackwell.

Hardiman, R.J. (1993) 'On becoming a participant: a view from an iconoclast'. Unpublished paper, Centre for Action Research in Professional Practice, University of Bath.

Harding, S. (ed.) (1986) *Feminist Methodology*. Milton Keynes: Open University Press.

Harvey, D. (1989) *The Condition of Post-Modernity*. Oxford: Basil Blackwell.

Haug, F. (1983) translated by Erica Carter (1987). *Female Sexualisation: a Collective Work of Memory*. London: Verso.

Hawkins, P. (1988) 'A phenomenological psychodrama workshop', in P. Reason (ed.) *Human Inquiry in Action: Developments in New Paradigm Research*. London: Sage.

Hegel, G. (1948) 'On love', trans. R. Kroner, in *Early Theological Writings*, trans. T.M. Knox. Chicago: University of Chicago Press.

Heron, J. (1971) *Experience and Method: an Inquiry into the Concept of Experiential Research*. Human Potential Research Project, University of Surrey.

Heron, J. (1981a) 'Philosophical basis for a new paradigm', in P. Reason and J. Rowan (eds) *Human Inquiry: a Sourcebook of New Paradigm Research*. Chichester: Wiley.

Heron, J. (1981b) 'Experiential research methodology', in P. Reason and J. Rowan (eds) *Human Inquiry: a Sourcebook of New Paradigm Research*. Chichester: Wiley.

Heron, J. (1985) 'The role of reflection in a co-operative inquiry', in D. Boud, R. Keogh and D. Walker (eds) *Reflection: Turning Experience into Learning*. London: Kogan Page.

Heron, J. (1988) 'Validity in co-operative inquiry', in P. Reason (ed.) *Human Inquiry in Action: Developments in New Paradigm Research*. London: Sage.

Heron, J. (1989) *The Facilitators Handbook*. London: Kogan Page.

Heron, J. (1992) *Feeling and Personhood: Psychology in Another Key*. London: Sage.

Heron, J. (1993) *Group Facilitation: Theories and Models of Practice*. London: Kogan Page.

Hillman, J. (1975) *Revisioning Psychology*. New York: Harper Collophon.

HMSO (1981) *Experience and Participation: Report of the Review Group on the Youth Service in England and Wales*. London: HMSO.

Hollway, W. (1984) 'Gender difference and the production of subjectivity', in J. Henriques, W. Hollway, C. Urwin, C. Venn and V. Walkerdine (eds) *Changing the Subject: Psychology, Social Regulation and Subjectivity*. London: Methuen.

Hollway, W. (1989) *Subjectivity and Method in Psychology: Gender, Meaning and Science*. London: Sage.

Horgan, J. (1993) 'The worst enemy of science: profile of Paul Karl Feyerabend', *Scientific American*, 268 (5): 16–17.

Houston, J. (1982) *The Possible Human*. Los Angeles: J.P. Tarcher.

Houston, J (1987) *The Search for the Beloved: Journeys in Mythology and Sacred Psychology*. Los Angeles: J.P. Tarcher.

Kaptchuk, T.J. (1983) *Chinese Medicine: the Web that has no Weaver*. London: Rider.

Kari-Oca Village Declaration (1992) Declaration from the World Congress of Indigenous Peoples on Territory, Environment and Development in Rio de Janeiro. Reprinted in *World Goodwill Newsletter*, No. 2, 1993.

Kaufmann, W. (1950) *Nietzsche: Philosopher, Psychologist, Anti-Christ*. Princeton, NJ: Princeton University Press.

Kegan, R. (1980) *The Evolving Self*. Cambridge, MA: Harvard University Press.

Kemmis, S. and McTaggart, R. (eds) (1988) *The Action Research Planner*. Victoria, Australia: Deakin University Press.

Kohler Riessman, C. (1987) 'When gender is not enough: women interviewing women', *Gender and Society*. 1 (2): 172–207.

Kolb, D. (1984) *Experiential Learning: Experience as the Source of Learning and Development*. London: Prentice Hall.

Kolb, D., Rubin, I.M. and McIntyre, J.M. (1979) *Organisational Psychology: an Experiential Approach*. London: Prentice Hall.

Kremer, J. (1992a) 'The dark night of the scholar: reflections on culture and ways of knowing', *ReVision*, 14 (4): 169–78.

Kremer, J. (1992b) *The Past and Future Process of Mythology*. Unpublished paper, California Institute of Integral Studies, San Francisco.

Kremer, J. (1992c) *Prolegomena Shamanica*. Red Bluff, CA: Falkenflug Press.

Krim, R. (1988) 'Managing to learn: action inquiry in City Hall', in P. Reason (ed.) *Human Inquiry in Action*. London: Sage Publications.

Kuhn, T. (1962) *The Structure of Scientific Revolutions*. Chicago: University of Chicago Press.

Laing, R.D. (1967) *The Politics of Experience*. New York: Ballantine Books.

Lather, P. (1986) 'Research as praxis', *Harvard Educational Review*, 56 (3): 257–77.

Lather, P. (1991) *Getting Smart: Feminist Research and Pedagogy Within the Postmodern*. New York: Routledge.

Lawson, H. (1985) *Reflexivity: the Post-modern Predicament*. London: Hutchinson.

Lefkowitz, M. (1992) 'The twilight of the Goddess', *The New Republic*, August 3: 29–33.

Lewin, K. (1946) 'Action research and minority problems', *Journal of Social Issues*, 2: 34–46.

Lewin, K. (1947) 'Frontiers of group dynamics: concept, method, reality in social science; social equilibria and social change', *Human Relations*, 1: 5–42.

Lewin, K. (1951) *Field Theory in Social Science: Selected Theoretical Papers*. New York: Harper & Row.

Lincoln, S.Y., and Guba, E.G. (1985) *Naturalistic Inquiry*. Beverly Hills: Sage.

Loevinger, J. (1976) *Ego Development*. San Francisco: Jossey Bass.

Long, A. (1992) *In a Chariot Drawn by Lions: the Search for the Female in Deity*. London: The Women's Press.

Lovelock, J.E. (1979) *Gaia: a New Look at Life on Earth*. London: Oxford University Press.

Luke, C. (1992) 'The Politicised "I" and Depoliticised "we": the politics of theory in postmodern feminisms', Paper presented to the *Conference on Gendered Culture: Educational Management in the 90's*, Victoria University of Technology, St Albans, Victoria, Australia.

Macy, J. (1989) 'Awakening to the ecological self', in J. Plant (ed.) *Healing the Wounds: the Promise of Eco-feminism*. London: Greenprint.

Marsh, P. and Fisher, M. (1992) *Good Intentions: Developing Partnership in Social Services*. York: Joseph Rowntree Foundation.

Marshall, J. (1984) *Women Managers: Travellers in a Male World*. Chichester: Wiley.

Marshall, J. (1989) 'Re-visioning career concepts: a feminist invitation', in M.B. Arthurs, D.T. Hall and B.S. Lawrence (eds) *A Handbook of Career Theory*. Cambridge: Cambridge University Press.

Marshall, J. (1993) 'Viewing organizational communication from a feminist perspective: a critique and some offerings', in *Communication Yearbook*, 16. Thousand Oaks, CA: Sage.

Marshall, J. (1994) 'Re-visioning organizations by developing female values', in R. Boot, J. Lawrence and J. Morris (eds) *Creating new Futures: a Manager's Guide to the Unknown*. London: McGraw-Hill.

Marshall, J. and Reason, P. (1994) 'Adult learning in collaborative action research: reflections on the supervision process', for Special Issue of *Studies in Continuing Education*, Research and Scholarship in Adult Education, 15(2): 117–32.

Maturana, H.R. and Varela, F.J. (1987) *The Tree of Knowledge: the Biological Roots of Human Understanding*. Boston, MA: Shambhala.

McClelland, S., Pat and Ann (1993) 'The art of science with clients: beginning collaborative inquiry in process work, art therapy and acute states', in H. Payne (ed.) *One River, Many Currents*. London: Jessica Kingsley.

Mies, M. (1983) 'Towards a methodology for feminist research', in G. Bowles and R.D. Klein (eds) *Theories of Women's Studies*. London: Routledge and Kegan Paul.

Mies, M. (1991) 'Women's research or feminist research? the debate surrounding feminist science and methodology', in M.M. Fonow and J.A. Cook (eds) *Beyond Methodology: Feminist Scholarship as Lived Research*. Bloomington: Indiana University Press.

Miller, J.B. (1976) *Toward a New Psychology of Women*. London: Penguin.

Mumford, L. (1957) *The Transformations of Man*. London: Allen and Unwin.

Neumann, E. (1973) *Origins and History of Consciousness*. London: Routledge and Kegan Paul.

Norberg-Hodge, H. (1991) *Ancient Futures: Learning from Ladakh*. San Francisco: Sierra Club.

Park, P., Brydon-Miller, M., Hall, B. and Jackson, T. (eds) (1993) *Voices of Change: Participatory Research in the United States and Canada*. Toronto: OISE Press.

Parker, F. (1991) 'Women at Hawkesbury Agricultural College', B.M. Braithwaite (ed.) *Challenge and Change: The History of Hawkesbury Agricultural College 1966–1991*, Hawkesbury Agricultural College Old Boys Union, Richmond, NSW.

Peters, D. (1994) 'Sharing responsibility for patient care', in U. Sharma (ed.) *The Healing Bond*. London: Routledge.

Plant, J. (ed.) (1989) *Healing the Wounds: the Promise of Eco-feminism*. London: Greenprint.

Poiner, G. (1991) *Women and the Academic Procession: Questions of Equality and Opportunity*. Working Papers in Women's Studies, No. 1 Women's Research Centre, UWS, Nepean. Kingswood, NSW.

Polanyi, M. (1958) *Personal Knowledge: Towards a Postcritical Philosophy*. London: Routledge and Kegan Paul.

Randall, R. and Southgate, J. (1980) *Co-operative and Community Group Dynamics . . . or your meetings needn't be so appalling*. London: Barefoot Books.

Reader, J. (1988) *Man on Earth*. London: Collins.

Reason, P. (ed.) (1988) *Human Inquiry in Action: Developments in New Paradigm Research*. London: Sage.

Reason, P. (1991a) 'Power and conflict in multidisciplinary collaboration', *Complementary Medical Research*, 5 (3): 144–50.

Reason, P. (1991b) Editorial, *Collaborative Inquiry*, 4: 3.

Reason, P. (1993) 'Reflections on sacred experience and sacred science', *Journal of Management Inquiry*, 2 (3): 273–83.

Reason, P. (1994) 'Co-operative inquiry, participatory action research and action inquiry: three approaches to participative inquiry', in N.K. Denzin and Y.S. Lincoln (eds) *Handbook of Qualitative Research*. Newbury Park CA: Sage.

Reason, P. and Hawkins, P. (1988) 'Inquiry through storytelling', in P. Reason (ed.) *Human Inquiry in Action: Developments in New Paradigm Research*. London: Sage.

Reason, P. and Heron, J. (1995) 'Co-operative inquiry', in J. Smith, R. Harré, and L. van Langenhove (eds) *Rethinking Psychology: Volume 2: Evolving Methods*. London: Sage.

Reason, P. and Marshall, J. (1987) 'Research as personal process', in D. Boud and V. Griffin (eds) *Appreciating Adults' Learning: from the Learner's Perspective*. London: Kogan Page.

Reason, P. and Rowan, J. (eds) (1981) *Human Inquiry: a Sourcebook of New Paradigm Research*. Chichester: Wiley.

Reason, P., Chase, H.D., Desser, A., Melhuish, C., Morrison, S., Peters, D., Wallstein, D., Webber, V. and Pietroni, P.C. (1992) 'Toward a clinical framework for collaboration between general and complementary practitioners', *Journal of the Royal Society of Medicine*, 86: 161–4.

Reich, W.R. (1972) *Character Analysis* (translated by V.R. Carfagno). New York: Simon and Schuster. (Original work published in 1945.)

Reinharz, S. (1981) 'Implementing new paradigm research: a model for training and practice', in P. Reason and J. Rowan (eds) *Human Inquiry: a Sourcebook of New Paradigm Research*. Chichester: Wiley.

Riley, D. (1988) *'Am I That Name?' Feminism and the Category of 'Women' in History*. Minneapolis: University of Minnesota Press.

Romanyshyn, R.D. (1989) *Technology as Symptom and as Dream*. New York: Routledge.

Rowan, J. (1981) 'A dialectical paradigm for research', in P. Reason and J. Rowan (eds) *Human Inquiry: a Sourcebook of New Paradigm Research*. Chichester: Wiley.

Rowan, J. (1989) *Subpersonalities: the People Inside Us*. London: Routledge.

Schon, D. (1983) *The Reflective Practitioner*. New York: Basic Books.

Schwartz, P. and Ogilvy, J. (1980) *The Emergent Paradigm: Changing Patterns of Thought and Belief*. Analytical Report No. 7, Values and Lifestyles Program, SRI International, Menlo Park, California.

Segal, L. (1986) *The Dream of Reality*. New York: Norton.

Shepard, H (1975) 'Rules of thumb for change agents', *OD Practitioner*, 7 (3): 1–5.

Shorter, B. (1987) *An Image Darkly Forming: Women and Initiation*. London: Routledge and Kegan Paul.

Sims, D.P.S. (1981) 'From ethnogeny to endogeny: how participants in research projects can end up doing research on their own awareness', in P. Reason and J. Rowan (eds) *Human Inquiry: a Sourcebook of New Paradigm Research*. Chichester: Wiley.

Skolimowski, H. (1986) 'The interactive mind in the participatory universe', *The World and I*, February, pp. 453–470.

Skolimowski, H. (1992) *Living Philosophy: Eco-philosphy as a Tree of Life*. London: Arkana.

Skolimowski, H. (1993) *A Sacred Place to Dwell: Living with Reverence Upon the Earth*. Rockport, MA: Element.

Skolimowski, H. (1994) *The Participatory Mind*. London: Arkana.

Smale, G.G. (1992) *Managing Change Through Innovation*. London: National Institute for Social Work.

Snyder, G. (1990) *The Practice of the Wild*. San Francisco: North Point Press.

Sogyal Rinpoche (1992) *The Tibetan Book of Living and Dying*. San Francisco: Harper.

Southgate, J. (1985) *Community Counselling Circles*. London: Institute for Social Inventions.

Spender, D. (1992) Comments recorded on ABC TV, *Four Corners: the Glass Ceiling*, 12/10/92, Australian Broadcasting Corporation.

Spretnak, C. (1991) *States of Grace: the Recovery of Meaning in the Postmodern Age*. New York: HarperCollins.

Srivastva, S., Obert, S.L. and Neilson, E. (1977) 'Organizational analysis through group processes: a theoretical perspective', in G.L. Cooper (ed.) *Organizational Development in the UK and USA*. London: Macmillan.

Stanley, L. (1991a) 'Feminist autobiography and feminist epistemology', in J. Aaron and S. Walby (eds) *Out of the Margins: Women's Studies in the Nineties*. London: Falmer Press.

Stanley, L. (ed.) (1991b) *Feminist Praxis: Research, Theory and Epistemology in Feminist Sociology*. London: Routledge.

Stanley, L. and Wise, S. (1983) *Breaking Out: Feminist Consciousness and Feminist Research*. London: Routledge and Kegan Paul.

Stanley, L. and Wise, S. (1991) 'Feminist research, feminist consciousness, and experiences of sexism', in M. Fonow and J. Cook (eds) *Beyond Methodology: Feminist Scholarship as Lived Research*. Bloomington and Indianapolis: Indiana University Press.

Steedman, C. (1986) *Landscape for a Good Woman: a Story of Two Lives*. London: Virago.

Steier, F. (ed.) (1991) *Research and Reflexivity*. London: Sage.

Stevens, B. (1970) *Don't Push the River (it flows by itself)*. Moab, UT: Real People Press.

Still, L.V. (1993) *Where To From Here? The Managerial Woman in Transition*. Sydney: Business and Professional Publishers.

Stone, M. (1978) *When God was a Woman*. San Diego: Harcourt Brace and Co.

Stone, M. (1992) *Ancient Mirrors of Womanhood: a Treasury of Goddess and Heroine Lore from Around the World*. Boston: Beacon Press.

Swimme, B. (1984) *The Universe is a Green Dragon*. Santa Fe: Bear and Co.

Swimme, B. and Berry, T. (1992) *The Universe Story: from the Primordial Flaring Forth to the Ecozoic Era – a Celebration of the Unfolding of the Cosmos*. New York: HarperCollins.

Tandon, R. (1981) 'Dialogue as inquiry and intervention', in P. Reason and J. Rowan (eds) *Human Inquiry: a Sourcebook of New Paradigm Research*. Chichester: Wiley.

Tandon, R. (1989) 'Participatory research and social transformation', *Convergence*, 21 (2/3): 5–15.

Tannen, D. (1990) *You Just Don't Understand: Men and Women in Conversation*. New York: Ballantine Books.

Tarnas, R. (1991) *The Passion of the Western Mind: Understanding the Ideas that have Shaped our World View*. New York: Ballantine.

Torbert, W.R. (1976) *Creating a Community of Inquiry: Conflict, Collaboration, Transformation*. New York: Wiley.

Torbert, W.R. (1981) Empirical, behavioural, theoretical and attentional skills necessary for collaborative inquiry', In P. Reason and J. Rowan (eds) *Human Inquiry: a Sourcebook of New Paradigm Research*. Chichester: Wiley.

Torbert, W.R. (1987) *Managing the Corporate Dream: Restructuring for Long-term Success*. Homewood, IL: Dow Jones-Irwin.

Torbert, W.R. (1991) *The Power of Balance: Transforming Self, Society, and Scientific Inquiry*. Newbury Park, CA: Sage.

Torbert, W.R. (nd) *Leadership and the Spirit of Inquiry*. Unpublished manuscript.

Traylen, H. (1989) *Health Visiting Practice: an Exploration into the Nature of the Health Visitor's Relationship with their Clients*. MPhil dissertation, School of Management, University of Bath.

Treleaven, L. (1991) 'Listening circles', *Collaborative Inquiry*, No. 6, December 1991, University of Bath.

Treleaven, L. (in preparation) *Unsettling Silences: Gendered Subjectivity at Work*. PhD thesis, Faculty of Humanities and Social Sciences, University of Western Sydney, Nepean, NSW, Australia.

Turner, F. (1980) *Beyond Geography: the Western Spirit Against the Wilderness*. New York: Viking.

Ulanov, A. (1983) 'The feminine in Jungian psychology and Christian theology', in Estelle Weinrib (ed.) *Images of the Self: the Sand Play Therapy Process*. Boston: Sigo Press.

Walkerdine, V. (1984) 'Developmental psychology and child-centred pedagogy', in J. Henriques (ed.) *Changing the Subject: Psychology, Social Regulation and Subjectivity*. London: Methuen.

Ward, K.B. and Grant, L. (1991) 'Co-authorship, gender and publication among sociologists', in M.M. Fonow and J.A. Cook (eds) *Beyond Methodology: Feminist Scholarship as Lived Research*. Bloomington: Indiana University Press.

Watts, A. (1963) *The Two Hands of God: the Myths of Polarity*. New York: George Braziller.

Weedon, C. (1987) *Feminist Practice and Poststructuralist Theory*. London: Basil Blackwell.

Whitaker, D.S. and Archer, J.L. (1985) 'An experiment in helping social work practitioners to design and conduct research', *Journal of Social Work Education* 4 (2): 3–8.

Whitaker, D.S. and Archer, J.L. (1987) *The Quality of Life in Residential Homes for the Elderly*. University of York, Social Work and Development Unit.

Whitaker, D.S. and Archer, J.L. (1989) *Research by Social Workers: Capitalizing on Experience*. Leeds: Council for Education and Training in Social Work.

Whitaker, D.S., Archer, J.L. and Greve, S. (1990) *Research, Practice, and Delivery: the Contribution of Research by Practitioners*. Leeds: Council for Education and Training in Social Work.

Whitehead, A.N. (1929) *Process and Reality*. Cambridge: Cambridge University Press.

Whitmore, E. (1990) 'Empowerment in program evaluation: a case example', *Canadian Review of Social Work*, 7 (2): 215–29.

Wilber, K. (1980) *The Atman Project: a Transpersonal View of Human Development*. Wheaton, IL: Quest.

Wilber, K. (1981) *Up from Eden*. New York: Anchor Press/Doubleday.

Index